Progressive Rhetoric and Curriculum

Progressive Rhetoric and Curriculum: Contested Visions of Public Education in Interwar Ontario considers the ways that progressivist ideas and rhetoric shaped early curriculum and structural changes to Ontario's public schools. Through a series of case studies, conceptual analyses, and personal reflections from the field, this volume shows how post-WWI era debates around progressive education were firmly situated within political, economic, social, and intellectual evolutions in the province and beyond. By framing contemporary educational rhetoric in light of historical concepts and arguments, *Progressive Rhetoric* adds to the ongoing historical examination of the meaning of progressive education in the modern age.

Theodore Michael Christou is an Associate Professor of Social Studies and History Education in the Faculty of Education at Queen's University, Ontario with a cross-appointment to the Department of History.

T0349527

Routledge Research in Education

For a complete list of titles in this series, please visit www.routledge.com/Routledge-Research-in-Education/book-series/SE0393

This series aims to present the latest research from right across the field of education. It is not confined to any particular area or school of thought and seeks to provide coverage of a broad range of topics, theories, and issues from around the world.

Recent titles in the series include:

Progressive Rhetoric and Curriculum

Contested Visions of Public Education in Interwar Ontario

Theodore Michael Christou

Routledge
Taylor & Francis Group

LONDON AND NEW YORK

First published 2018 by Routledge

2 Park Square, Milton Park, Abingdon, Oxfordshire OX14 4RN
52 Vanderbilt Avenue, New York, NY 10017

Routledge is an imprint of the Taylor & Francis Group, an informa business

First issued in paperback 2019

Library of Congress Cataloging-in-Publication Data
A catalog record for this book has been requested

ISBN: 978-1-138-55817-5 (hbk)
ISBN: 978-0-367-28166-3 (pbk)

Typeset in Sabon
by Apex CoVantage, LLC

It is, then, the responsibility of educators of every grade and rank, from the primary school to the university, to acquaint themselves with the facts of the present day world, and if possible, to determine a philosophy adequate for the construction of that new society which may emerge from the present chaos.

Joseph McCulley, "Education in a Changing Society,"
The Canadian School Journal (January, 1932), p. 60

Contents

Acknowledgments

I wish to acknowledge the family, friends, colleagues, and various funding sources that supported this project over many years in various and sundry ways.

I am grateful to the many libraries and archives that were eminently useful and generous with their resources throughout the research process.

I am in debt to the editors and reviewers of this manuscript for their diligence.

It is a privilege to devote a life to educational pursuits. I am hopeful that this is of use to students and researchers wondering how things ended up as they have and imagining how they might be.

Ἀγαπήσω σε, Κύριε, ἡ ἰσχύς μου. Κύριος στερέωμά μου καὶ καταφυγή μου καὶ ῥύστης μου. Ὁ Θεός μου βοηθός μου, ἐλπιῶ ἐπ᾽ αὐτόν, ὑπερασπιστής μου καὶ κέρας σωτηρίας μου καὶ ἀντιλήπτωρ μου.

Introduction

Who Is Not a Progressive Reformer, Anyway?

> The meaning of progressive education, as the term is used in recent educational writings, is not easy to define. It is in the nature of the word that the types of educational activity to which it is applied should continually vary.[1]

Progressive education as a historical subject evokes Meno's paradox.[2] In Plato's celebrated dialogue, *Meno*, the title character approaches Socrates and asks him a series of questions regarding virtue. Can it be taught? If it cannot be taught, can it be acquired by practice? If neither, is it an aspect of human nature inherent to us? Socrates, being Socrates, does not answer any of the three questions and, instead, engages Meno with a series of challenges of his own devise. First, he challenges his young interlocutor to define virtue. Meno responds by listing a series of virtues appropriate for men, women, and children. Socrates balks at the response. It is as if I asked you to define the nature of a bee and, instead, you listed the various types of bees that exist, chides the philosopher. Socrates persists in systematically unraveling the young man's a priori assumptions and presumptions regarding the subject at hand, virtue. The standard fare for Plato's dialogues, in other words.

Meno is flummoxed as he confronts a dilemma. Socrates believes that he knows nothing, so he questions everything. Even if Meno is able to define virtue accurately, Socrates will still question this definition. Herein lies the paradox: if one knows the answer to a question, there is no need to ask. If one does not know the answer to a question, and if one questions everything, the answer will never be wholly recognized as it will be perpetually subjected to inquiry. Knowledge is always partial, at best, or intermediary.

Progressive education, then, is something akin to virtue (which is not to say that it is virtuous). We have tried to define it. We have framed it historically and, somewhat more begrudgingly, contemporaneously, we have projected it into the future, normatively imagining the world to come. We have, like Meno, listed its types and its kinds. Still, we wrestle with its very nature.

Previously, I have argued that progressive education could be understood in terms of three core beliefs: a) the individual student is more important than any other factor; b) learning is an active process; and c) schools ought to reflect contemporary society. This definition followed from John Dewey's critique of progressives, who he cautioned not to define themselves merely in opposition.[3] Tell us who you are, not who you aren't, Dewey stated. Examining educational journals and various other historical sources within the province of Ontario, I found that progressives did a lot of telling others and themselves what they disliked. They railed against the traditional curriculum and subject matter that was taught to all students regardless of who they were and what they wanted. They bemoaned the seemingly passive forms of learning that involved reading, memorizing, and regurgitating responses on tests and uniform examinations. They grumbled that society had changed and that schools remained fixed in the same epoch in which they had been established. These three complaints led to my own, tripartite definition, which restated in positive terms the concerns of Ontario's progressivists.

I termed the three core beliefs *domains* to signify that these were the common ground that all progressives treaded. Distinct from these domains were three *themes*: a) child study/developmental psychology; b) social efficiency; and c) social meliorism. These interests were borrowed from Herbert Kliebard's seminal work, *The Struggle for the American Curriculum*.[4] Kliebard, seeing how historians and educationists continued to wrestle with the subject of what *progressive* meant and means, decided that the term itself was useless and troublesome. Instead, he argued that there were competing interests, each with their own set of protagonists and perspectives, vying for control over the curriculum, which he represented using the metaphor of a giant battlefield.

Enthralled with Kliebard's work, I set out to test his model on the Canadian context, concentrating on my home province of Ontario. What I found, was that these interest groups, while real, were all merely themes of educational progressivism. They were akin to the various *types* of virtues that Meno listed off when he struggled to understand Socrates' request for a definition of virtue. All progressives believed that education had to be, as noted above, focused on the individual, active in its implementation, and nested in contemporary life. Yet, there was no consensus regarding what this actually meant. Thus, I concentrated on the three domains of progressivist education while demonstrating how each of the three interests variously understood or interpreted what it meant to be progressive. As a model, this approach was inclusive of common beliefs as well as disputed perceptions.

I was fairly certain that I had solved the problem of progressive education, at least within the context under examination. Then, whilst on sabbatical from my work at Queen's University, I decided to tackle the Herculean task of making sense of my filing cabinets. The state of these was—and, sadly, remains—horrendous, crammed to the extent that there was no room for the odd piece of correspondence or thank you card to fit. I uncovered a series of stuffed, hanging folders titled *The School* and *The Canadian School Journal*.

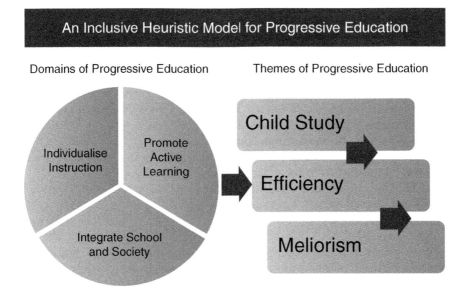

An Inclusive Heuristic Model for Progressive Education

Domains of Progressive Education   Themes of Progressive Education

Individualise Instruction

Promote Active Learning

Integrate School and Society

Child Study

Efficiency

Meliorism

These were the two primary sources used extensively in my previous study, both professional journals published throughout the interwar period in Ontario during the school year (September to June). The photocopied pages were dog eared, scribbled upon, highlighted, and dressed with neon sticky notes. Flipping through the sources, I noted that I had gathered a great deal more data than I had used. This is ever the case, as all historians and scholars know too well. I should do something with this one day, I thought.

More recently, preparing to teach a doctoral course titled Contemporary Curriculum Theory, I began the beguiling task of developing a reading list. This task, obviously, involves a great deal of reading. I began with Plato, because there is nothing so contemporary as classical philosophy. When I reached the *Meno*, I was dumbfounded.

Back to my filing cabinet. Back to *The School*. Back to *The Canadian School Journal*. Back to interwar Ontario. Back to progressive education. This time, I have toppled the structure that framed my 2012 work. Rather than begin with the common domains of progressivist thinking, I begin with the themes—those interest groups that interpret and define the terrain. I think about progressivism writ large more broadly, and I consider progressivist ideas as they are framed today within the popular parlance of the twenty-first century.

Once again, I situate myself as a former public school teacher, who in the midst of my career in Canada's largest school board, needed historical help to make sense of real problems of instruction. I was awash in novelty. Throughout my first year of teaching, many things did appear new and novel. But by my third year I began to have serious doubts. How much of what was touted with much fanfare by educationists was just old wine in new skins? Was I, in the microcosm of a third-grade classroom, the product of an evolving and improving system of schooling? Were we, teachers and educationists, regressing, progressing, or doing nothing of the sort. Even if I were to assume the progress part of this equation, I could not see the direction in which this progress proceeded. I heard a curmudgeon tell me that he had seen it all before, and was not interested in seeing it anew, once more. Alfred North Whitehead famously demarked that history was a footnote to Plato, signifying his indebtedness to the past. Cantankerously, I suppose, he could have told us to stick our heads in the sand instead, since naught was new and our intimations of progress in scholarship were frail.

I had completed a 2-year teacher education program at a time when such programs were 8 months long and, not once, did I encounter a course in the history or in the philosophy of education.[5] Why not? I asked this at the time and I have asked it again in retrospect, having received no answer. Yet this question, which began burrowing in me as a graduate student, thoroughly harassed me as a teacher with tenure and all the security for which I could ask. I turned to history. And, again, I turn to the theme of progressive education as a force that transformed public schooling in Ontario and as a remarkably underexplored subject considering our proclivity for pendulums and for the swinging between modernity and tradition in Canadian educational thought.

"Education," Joel Spring noted, "like democracy, is something everyone in America says they support, but exactly what they mean by education is never clearly stated."[6] Historically, the meanings of progressive education—of schooling writ large, we might say—are just as problematic. While the two World Wars represent historical breaking points that dramatically altered the socio-political character of the context examined here, the Great Depression of the 1930s, which nurtured the belief that educational reform could bring about economic and social change, features rather largely.[7] What is more, by the early 1930s, the dominant educational discourse in all the provinces was beginning to be influenced by progressive ideas of democracy and education.[8] By the end of the First World War, the social and economic effects of a sudden, dramatic increase in immigration and urbanization had taken hold across Canada. The Second World War provoked great change across the country, influencing notions of citizenship and the role of education in shaping a polity.[9]

Progressive education, because it embraces multiple, often contradictory, movements, has been difficult to define clearly. The various manifestations of progressive education are bound together by the oppositional stance that they take to traditional and to conservative pedagogical practices, including rote memorization of academic content that is neither differentiated nor explicitly related to the actual lives or future ambitions of students.[10] I have remained particularly interested in the discourses surrounding the different manifestations of progressive education. Historically, there has been a gap between expressed aims or objectives and actual policy changes and classroom practice.[11] Various historians have used that reality to disregard the language surrounding educational affairs and concentrate on schooling as experienced and as enacted. I, conversely, focus not on policy and practice, but on the rhetoric of schooling, which shapes our popular imaginary. In many instances, John Dewey hides as a specter, which is relatively commonplace when we imagine the landscape of twentieth-century educational reform.[12]

I look here at the Canadian province of Ontario, yet it is important to acknowledge the multifaceted and international scope of progressive education. As a movement, it is tied to a larger wave of progressivism sweeping across society in the final decades of the nineteenth century and in the first half of the twentieth century.[13] Progressive education, then, is an idea imported into the Ontario context. It is in no way autochthonous to this space. Yet, its own development, trajectory, and relentless pendulum swinging is a case in point.

Progressivism and Progressive Education

What does progressivism writ-large mean in relation to the Canadian context? What was the *progressive era*? James T. Kloppenberg represents progressivism as a "body of ideas cut loose from its moorings in the liberal tradition."[14] This entailed the renouncing of "atomistic empiricism, psychological hedonism, and utilitarian ethics" along with greedy individualism.[15] Progressive visions of a welfare state, Kloppenberg argues, were intimately linked to the conception of a socialized individual "whose values are shaped by personal choices and cultural conditions."[16]

So-called progressives were not of one sort. New Liberalism, which was influenced by evolutionary theory, Social Darwinism, and the unclenching of religious authority, was not the only impetus for the rise of progressivist thought.[17] This was not an entirely secular movement, despite its Darwinian tones. Bruno-Jofré analyzed how social gospelers embraced progressive education and, in part, John Dewey's pedagogical themes to develop their educational conceptions.[18] She demonstrated that the confluence of the social gospel and progressive educational thought nourished regenerative and redemptionist views of education that were moved to the missionary realm.[19] Bruno-Jofré's work rejuvenated themes explored by an influential American religious educator and a follower of Dewey, George Coe. Coe, whose work was used in both U.S. and Canadian seminaries, integrated Deweyan educational theory with themes that are related to the social gospel movement.[20] Daniel Tröhler, examining the linkages between Dewey's pragmatism and the Protestant mentality, argued that the provocations of modernity were negotiated in terms that were not entirely secular.[21] The social gospel, also preoccupied with the notion of a socialized individual, "sought to apply the Christian message of salvation to society as well as to the individual in an urban, industrial age."[22]

The picture that emerges of the progressive period is one "populated by hybrid discourses" constellated and interacting in multiple spaces.[23] Dewey, a popular, although not imaginary, figurehead of the progressive era in education, put forward a theory of education that could deal with the devastation wrought upon society by industrial capitalism.[24] His seminal influence on pedagogy can, in large measure, be attributed to his theories' ability to *encompass the terrific diversity* of the progressive movement. Dewey's ideas, consequently, appealed to and were adopted by many groups, enabling their interaction with multiple and often divergent interests, contexts, and motivations.[25] Interpretations of Deweyan educational theory, then, like interpretations of progressivism writ large, were reformulated, reframed, and reconstructed continuously as they are mediating between values of modernity and of tradition."[26]

The largely reconstructionist and regenerative tides in education were not unilaterally modernist or, even, progressive. This is because the very general sense of modernity implied more than the "replacement of Victorian society—agrarian, religious, adhering to a rigid set of philosophical and moral codes—with the modern age: industrial, secular, and anti-philosophical."[27] Modernization, encompassing socio-economic, educational, and political reforms, encompassed ideological and philosophical changes. These represented a value system "more attuned to a secular and materialist society. It involves the subsuming of the moral and 'humane' values of former times and the emergence of new attitudes and values consistent with an industrial, technological and consumer society."[28] Bluntly put, the old order and traditions of education did not roll over and die. Its critiques of modernity, while evident in the interwar period, become increasingly pronounced and prominent in the decades following the Second World War.[29]

Like the progressives, the anti-modernists, anti-progressives, and humanists were not a monolithic entity. Principally, they were academics and public intellectuals, "devoted to their individual intellectual specializations. As a result, they were eclectic and sometimes even haphazard in their considerations of the ramifications of modernity."[30] So even as the tide of progress swept over and subsumed the traditional academic curriculum, the classics, and the canon, defenses of a liberal arts education steeped in the humanities opposed the swell of modernity. This opposition, largely representative of the classical or Arnoldian conception of education, was largely established and modeled in Ontario's universities. In the words of A. B. McKillop, "the culture of utility gained a secure foothold in the institutions of higher education in the province . . . but it was not yet a dominant one."[31] As McKillop demonstrated, the humanities "remained the formal base of the scholarly pyramid."[32]

The sources reveal that here, amongst academics, raged the debates surrounding the necessity of Greek and Latin in the schools, as well as the content and place of Departmental examinations as prerequisites for university study. With respect to the elementary schools in Ontario, the sources reveal an increasing humanist concentration on public and school libraries. Arguments for the inclusion of libraries in schools emphasize the significance of the classics, the canon of best books, and the enjoyment of life in leisure. A liberal education could still be pursued by the general public, with some degree of solitude and a modicum of free time to read and reflect, could still be pursued in the public libraries, which were championed even as the classics were in retreat within the school curricula.

The humanists, these advocates of a liberal education steeped in good literature, like the progressivists, were not of one sort. What seemed to bound them was a belief that progressive education led to rampant individualism, a decline in the mastery of content knowledge, disregard for authority and tradition—the decline of literary authority is not inextricable for authority as we might understand it on a larger scale—weakened family structure, disrespectful questioning of authority, a lack of discipline, and a decline in patriotism and respect for national icons.[33] This, juxtaposed with the rhetoric promoting progressive educational reform because it would save schools from conformity, bureaucracy, impersonal approaches to teaching and learning, and the oppressive demands of a rigidly academic curriculum represents quite a conundrum for historians. This conundrum is also particularly contemporary.

"On its educational side," Herbert Kliebard explains, humanism—which he termed the educational lobby that challenged the various lobbies advocating for progressivist curriculum reforms—"has come to be associated with a set of subjects, a segment of the school curriculum, believed to have the power to stir the imagination, enhance the appreciation of beauty, and disclose motives that actuate human behaviour."[34] This explanation appears to confirm John Dewey's remark that "humanism is a portmanteau word."[35] Kliebard interpreted this term as signifying a term that "packs together a variety of meanings," drawing from the study of Latin and Greek, language, literature, and the arts.[36] Humanism in this context seemed as amorphous as progressivism.

Faculty Psychology and Mental Discipline

The underpinnings of the curriculum theory espoused by humanists lay in a belief that individuals had particular intellectual faculties, which could be exercised and disciplined through educational activity. Faculty psychology was based on the understanding that humans had "various faculties of the mind, such as memory, imagination, and reasoning."[37] In a corresponding sense, mental discipline argued that "certain subjects of study had the power to invigorate the various faculties," all of which needed to be harmoniously developed.[38] Different parts of the mind, like muscles in the body, required conditioning, testing, and stretching to build overall strength in reasoning.

The traditional curriculum, humanists argued, strengthened the mind. In the words of L. J. Crocker, this gave individuals "power to interpret our own society."[39] "The chief emphasis, although not the only emphasis of the school should be on intellectual development," posited Dr. R. B. Liddy, Professor of Psychology at the University of Western Ontario, "and we must continue to emphasize the fact that the primary scholastic function is intellectual education. W. H. Fyfe, Classicist and Principal of Queen's University, put the matter boldly, noting that modern school reforms were: "Largely inspired by the false motive of producing factory-fodder."[40] Fyfe argued that education that concerns itself primarily with directly training, rather than broadly educating, is myopic. As late as 1930, in a speech to incoming students, he noted "the function of a university . . . [was] to aid human beings in the growth of character, in the healthy development of all their faculties, physical, mental, moral, aesthetic, and spiritual."[41]

As noted above, progressivist reforms challenged many of the structural aspects of schooling, transforming curricula, consolidating schools, loosening examination standards, reducing the emphasis upon textbooks, and introducing new subjects of study such as health and social studies. The development of auxiliary education, an antecedent to special education programs, which manifest an increased concern with mental (intelligence) testing, inclusion, and differentiated programs of instruction, further challenged the underpinning philosophy of faculty psychology.[42] By the mid-1920s, mental testing was acknowledged as the most important factor in educational reform, altering the ways that administrators and educationists thought of the purposes of schooling with respect to individuals of differing abilities.[43]

Yet faculty psychology had deep roots; the training of mental faculties persisted as an educational aim. Disciplines of study served, in an almost literal sense, as training ground for the various faculties of mind. The mind could, in an almost literal sense, be disciplined by the various disciplines of study. History, for instance, served a vital role in the curriculum, "developing the logical faculties," as well as memory and imagination.[44]

Further, humanists argued that school curricula had a seminal role to play in the preservation of the cultural heritage of Western civilization. As Herbert Kliebard notes, this conception took "its cue not from the vagaries of children's interests, nor their spontaneous impulses, but from the great resources of civilization."[45] In their 1947 text, *The Humanities in Canada*, Watson Kirkconnell and A.S.P. Woodhouse outlined a comprehensive vision of liberal education, which was one that related to every citizen.[46] The humanities were at the root of Western culture, and thus were relevant to all people within that culture. They were conceptualized as preserving the very best aspects of literary, linguistic, artistic, historical, religious, and philosophical tradition. The world was forever evolving, and these traditions were a firmament that steadied the mind and soul.

Greek and Latin, for example, were seminal influences on modern English language and literature. As A. B. McKillop demonstrates, scholars of the Classics and the Humanities such as University of Toronto Professor Maurice Hutton "viewed their students as the spiritual heirs of Greece and Rome and sent them to examine the foundations of their common culture."[47] In line with this, a *Group of Classical Graduates*, which was thought to include Maurice Hutton, expressed the following statement in a 1929 publication for which University of Toronto president Sir Robert Falconer wrote the foreword:

> The fundamental unity of Greco-Roman culture is accepted as a starting-point. The Greeks are important as the discoverers of the main forms of European thought and expression; the Romans, as the first of a long series of European peoples whose lives have been enriched by the reception of Greek culture, and also as the architects of that institutional framework within which Greek culture was preserved and perpetuated; both together as the *fons et origo* of much that is still current and vital in the life of Europe and the West.[48]

The traditional curriculum and its philosophical basis, in other words, were vital to a healthy, balanced, and enriching life. The Group of Classical Graduates thumbed their noses at critics who argued that the classical languages had to demonstrate their usefulness within a modern and progressive context of schooling: "utility simply consists in the fact that it provides a balanced development of the mind."[49]

E. D. MacPhee, a Psychologist at the University of Toronto, used the educational journal *The School* to argue that the traditional curriculum was rooted in the Enlightenment tradition, noting John Locke, whose

> general educational theory has been described by the term 'disciplinary.' Locke conceived of education . . . as being properly discipline, whether of the body or mind. He was aided, in so far as mental factors go, by a 'faculty' psychology.[50]

Mind, for example, was a term describing entities such as attention and memory. Each functioned more or less independently of the other, and each could be trained, or disciplined, with appropriate mental exercises. McPhee does not trace the idea of mental discipline to its actual roots in classical Greek and Roman ideas about exercise and discipline; these were derived in their own right from a way of thinking about physical exercise and the strengthening of bodies.

Fyfe corroborated the belief that classical ideas and sources were vital dimensions to education and schooling:

> Without some knowledge of Greek and Roman history and literature, it is inevitably difficult to appreciate fully our own literature and our own history. Despite the distance in time and space, the influence of Athens and of Rome is still effective in our thought, our language, our legal and political institutions.[51]

In the words of one teacher writing in *The School*, great literature helped to liberate the soul from the mundane aspects of modern existence; children's lives were overly structured by routine, and "the way to escape this mechanization is to read widely."[52] The habit of reading widely and well needed to be cultivated early in children's lives through school work, otherwise "that taste probably never will be acquired."[53] In other words, one purpose of schools was "refining the taste and enlarging the knowledge of the young."[54] Progressivists, looking only to modern life, could not achieve these aims.

Even as humanists appealed to classical culture and traditions, these were increasingly subjected to scrutiny within a context that was at best forward-looking and at worst fixated upon the extant world and its shifting landscapes. What is more, humanism was increasingly associated with elite culture and society. As Kliebard has noted, this was particularly unfortunate within a climate that was, at the very least rhetorically, largely intent on dismantling extant hierarchies and structures. Humanism, according to Kliebard:

> Coincided, not accidentally, with the rise of a highly restricted class of cultivated aristocracy, a class capable of rarified tastes, who was removed from the world in which the vast majority of Europeans lived. Humanistic education had its origins in a world where education served mainly as an adornment to courtly life. Without denying the value of that adornment to those privileged to enjoy it, humanistic education was never an education for power or even, for that matter, for survival.[55]

A liberal education was thus viewed as a privilege that did not serve the needs of Ontarian society writ large.

It was not until the 1920s that most children in Ontario attended high schools, mandated by the Adolescent School Act of Ontario, which took effect on January 1, 1921, raising the age of compulsory attendance from 14 to 16 years of age.[56] Still, students had to pass examinations set by the Department of Education for entrance into secondary school studies.[57] Departmental examinations were also the defining mark for graduation from high school and entrance into university studies. The exams, then, were a sort of filter for the progression of students through the system of schooling and into universities, where the humanistic curriculum was enthroned.

As increasing numbers of students entered the public, secondary, and postgraduate schools, the hold of humanism, once upheld for the elite in society, slipped.[58] Yet, humanists argued, only a relatively small part of the population had ever studied the classics and enjoyed a liberal education. These had been the privilege of an elite minority, yet education had now expanded to include the entire population of the province. What role could the classics play in Ontario's educational system? The province was, it was acknowledged, in the midst of "a tremendous democratic experiment. We have been trying to educate whole classes of people never reached by a secondary education before . . . [and] into homes that have no cultural background and no educational standards."[59]

It was only a minority of students who attended high school at the start of the twentieth century and it was an even smaller minority that would graduate to the university system.[60] It was within that university system in Ontario that a commitment to liberal education was entrenched, at least throughout the interwar period.[61] Yet, in Ontario, the majority of students who entered Ontario Universities passed entrance exams to high school, pursued an academic stream in a collegiate institute, took a five-year stream (grades 9–13), passed the Departmental exams, and took a course in Latin in order to qualify.[62]

Humanists, whilst arguing that intellectual development of students' mental faculties would pay dividends for the future well-being of Canadian society, failed to acknowledge the concerns of society at large. When education was the privilege of a relatively small, somewhat elite, tranche of society, intellectual formation and training in the classics was generally uncontested. Once schools were charged with the responsibility of serving every citizen regardless of gender, class, and heritage, a liberal education in and of itself was no longer sufficient. Humanists argued that it would take time, "possibly several generations, for the educational leaven to permeate the whole lump," yet the demands of the twentieth century could no longer be addressed by Greek, Latin, literature, and history.[63]

How could knowledge of Homer or Thucydides serve everyone in their future work places? Humanists answered this question by appealing to the notion of leisure time. One did not work all day, every day. The intelligent use of one's leisure time could cultivate a richer and deeper understanding of life and its meanings. Students, as an article penned in 1931 for *The School* noted, had to "discover the most profitable ways of using the leisure hours that are sure to come to them shortly. Many of them will devote much of this free time to the pursuit of pleasure."[64] Herbert Spencer's seminal work, *What Knowledge is of Most Worth*, which won wide appeal in educational circles across North America, listed the activities enjoyed during leisure time as one of five worthwhile educational aims.[65] Leisure is not common parlance today in educational parlance, yet its significance for the humanist educationists in interwar Ontario was noted repeatedly in the province's educational journals.

What is more, humanists argued that the study of classics was the key to unlocking a richer and deeper understanding of present life, language, and meanings. Charles Ewing, a teacher in Oshawa, Ontario, argued that study of the classical languages "sheds light at every turn on our own tongue," and was useful for the uncovering the derivation of modern terms used commonly in science and in literature.[66] These claims would be heavily contested, particularly as a series of studies demonstrated that the "direct utility values of classics" was largely limited to the study of particular types of prose or fields and, as a consequence, was of no particular interest to the public at large.[67]

The transferability of classical learning to contemporary life, humanists retorted, depended on the manner of instruction, not on the subject matter itself. No subject or discipline was inherently applicable when a universal rubric is applied, although the teacher played an important role in demonstrating how school studies could relate to life outside of the school. "Transfer depends more on the method of presentation," explained E. J. Transom, a teacher from Central Public School in Timmins, "than on the subject matter involved."[68] Yet, this argument had little traction. Instruction was increasingly understood as being most applicable when it was context and content specific. This argument was reinforced by studies by experimental psychologists. As an editorial article in *The School* put the matter, education needed to depend upon "*direct* instruction and discussion. There is little or no transfer from classics or mathematics or science, as far as interest in and knowledge of world affairs are concerned."[69]

The Progressivist Triumph

While the high-water mark of Ontario's progressivist reformists was 1937, the year the Ministry of Education under the leadership of Duncan McArthur introduced its first *Revised Programme of Studies* for the elementary public schools of Ontario, the tide had turned dramatically following the First World War.[70] The Great War was the catalyst for "permanent rupture of a civilization; the war in fact became a metaphor for it: 'the Great Divide.' "[71] The First World War had caused a "considerable narrowing of the intellectual field," explained Queen's University's Ernest Scott, "we find ourselves in a world pre-occupied with the present, and the studies we once associated with the higher culture will be more and more crowded out."[72] Yet, despite the curriculum ferment in the humanities, McKillop has noted: "the pronouncements of Ontario university leaders between the wars on the meaning of a liberal education recapitulated, as often as not, the broad idealism of the pre-war years."[73]

Sir Arthur W. Currie, President and Vice-Chancellor of McGill University, for example, reminded his audience at the Ridley College Old Boys' Association Banquet on December 3, 1932 that they should never forget that the main goal of education "must be what it always was—to pass on the full heritage of the civilization."[74] The context of the talk speaks volumes. Classics was, in real and perceived senses, the domain of an exclusive group. The transmission of Western civilization's heritage, which the humanists proclaimed, could not be applicable to everyone or, even, to the majority of Canadians. Currie implored his audience never to "underestimate the solidity and permanence of that heritage."[75] It was not until the late 1930s that such proclamations favouring liberal education and the classical subjects would decline.[76] This coincides with the triumph of progressivist ideas, at least with respect to the formal curriculum. What has been examined above is largely the lead up to this triumph. A decade after the introduction of the *Revised Programme*, Kirkconnell and Woodhouse expressed concern that increased advocacy for progressivist educational ideas had dramatically altered Canada's intellectual landscape: "the flight from the classics which has been a mark of the twentieth century" they concluded.[77] McKillop, offering a caveat, argued: "nevertheless, classics survived, if dethroned and generally diminished."[78] Here, humanism is equated with the classical languages rather than to the general intellectual framework in which they belonged, which included faculty development and encyclopedic learning as educational aims.

By 1935, Latin had been removed as a compulsory subject of study either in Ontario's secondary schools, nor was it even offered as a subject of study in the technical and commercial schools.[79] It was not required by the Department of Education for High School graduate diplomas or for admission to the normal schools. Also, students could enter any of Ontario's universities without Latin and enroll in the Faculties of Applied Science, Household Science, and Forestry. Within the Faculty of Arts, the Commerce program did not have Latin as a prerequisite. Middle School Latin was required in all other areas in the Faculty of Arts, as well as within the Faculties of Medicine and Dentistry in Ontario's universities. Upper School Latin remained a requirement for University Honours programs.[80]

Soon afterwards, "Latin was denied to students in the first year in the secondary school system (grade nine); Greek was limited to two schools."[81] These reforms "invariably undercut enrolment in classics programs throughout the province, even at the University of Toronto."[82] The humanities never recovered their position in the province's schooling. As Kliebard notes, "these, it turns out, are the very subjects that have suffered the steepest decline."[83]

Humanism was diminished, but not vanquished by the rise of progressivist educational ideas. There are aspects of humanist curriculum theory underpinning educational practice today, sometimes tacitly. Mathematics textbooks maintain practice drills and exercises, vestiges of a philosophical and psychological outlook that sought to discipline the mind. Students study literature, notably Shakespeare, thought to be exemplary, indicative of a residual concern for the transmission of classic texts that connect the student to the tradition of ideas and language, which are seminal to Western educational traditions. History courses have moved from a Great Man model, where the heroics and exploits of archetypal figures transform through their actions the social landscape, but not to the extent that figures such as Abraham Lincoln, Sir John A. MacDonald, and Martin Luther King are not socializing forces, standing as paragons of citizenship and virtue within public school curricula and classrooms.

Ontario's humanists pursued an educational vision that sought to weave balance between industry and leisure. They based their arguments on a psychological theory that they traced back to antiquity, which faltered in the face of evidence that empirical psychologists brought to the bear about the way that students learn and the relationship that this learning has upon other domains of life, and yet this theory envisaged education as a broadening of the human capacity to live well and thoughtfully in life. Training for work, and work itself, were important in life, but they were not life itself. In a rapidly evolving and increasingly complex world, tradition offered a foundation that would offer all students a common basis of ideas and knowledge. This basis was not cosmopolitan or multicultural, and it has historically been tied to the education of an elite few; it offered a counterpoint to forward-looking, progressivist educational reform agenda, which sought to align schools more closely to the mutable world of the present.

Not everyone was, or is, a progressive. While pervasive, progressivist rhetoric has been contested throughout the twentieth century and it remains contested today. A case in point is the venerable figure of Hilda Neatby, who surveyed Canadian school curricula and methods of schooling in the 1950s, declaring that they were wanting with respect to intellectual rigour and mental discipline.[84] Humanists had anticipated her critique decades earlier. Yet, as Neil Sutherland argues: "Neatby accurately characterized Canadian education not only as it was in the 1950s, but as it had been over the whole of the twentieth century: it did not and had never done much to train the minds it served."[85] In Sutherland's view, "formalism," the traditional methods and disciplines of school, persevered despite all progressivist reforms to the structures of schooling: curricula, school buildings, examinations, and textbooks.[86]

Humanist curriculum theory persevered into the 1950s and well into our own century, even as they never reached the lofty academic aims that they strove to achieve. Neither progressivist nor humanist education triumphed over the other, and both fell short of their purported ideals. This conclusion is corroborated by Paul Axelrod, who went to elementary school during the decade that followed the publication of Neatby's critique of progressivist educational reforms, yet found that her critiques did not match up with his memory of his own schooling experiences:

> I simply didn't recognize the progressive, "child-centred" system of education which she claimed was rampant in Canada during my childhood. "In an age without standards," she wrote, educators apparently believed that children could only learn when they were "happy" '. . . . My fellow educational historians, in the main, have concluded that Hilda Neatby was wrong about the nature of Canadian schooling in the post-World War II period. Robert Stamp, George Tomkins, Neil Sutherland, and Bob Gidney, among others, contend that tradition rather than progressivism characterized education in the 1950s.[87]

The empirical question regarding the extent to which schools were progressivist or traditional in their practice is an open one.[88] Yet, the structural changes to public schooling deeply unsettled Ontario's humanists, and their challenge to progressivist thinking was vocal, if not concerted and unified as a single lobby.

Historical perspective is needed to guide educational policy in Ontario today and to steady the weight that swings rhetorically and ideologically between progress and tradition. Public education in the province has served many purposes; it has pursued visions, revised these, and, in instances, made old ideas new again.[89] Its history is an inimitable aspect of its present. Understanding how and why aspects of Ontario's schools look the way they do is foundational research that will facilitate important decisions regarding what education ought to do and how it might do so. This book explores the history of curriculum and policy over a formative period in its history and situates public education within a broader examination of Ontario as an intellectual and social space.

It emerges from a need to understand the evolution of Ontario's educational history, as it relates to the ongoing tension between progress and tradition that has driven curriculum and policy reform.[90] This tension is characterized here as the predominant feature of educational history over the past century and one that persists today. Variously, progressive education has been described as the seminal force for reform in the twentieth century and as the cause of all the ills plaguing contemporary schooling.[91] Progressivists, as well as their discontented critics, have shaped the landscape of educational reform in Ontario since the start of the twentieth century, when the traditional rhetoric and structure of public schooling began to undergo dramatic change.[92] This research project contextualizes educational reform, past and present, in light of a social, political, and economic climate of change and of progress.

As the Canadian Council on Learning has noted, there have been numerous reversals in educational policy in Ontario, each serving to swing the pendulum of public education in a direction previously explored, then abandoned.[93] Educational history is a record of past experience with curriculum and policy reforms but, further, it can be a means of telling the story of how a province responds to modernity and shapes the vision of public schooling in accordance with its collective vision of the public good. The impact of this research extends beyond the humanities and social sciences, as it has direct implications for public policy, administration, and governance of education. History of education informs each, even as it reflects on education, as a public good, shapes communities and is in turn shaped by competing visions of how children ought to prepare for the present and face the future.

By 1919, educationists in the province anxiously engaged the new century, and a progressivist movement arose in education, which endeavoured to shake off the yoke of traditional schools associated with the Victorian era.[94] Progressive education came into its own and amidst radically altered perceptions of what it meant to be Canadian and what the purposes of schooling ought to be.[95] Various upheavals during the Depression, the two

World Wars, and their aftermaths each stoked the tensions between progressivist and traditionalist approaches to public education.[96]

The 21st Century Learning, as it is labeled today, embraces the core tenets of progressive education, particularly the anxiety concerning the role of education within a rapidly transforming world; its rhetoric is profoundly effective in shaping contemporary policy, practice, curricula, and funding models.[97] The Ministry of Education in Ontario is actively promoting the idea that the province is on the "cusp of a new era of learning," which is ushered in by new technologies, new media, and new research on the nature of the child.[98] Societal and technological change has moved inexorably forward, yet schools have stayed the same, progressivists argue today, even as they have in the past.[99] A new, progressive education is called for once more, to meet a new, progressive age.

During each progressivist wave, resistance has been encountered. Countering the arguments of progressive education have been educational stakeholders that stood by the steadying powers of tradition.[100] The decline of Greek and Latin, the reforms to examination systems and textbooks, the adoption of open classrooms and reformed mathematics, and the increased embracing of computer technologies—to name only a few points of contention—have been resisted forcefully over the past century.[101] Tradition has been portrayed as a pejorative, and progressivist educators have been depicted as petulant youth.[102] The tension between the two is not only persistent, it is the very core of the ongoing pendulum swinging, which has often epitomized educational reform in popular and in academic literature.[103] Literature examining this tension has blossomed in the United States, but it has not been adequately considered within the Canadian context, which is decidedly partisan or agnostic.[104]

"One of the disturbing characteristics," of educational research, Herbert Kliebard noted, "is its lack of historical perspective. New breakthroughs are solemnly proclaimed when in fact they represent minor modifications of early proposals, and, conversely, anachronistic dogmas and doctrines maintain a currency and uncritical acceptance far beyond their present merit."[105] Disciplinarily, history of education offers the opportunity to hold the world that we take for granted and to subject it to critical scrutiny.

Historical contexts and questions may be more amenable to scrutiny than contemporary ones. There is often strangeness to historical settings that we cannot see in our own, and this permits us to evaluate matters in a different light.[106] Kliebard's position follows from that of Emile Durkheim, who held out the promise that studying history taught us neither to revel in the past, nor to be seduced by whatever is new or technological. History leads us "away from the prejudices both of neophobia and neophilia: and this is the beginning of wisdom."[107] Neophilia is best exemplified by the promise of progress exemplified by educational technologies and social media. Neophobia is personified by the debates raging in mathematics and language education, wherein the results of international standardized examinations (e.g., PISA, the Program for International Student Assessment) result in ranking of countries and provinces and provoked anxieties about school effectiveness. Ontario's educationists have been consistently torn between a polemic discourse, both progressivist and traditional.

Notes

1. "Editorial Notes: Progress in Education," *The School* (November 1930), p. 213.
2. Plato, "Meno," in *Plato, IV*, trans. W.R.M. Lamb (Cambridge: Harvard University Press), pp. 259–372.
3. John Dewey, *Experience and Education* (New York: Touchstone, 1938).
4. Herbert M. Kliebard, *The Struggle for the American Curriculum, 1893–1958* (New York and London: RoutledgeFalmer, 2004).
5. Presently, all teacher education programs in Ontario are either two years, or four terms, in length.
6. Joel Spring, *Education and the Rise of the Corporate State* (Boston: Beacon Press, 1972).
7. Lynn S. Lemisko and Kurt W. Clausen, "Connections, Contrarieties, and Convulsions: Curriculum and Pedagogical Reform in Alberta and Ontario, 1930–1955," *Canadian Journal of Education* 29, no. 4 (2006), pp. 1097–1126.
8. Rosa Bruno-Jofré, "Citizenship and Schooling in Manitoba: 1918–1945," *Manitoba History* (1998/1999), 36, pp. 26–36; Robert Patterson, "The Implementation of Progressive Education in Canada, 1930–1945," in N. Kach, K. Mazurek, R. S. Patterson and I. DeFavery (Eds.), *Essays on Canadian Education* (Calgary: Detselig, 1986), pp. 79–93; Amy von Heyking, *Creating Citizens: History and Identity in Alberta's Schools, 1905 to 1980* (Calgary: University of Calgary Press, 2006).
9. Paul Axelrod, "Beyond the Progressive Education Debate: A Profile of Toronto Schooling in the 1950s," *Historical Studies in Education* 17, no. 2 (2005), pp. 227–241; Ken Osborne, "Teaching History in Schools: A Canadian Debate," *Journal of Curriculum Studies* 35, no. 5 (2003), pp. 585–626.
10. Lawrence Cremin, *American Education: The Metropolitan Experience, 1876–1980* (New York: Harper & Row, 1988).
11. Bruno-Jofré, "Citizenship and Schooling in Manitoba"; Axelrod, "Beyond the Progressive Education Debate".
12. William Hayes, *The Progressive Education Movement: Is It Still a Factor in Today's Schools?* (New York: Rowman & Littlefield Education, 2006).
13. Kevin J. Brehony, "A New Education for a New Era: The Contribution of the Conferences of the New Education Fellowship to the Disciplinary Field of Education, 1921–1938," *Paedagogica Historica* 40, no. 5 (2004), pp. 733–755.
14. James T. Kloppenberg, *Uncertain Victory: Social Democracy and Progressivism in European and American Thought, 1870–1920* (New York: Oxford University Press, 1986), p. 298.
15. Ibid.
16. Ibid., p. 299.
17. For further reading on 'new liberalism' in the British and North Atlantic contexts, see Daniel Rodgers, *Atlantic Crossings: Social Politics in a Progressive Age* (Cambridge: Belknap, 1999); Kloppenberg, *Uncertain Victory*.
18. Rosa Bruno-Jofré, "To Those in 'Heathen Darkness': Deweyan Democracy and Education in the American Interdenominational Configuration," in *International Standing Conference for the History of Education, July 2007* (Hamburg: University of Hamburg, 2008), p. 11.
19. Ibid.

20. George A. Coe, *A Social Theory of Religious Education* (New York: Charles Scribner's Sons, 1927). In the interwar period, the tensions between public and religious educators are discussed, in David P. Sertran, "Morality for the 'Democracy of God': George Albert Coe and the Liberal Protestant Critique of American Character Education, 1917–1940," *Religion and American Culture* 15, no. 1 (2005), pp. 107–144.
21. Daniel Tröhler, "The 'Kingdom of God on Earth' and Early Chicago Pragmatism," *Educational Theory* 56, no. 1 (2006), pp. 89–105.
22. Bruno-Jofré, "To Those in 'Heathen Darkness'," p. 1.
23. Ibid.
24. David K. Cohen, "Dewey's Problem," *The Elementary School Journal* 98, no. 5 (1998), pp. 427–446.
25. Lawrence Cremin, "John Dewey and the Progressive Education Movement, 1915–1952," in Reginald D. Archambault (Ed.), *Dewey on Education* (New York: Random House, 1961), p. 13.
26. The realms where values constellate and interact are many, including pedagogical theory and religious doctrine.
27. Philip Massolin, *Canadian Intellectuals, the Tory Tradition, and the Challenge of Modernity, 1939–1970* (Toronto: University of Toronto Press, 2001), p. 3.
28. Ibid., p. 4.
29. Among the most prominent postwar Canadian critics of modernity are George Grant, Marshall McLuhan, Northrop Frye, Vincent Massey, Donald Creighton, Harold Innis, and Hilda Neatby.
30. Massolin, *Canadian Intellectuals, the Tory Tradition, and the Challenge of Modernity, 1939–1970*, p. 5.
31. A. B. McKillop, *Matters of Mind: The University in Ontario, 1791–1951* (Toronto: University of Toronto Press, 1994), p. 325.
32. Ibid.
33. Hayes, *The Progressive Education Movement.*
34. Herbert Kliebard, "The Decline of Humanistic Studies in the American School Curriculum," in *Forging the American Curriculum: Essays in Curriculum History and Theory* (New York and London: Routledge, 1992), p. 3.
35. John Dewey, "Whither Humanism," *The Thinker* 2 (1930), p. 9.
36. Kliebard, "The Decline of Humanistic Studies," p. 3.
37. Ibid., pp. 7–8.
38. Ibid., p. 7.
39. Ibid., p. 655.
40. W. H. Fyfe, "Science in Secondary Education," *The School* (April, 1934), p. 653.
41. W. H. Fyfe, *Inaugural Address* (October 24, 1930), W. H. Fyfe Papers, Box 2, File 9, Queen's University Archives.
42. Jason Ellis, *Backward and Brilliant Children': A Social and Policy History of Disability, Childhood, and Education in Toronto's Special Education Classes, 1910–1945*. Ph.D. diss. (York University, 2011).
43. Ibid.
44. A. J. Husband, "The Teaching of History in the Secondary School," *The School* (December, 1931), p. 308.
45. Kliebard, "The Decline of Humanistic Studies," p. 17.
46. Watson Kirkconnell and A.S.P. Woodhouse, Eds., *The Humanities in Canada* (Ottawa: The Humanities Research Council of Canada, 1947), p. 203.
47. McKillop, *Matters of Mind*, p. 465.
48. *Honour Classics in the University of Toronto* (Toronto: University of Toronto Press, 1929), p. 29, italics in original text.
49. "The Report on Latin," *The School* (June, 1935), p. 866.

50. E. D. MacPhee, "The Value of the Classics," *The School* (October, 1927), p. 111.
51. Ibid.
52. S. Silcox, "The Teacher's Book Shelf," *The School* (March, 1930), p. 470.
53. Arthur A. Lowther, "A Vocational School Literature Course," *The School* (September, 1926), p. 53.
54. J. W. Brown, "The School Library," *The Canadian School Journal* (January, 1934), p. 8.
55. Kliebard, "The Decline of Humanistic Studies," p. 6.
56. Robert Stamp, *Ontario Secondary School Program Innovations and Student Retention Rates: 1920s–1970s* (Toronto: Ministry of Education, 1988), p. 8.
57. Ibid., p. 4.
58. Postgraduate schooling was predominately in the hands of universities and normal schools.
59. Charles M. Ewing, "The Case for Latin in the High Schools," p. 101.
60. R. D. Gidney and W.P.J. Millar, *How Schools Worked: Public Education in English Canada, 1900–1940* (Montreal and Kingston: McGill-Queen's University Press, 2012). The authors argue: "Today, Canadians pretty much take it for granted that a complete high school education takes four years, that most young people will complete those four years, and that there will be diversified programs of studies catering to a wide range of interests and abilities," 217.
61. McKillop, *Matters of Mind*. The author notes: "The rise in importance of professional programs took place, at first, as a way of educating an expanding middle class in ways that were meant to be complementary to it. In these years the culture of utility gained a secure foothold in the institutions of higher education in the province. It was becoming an influential academic force, but it was not yet a dominant one. The humanities, as will be seen, remained the formal base of the scholarly pyramid," 325.
62. See Gidney and Millar, *How Schools Worked*, pp. 217–270. Ontario was the only province that included a mandatory four-year stream (Grades IX to XII) and a "senior matriculation year," which was Grade XIII. It was not the mid-1930s, under the leadership of Duncan McArthur, Minister of Education in the province under a Liberal government, that Departmental examinations were loosened as criteria for matriculation and that Latin was made an elective course for graduation.
63. Ibid.
64. W.E.M. Aitken, "The Use of a High School Library," *The School* (March, 1931), p. 614.
65. Herbert Spencer, *Progress: Its Law and Cause in Education: Intellectual, Moral, and Physical* (1890). Beside leisure, the most worthwhile learning concerned activities that: a) directly affect self-preservation; b) indirectly serve the same end; c) concern the rearing and upbringing of children; and d) relate to appropriate social interactions.
66. Ewing, "The Case for Latin in the High Schools," p. 100.
67. See, for instance, MacPhee, "The Value of the Classics".
68. E. J. Transom, "Time Off for Thinking," *The School* (March, 1941), p. 607.
69. "Editorial Notes: Education for Citizenship," *The School* (June, 1936), p. 823.
70. Christou, "The Complexity of Intellectual Currents." A *Revised Programme* for secondary schools would be issued in 1938, and both documents would be revised and reissued in 1942 and 1943, respectively.
71. McKillop, *Matters of Mind*, p. 454.
72. Ernest F. Scott, "The Effects of the War on Literature and Learning," *Queen's Quarterly* 27 (December, 1919), pp. 147–153.
73. McKillop, *Matters of Mind*, p. 457.

74. Currie, "Address," p. 6.
75. Ibid.
76. Paul Axelrod, *Making a Middle Class: Student Life in English Canada During the Thirties* (Montreal and Kingston: McGill-Queen's University Press, 1990), pp. 39–41.
77. Watson Kirkconnell and A. S. P. Woodhouse, *The Humanities in Canada*, p. 46.
78. McKillop, *Matters of Mind*, p. 463.
79. Committee of the Classical Section of the Ontario Educational Association, "The Report on Latin," *The School* (June, 1935), pp. 865–871.
80. Ibid.
81. McKillop, *Matters of Mind*, p. 463.
82. Ibid.
83. Kliebard, "The Decline of Humanistic Studies," p. 3.
84. Hilda Neatby, *So Little for the Mind* (Toronto, ON: Clarke, Irwin, 1953).
85. Neil Sutherland, "The Triumph of 'Formalism': Elementary Schooling in Vancouver From the 1920s to the 1960s," *BC Studies* nos. 69 and 70 (Spring–Summer, 1986), p. 176.
86. Ibid.
87. Paul Axelrod, "Beyond the Progressive Education Debate: A Profile of Toronto Schooling in the 1950s," *Historical Studies in Education* 17, no. 2 (2005), p. 228.
88. Ibid. With respect to this question, Axelrod argues that the historical truth lay in an amalgam, which mixed both extremes: "Rather than a case of either progressive or traditional education, school policy was an amalgam in which educators were using available and emerging tools to address the perceived instructional needs of a ballooning population.
89. George S. Tomkins, *A Common Countenance: Stability and Change in the Canadian Curriculum* (Vancouver: Pacific Educational Press, 2008).
90. Hugh Oliver, Mark Holmes, and Ian Winchester, Eds., *The House that Ryerson Built: Essays in Education to Mark Ontario's Bicentennial* (Toronto: OISE Press, 1985).
91. The debate concerning the relative merits of progressive education in Ontario's schools is both long-standing and divisive. See, for instance, "The Aims of Education," *Canadian School Board Journal* (June, 1928), pp. 4–6; "Editorial Notes: Progress in Education," *The School* (November, 1930), pp. 213–215; Frank T. Sharpe, "What Would I Do If I Left School Under Present Conditions?" *The Canadian School Journal* (October, 1933), pp. 355–358; F. P. Gavin, "Recent Social Changes and the Schools," *The Canadian School Journal* (May, 1935), pp. 134–135; J. Donald Wilson, Robert M. Stamp, and Louis-Philippe Audet, Eds., *Canadian Education: A History* (Toronto: Prentice-Hall of Canada, 1970); Ken Osborne, "Teaching History in Schools: A Canadian Debate," *Journal of Curriculum Studies* 35, no. 5 (2003), pp. 585–626.
92. Lynn S. Lemisko and Kurt W. Clausen, "Connections, Contrarieties, and Convulsions: Curriculum and Pedagogical Reform in Alberta and Ontario, 1930–1955," *Canadian Journal of Education* 29, no. 4 (2006), pp. 1097–1126; Patrice Milewski, "Positivism and Post-World War I Elementary School Reform in Ontario," *Paedagigica Historica* 48, no. 5 (2012), pp. 728–743.
93. Canadian Council on Learning, *Changing Our Schools: Implementing Successful Educational Reform* (2009). Accessed at: www.edu.gov.on.ca/eng/policyfunding/memos/jan2009/LessonsinLearning.pdf.
94. Theodore Michael Christou, "The Complex of Intellectual Currents: Duncan McArthur and Ontario's Progressivist Curricular Reforms, Paedagogica Historica," *Paedagogica Historica* 49, no. 5 (2013), pp. 677–697.

95. Robert Patterson, "Society and Education During the Wars and their Interlude: 1914–1945," in J. Donald Wilson, Robert M. Stamp, and Louis-Philippe Audet (Eds.), *Canadian Education: A History* (Toronto, ON: Prentice-Hall of Canada, 1970).

96. John Herd Thompson and Allen Seager, *Canada, 1922–1939: Decades of Discord* (Toronto, ON: McClelland and Stewart, 1985).

97. Michael Fullan, *Great to Excellent: Launching the Next Stage of Ontario's Education Agenda* (2012). Accessed at: www.edu.gov.on.ca/eng/document/reports/FullanReport_EN_07.pdf.

98. See, for instance, Ministry of Education, Ontario, *21st Century Teaching and Learning* (2014). Accessed at: www.edu.gov.on.ca/eng/policyfunding/memos/feb2014/QuickFactsWinter2014.pdf.

99. Theodore Christou, "Schools Are No Longer Merely Educational Institutions: The Rhetoric of Social Efficiency in Ontario Education, 1931–1935," *History of Education* 42, no. 5 (2013), pp. 566–577.

100. Theodore Christou, "We Find Ourselves in the World of the Present: Humanist Resistance to Progressive Education in Ontario," *History of Education Quarterly* 55, no. 3 (2015), pp. 273–293.

101. See, for instance, Katie Gemmell, *The Impact of Progressive Education on Roman Catholic Schools in the Archdiocese of Vancouver, 1924–1960*. Ph.D. diss. (University of British Columbia, 2015).

102. Theodore Christou, "Progressivist Rhetoric and Revised Programmes of Study: Weaving Curricular Consistency and Order Out of Diverse Progressivist Themes in Ontario, Canada," *Curriculum History* 13, no. 1 (2014), pp. 61–82.

103. Alan Sears, "Historical Thinking and Citizenship Education: It Is Time to End the War," in P. Clarke (Ed.), *New Possibilities for the Past: Shaping History Education in Canada* (Vancouver: UBC Press, 2011).

104. Recent studies from the United States include Jack Schneider, *From the Ivory Tower to the Schoolhouse: How Scholarship Becomes Common Knowledge in Education* (Cambridge: Harvard Education Press, 2014); Larry Cuban, *Inside the Black Box of Classroom Practice: Change Without Reform in American Education* (Cambridge: Harvard Education Press, 2013); Frederick M. Hess, Ed., *When Research Matters: How Scholarship Influences Education Policy* (Cambridge: Harvard Education Press, 2008). Canadian scholarship has tended to aggravate the tension, Hilda Neatby, *So Little for the Mind* (Toronto: Clarke, Irwin & Company, 1953), or to avoid it, either explicitly, Paul Axelrod, "Beyond the Progressive Education Debate: A Profile of Toronto Schooling in the 1950s," *Historical Studies in Education* 17, no. 2 (2005), pp. 227–241 or tacitly, R. D. Gidney and W.P.J. Millar, *How Schools Worked: Public Education in English Canada, 1900–1940* (Toronto: University of Toronto Press, 2012).

105. Herbert M. Kliebard, "Why History of Education?" *The Journal of Educational Research* 88, no. 4 (1995), p. 195.

106. Kliebard, "Why History of Education?," 195.

107. Émile Durkheim, *The Evolution of Educational Thought: Lectures on the Formation and Development of Secondary Education in France* (London: Routledge and Kegan Paul, 1977), p. 9.

1   Ontario in the Interwar Period

Progressive Education for a Progressive Age

I could discuss here the semantic problems raised by the epithet 'progressive', but I prefer to examine schools which were considered radical at the time of their foundation and since.[1]

Interwar Ontario presents a context ripe with complexity, contradictions, and socio-economic crises. Two Great Wars fought in large part for the sake of democracy and freedom bracketed nearly three decades of tension and change. Ontario was undergoing dramatic changes in the domains of public policy, labour, economic strategy, and political organization. In terms of the economic complex, for example, the idea of a new industrialism was interwoven with *modern* technological possibilities or innovations in the domains of fuels (petroleum, natural gas, hydroelectric), motive powers (combustion engines), transport (airplanes, trucks, cars), structural materials (aluminum, light alloys, alloy steels), and industrial processes (synthetic materials).[2]

The rapid and dramatic rise of automobile use in the province demonstrates one part of Ontario's modernization and change. The traffic of horse-drawn carriages dropped from 50 percent to 3 percent of transportation in the province in only eight years between 1914 and 1922.[3] This necessitated increasing public regulation, including driver licensing (instituted in 1927) and regulation (speeding, reckless walking, and parking).[4] Rising automobile use also made necessary public planning policies such as those promoting the development of city parks that would provide children with safe places to play off the streets and those redesigning and broadening roads.[5] There was never one single impetus for these changes but a long succession of disappointments contributed to the growing unease and unrest of Canadians.[6]

Within this context of economic uncertainty, the federal government funding of public works projects to stimulate economic recovery and employ citizens are examples of progress towards interventionist models of government and the fostering of a welfare state.[7] The fostering of a welfare state in the interwar period marks a change in the relationship between government and citizenry.[8] The welfare state, as we presently understand it, had not been invented. It would be years before British economist John Maynard Keynes's ideas concerning interventionist economic policy would cross the Atlantic and influence Canadian fiscal planning. Keynesian economics, as exemplified in Franklin Delano Roosevelt's New Deal legislation, argued that the injection of stimuli into the economy could trigger recovery by mitigating the shrinking effects of recessions and depressions.[9]

Classic, laissez-faire economics as practiced in Ontario dictated that the markets would adjust themselves without intervention. To avoid deficit, governments needed to cut back spending. By 1934, provincial funding to schools had plummeted by a third.[10] Administrators debated and experimented with a number of ways to increase the efficiency of schools in buildings that were over capacity. So-called staggered classes were promoted regularly in the educational journals as a quick and easy fix to the issue of overcrowding. The school plant, like a factory, needed to maximize its efficiency and could do so by staggering the time of day that groups of students used it.[11] The school day could begin earlier in the morning to accommodate the first of two cohorts, which would have a shorter lunch period and fewer breaks but would finish the day sooner. The second cohort would enter the school in the early afternoon and, following a schedule as efficiently planned as the first group, would finish classes by nightfall.[12]

Rotary classes were instituted in other schools as a solution. Groups of students would begin the day in a homeroom wherein they would receive their mandatory training in core subjects such as language and arithmetic. After a lunch break, they were to rotate through the school plant on a tight schedule, making efficient use of all the classrooms and available staff. The rotary system became a mainstay of Ontario schools, still the dominant model in most intermediate schools.[13]

These intermediate institutions were a third creation of creative administrative minds in the Ontario Department of Education. They had already been set up in many States and Provinces, including British Columbia as a means of bridging the divide between elementary and secondary schooling.[14] Intermediate schools catered to a new stage of learner between the ages of roughly 12 and 15, the adolescent. These schools appealed to administrators because it would download students from the high schools, where teachers were paid the most.[15] Intermediate school teachers would be paid as much as elementary teachers were paid. Further, in the middle school, teachers and administrators could provide vocational guidance to students and parents, helping them to decide on future employment thereby increasing their efficient movement from the system.[16]

Ontario's Department of Education, a highly centralized ministry, was eager to extend the educational franchise to rural and immigrant populations even when the Depression forced expenditures to contract.[17] The global economic collapse intensified the discourse concerning the need for educational reform that would bring the schools closer to society and improve social and economic spaces.[18] Nevertheless, it was only until a Liberal government led by Mitchell Hepburn won power in 1934 that "it was only when a new Liberal government ascended to power in 1934 that the Department of Education became "more receptive" of pedagocial reform to the public schools."[19] Yet, despite any progressivist proclivities that were at play, loyalty to the British Empire and to the idea of Anglo-conformity served as contextual limitations to the extent that Ontario could rewrite its curriculum. When the Programme of Studies was eventually rewritten, and distributed publicly in 1937, it would refer most distinctly to British curricular reforms undertaken in the same decade rather than to its most likely influences. These were, most immediately, the province of Alberta which had preceded Ontario in haste to initiate progressivist curricular reform, and, most vitally, various contexts within the United States.[20]

An historiographic review of progressive education has been achieved elsewhere.[21] Here, I attempt a broader definition of progressivism as it relates to education. To a particular extent, the answer will always be subject to an individual's perspective. As J. B. Bury notes, the term means "moving . . . in a desirable direction."[22] From here come its decidedly favourable connotations. One is presumed to progress towards the good. The limits of this definition are abundant, and clear.

As many of the traditional underpinnings of Victorian society were being questioned or dismantled, progressive educationists initiated a process directed at public schooling that involved breaking up of the classical, academic, and humanistic curriculum across Canada and in the United States as well.[23] The progressivists considered here were of the mindset that Ontario's schools were discordant with reality. Massive urbanization, industrialization, and immigration had transformed the province's physical and social appearance within a few generations. Wars had rattled faith in humanity, while the Depression provoked profound questioning of the economic and social underpinnings of the state. One could look backwards and forwards and simultaneously as how life could get worse and imagine how humanity could get better.

At this nexus in time, there was a general sense emerging that the world was unmoored from its distinctly Victorian bonds. The world was "neither well ordered nor harmonious. Instead of conforming to the Great Chain of Being or Newton's vision of regularity, the only law of nature was the struggle to survive."[24] In this context, and:

> Only if natural selection could be interpreted as a progressive process developing higher from lower forms of life could Darwinism be assimilated into a religious cosmology. The Great Chain of being might have been unfastened from eternity, but the comforting thought of progress offered some escape from the otherwise bleak prospects of defending faith without relying on the Bible or nature's harmonious order as evidence of divine purpose.[25]

Developments in science, and horrific experiences with war and financial destitution contributed to the sense of unease that life was not romantic, peaceful, and ordered.

This partly explains the profound impact of John Dewey's thought in the educational world, for while acknowledging the contingencies and precariousness of life, he gave voice to a truth that could be "created on earth by man's thought, reason, and activity."[26] For progressives, it goes without saying that progress could be achieved. The world was profoundly altered, but schools were utterly out of pace. They had not sufficiently adapted to a world rocked by all that was shaping it, in a Darwinian sense. The progressives, by and large, focused on that perceived gap between the traditional schools that were funded by the public and this world to come, which was no simulacrum to the world that engendered them. "Today," reported *The Canadian School Journal*, citing William James Cooper, United States Commissioner of Education, in a circular distributed by the U.S. Department of the Interior, "we live in a complex civilization which it is necessary to understand to be adjusted to it. Schools are the means by which we accomplish this period of adjustment."[27]

"We drift," announced Walter Lipmann in *Drift and Mastery* (1914), "unsettled to the very roots of our being."[28] Lipmann dances on the very thread of the tension that drove, and still does, educational reform discourse. He hints that he has faith in progress even as he acknowledges that the world is shifting. As the world shifted, and social life shifted apace, it seemed that public education was, as James Kloppenberg noted, "out of phase with reality."[29]

His analysis was prescient. Application of the "rubric of progressivism"[30] is concurrently appropriate and difficult. Etymologically,

> The word "progressive" first entered British political discourse in the late 1880s, when social and municipal reformers adopted it to designate their "advanced" position while distinguishing themselves from the imperialism of the Liberal party at the national level.[31]

In Britain, a group of intellectuals called the Rainbow Circle began meeting at a location called the Rainbow Tavern and established a publication, *The Progressive Review*, in 1896. In the United States, the Progressive People's party was founded in 1910. Its Progressive party's first presidential candidate was Theodore Roosevelt in 1912 and thereafter, Herbert Croly and Walter Lipmann established *The New Republic* in 1914, identifying themselves with the progressive movement.[32] In Canada, the Progressive Party had its roots in the politics of compromise of the Wilfred Laurier government; it was formed largely from the United Farmers candidates under the leadership of Thomas Crerar in 1919.[33]

That same party was splintered by the absence of a unified and coherent reform thrust. Doug Owram has rightly argued that "the progressive movement scattered in different directions politically as it had intellectually."[34] Kloppenberg noted that its "appearance of neatness is deceptive."[35] What is more:

> *The New Republic* largely discontinued its use of the word progressive after 1916, and the progressive label all but disappeared in Britain and Germany after World War I. The French use of the term indicates even more clearly the perils of using static categories for slippery historical phenomena . . . [progressivism] became a rather awkward synonym for reaction. British progressives denounced the Liberal party as excessively expansionist while German progressives denounced the National Liberal party as insufficiently expansionist. American progressives, to complicate matters further, ranged themselves on all sides of foreign policy issues.[36]

There is seemingly little on the surface that would allow educationists to see progressive as aspects of a singular movement:

> It makes more sense, even within a single nation, to discuss *progressivisms* in the plural than to attempt an inclusive definition of an essential or normative progressivism. By using the word, I am not arguing that only these thinkers merit designation as progressives. They represent one species among many of a political genus . . . and they figure prominently in this analysis not because of their typicality but because of the unusual incisiveness of their ideas.[37]

Notwithstanding these claims, it seems that progressivists were aligned by their fervent opposition to traditional schools. These, as caricature or instance might belie, cared more for the curriculum than they did for individual students, they ignored social change and were rooted in the interests of a world that was past. What incriminated them most, perhaps, was the sense that they were pedagogically driven towards rote memorization and modes of learning that were deemed passive or regurgitative. As a response, Canada's progressivist educationists responded by reversing each of these three shortfalls. Progressive education was to be focused on the individual student's interests, it would relate to contemporary society and its needs and, methodologically, it would engage students actively in the process of learning.

Never has an old argument been so new. Perhaps the alternative is true, also. Schools were envisaged as the means of bridging what Robert Stamp termed "gap between school and community, between the focus of the Ontario curriculum and the realities of Ontario society."[38]

Change was progress. And progress was desirable. In Bury's view, the process of progress:

> Involves a synthesis of the past and a prophecy of the future. It is based on an interpretation of history which regards men as slowly

advancing—*predemtin progredientes*—in a definite and desirable direction, and infers that this progress will continue indefinitely. And it . . . must be the necessary outcome of the psychical and social nature of man; it must not be at the mercy of any external will; otherwise, there would be no guarantee of its continuance and its issue, and the idea of Progress would lapse into the idea of Providence.[39]

As an Ontarian school inspector would note in 1934, "movements are not all of the past, but we are in the midst of them today and our senior pupils should be encouraged to read of and know them."[40] These were indicative of that schools could align more neatly with contemporaneity and be made into a "miniature of society."[41]

The pedagogical turn towards active learning deserves more discussion. Education was being defined as an active experience, not a process of acquisition. Living life was the test of how well an education could work. "Meaning is woven into the fiber of experience," is the most apt term to encapsulate the zeitgeist.[42] The schools were akin to a larger laboratory of life, and the way one lived would be the greatest test of their education. The ethos is entirely Deweyan and, simultaneously, it bears the mark of Aristotelian ethics.

In *School and Society*, a text that was initially designated as a series of lectures to parents at the Chicago Laboratory School and, consequently, remarkably accessible, John Dewey distills the progressivist attention to active learning:

> Some few years ago I was looking about the school supply stores in the city, trying to find desks and chairs which seemed thoroughly suitable from all points of view—artistic, hygienic, and educational—to the needs of the children. We had a good deal of difficulty in finding what we needed, and finally one dealer, more intelligent than the rest, made this remark: "I am afraid we have not what you want. You want something at which the children may work; these are all for listening."[43]

Dewey's derision towards the attitude that schooling is acquisition of knowledge versus the construction of knowledge is one thoroughly appropriated by Ontario's progressivist educationists. Despite this apparent agreement, what a curriculum focused on activity could mean in theory and it implementation remained contentious and it is, even today, debatable.

What of the focus upon the individual child? In the words of Thornton Mustard, who led the committee charged with studying a reorganizing of Ontario's curriculum: "The focus of attention is shifted from content to child, and form the child in general to the individual child . . . the factory system of mass production is replaced by something approaching the care and study of the craftsman and artist."[44] In the bigger picture, particular emphases on any aspect of progressivist reform did not appear to Canadian educationists. They did not represent competing interests insomuch as they each attempted, in their own way, to make sense of the perceived and urgent need for reform to school. Donalda Dickie, a pivotal figure in Alberta's educational reforms and a remarkably influential educator in the national landscape, exemplified how the themes of progressive education intertwined, arguing that the "task of modern education" was "threefold," bringing together the development of individual's talents, training in their social existence, and cultivation of the skills that they would find necessary in their future workplaces.[45] Ontario's progressives were at the same time a disparate group and aligned in particular ideological concerns.

Notes

1. W.A.C. Stewart, *The Educational Innovators: Progressive Schools, 1881–1967* (New York: St. Martin's Press, 1968).
2. W. T. Easterbrook and H.G.J. Aitken, *Canadian Economic History* (Toronto: University of Toronto Press, 1990).
3. Peter A. Baskerville, *Ontario: Image, Identity, and Power* (Toronto: Oxford University Press, 2002).
4. Ibid.
5. Ibid.
6. John H. Thompson and Allen Seager, *Decades of Discord, 1922–1939* (Toronto: McClelland and Stewart, 1985).
7. Robert Bothwell, *The Penguin History of Canada*; Thompson and Seager, *Decades of Discord* (Toronto: Penguin, 2006).
8. Doug Owram, "The Government Generation: Canadian Intellectuals and the State, 1900–1945." *The Canadian Historical Review* 68, no. 3 (1987): 465–468.
9. Ibid.
10. Robert Stamp, *The Schools of Ontario, 1876–1976* (Toronto: University of Toronto Press, 1982).
11. Ibid.
12. Ibid.
13. Ibid.
14. Ibid.
15. Ibid.
16. Ibid.
17. Lynn S. Lemisko and Kurt W. Clausen, "Connections, Contrarieties, and Convulsions: Curriculum and Pedagogical Reform in Alberta and Ontario, 1930–1955," *Canadian Journal of Education* 29, no. 4 (2006): 1097–1126.
18. Ibid.
19. Ibid., p. 1106.
20. Ontario Department of Education, *Programme of Studies for Grades 1 to 6 of the Public and Separate Schools* (Toronto: The King's Printer, 1937), pp. 5–6. Cited in Lemisko and Clausen, p. 1106.
21. Theodore Christou, *Progressive Education: Revisioning and Reframing Ontario's Public Schools, 1919–1942* (Toronto: University of Toronto Press, 2012).
22. J. B. Bury, *The Idea of Progress: An Inquiry into Its Origin and Growth* (New York: Dover Publications, Inc., 1932), p. 2.
23. David Tyack, *The One Best System: A History of American Urban Education* (Cambridge, MA: Harvard University Press, 1974).
24. James T. Kloppenberg, *Uncertain Victory: Social Democracy and Progressivism in European and American Thought, 1870–1920* (New York: Oxford University Press, 1986), p. 23.

25. Ibid.
26. Ibid., p. 43.
27. "Educational News," *The Canadian School Journal* (November, 1933), p. 403.
28. Walter Lipmann, *Drift and Mastery* (New York: Macmillan, 1914), p. 196. Accessed September 12, 2008 at: www.podmonkeyx.com/Walter_Lippmann/article.asp?articleID=58.
29. Kloppenberg, *Uncertain Victory*, p. 43.
30. Ibid., p. 300.
31. Ibid.
32. Ted V. McAllister, *Revolt Against Modernity: Leo Strauss, Eric Voegelin & the Search for Postliberal Order* (Lawrence, KS: University Press of Kansas, 1996), pp. 58–68.
33. Craig Heron, *The Workers' Revolt in Canada, 1917–1925* (Toronto: University of Toronto Press, 1998).
34. Owram, *The Government Generation*, p. 114.
35. Kloppenberg, *Uncertain Victory*, p. 300.
36. Ibid.
37. Ibid., my italics.
38. Stamp, *The Schools of Ontario*, p. 165.
39. Bury, *The Idea of Progress*, p. 5.
40. "Inspector's Report," in *The Annual Report of the Minister of Education to the Government of Ontario* (1931), p. 96.
41. C. C. Goldring, "The Work of a Principal," *Educational Courier* (June, 1933), p. 8.
42. Kloppenberg, *Uncertain Victory*, p. 4.
43. John Dewey, *The School and Society* (Chicago: University of Chicago Press, 1907), pp. 47–48.
44. Thornton Mustard, "The New Programme of Studies," *Educational Courier* (October, 1937), pp. 8–10.
45. Donalda Dickie, "Education Via the Enterprise: The Task of Education," *The School* (September, 1940), p. 3.

2 Child Study as an Aspect of Progressive Education

Concentrating on the Individual Student

Human childhood, lasting about twenty years, is a period of exploration, not of crystallization . . . Youth is a period for making mistakes. We learn by making mistakes, and the human being is more fortunate than lower animals in having the longest period in which to make mistakes with more or less impunity.[1]

Herbert Kliebard identified the child study (or, developmentalist) interest group as a distinct entity within the progressive movement, which held an almost romantic faith in nature and in the unfolding stages of child development. The developmentalists, he argues, traced their "ancestry as far back as Comenius, most prominently to Rousseau, and then to the work of Pestalozzi and Froebel."[2] Pedagogically, the orientation, which was geared principally towards the scientific and psychological understanding of human development, had as a central principle of striving "first of all to keep out of nature's way."[3]

In the United States, G. Stanley Hall, the key figure of the early child study movement, stressed two aims. The first was "nothing less than to create an exacting science of human nature . . . secondly, he dreamed of revolutionizing the practice of schooling by firmly rooting school practice in science rather than in speculation and tradition."[4] The self-proclaimed "Darwin of the mind,"[5] Hall aggressively campaigned for the "drive to make psychology into an experimentally based science" and used this as leverage to gain leadership of "what were regarded as the progressive forces in American Education."[6] His emphases on health, activity, nature, and laboratory study were reflected, as we shall see, in the Ontario child study scene.

It is prudent to reiterate that Kliebard's approach to the developmentalist interest group differs from that of both David Labaree's and David Tyack's. These two historians described two variations of progressive educators: the pedagogically and the administratively oriented reformers. According to Labaree, "the heart of the tale is the struggle for control of American education in the early twentieth century between two factions of the movement for progressive education."[7] The developmentalists, both Tyack and Labaree argued, were scattered amongst those two groups. They were principally concerned, in other words, with either classroom practice or with administrative matters: "the conservative and social efficiency groups fit more or less within the administrative category and the liberal and social reconstructionist groups fit roughly within the pedagogical, with child development straddling the two."[8]

This chapter examines the educationally progressive interest in the individual's biological and psychological aspects. The child, here, is principally seen from an organic lens and interpreted in naturalistic rhetoric. In the words of the General Secretary for the Big Brother Movement in Toronto:

> Teachers should be more like gardeners than mechanics. Knowledge of the forces of life adjustment show us where we may improve the conditions for growth. As a gardener gives water, controls insect pests, lifts a stone around which a young plant is trying to grow, so should we study each of your young charges, plan and direct them for the very best that life has to offer.[9]

Child study, stressing mental hygiene, social adjustment, and developmental psychology, then, offered a distinct orientation towards the individual; it represents a *kind* of progressive education in Ontario. "The main emphasis in the technique we have to offer will, therefore, be upon prevention rather than cure, to grasp certain principles, which can be utilized to facilitate the normal adjustment process,"[10] explained Drs. Blatz and Bott.[11]

An actual stress on physical health and well-being as a preventative measure was a related matter, promoted by parents, school medical inspectors, and the province's Division of Child Hygiene.[12] "Proper growth and development" of children depended upon sanitary schools, clean homes, appropriate levels of exercise, and a healthy diet.[13] "Progress" in terms of health promotion would require widespread "propaganda" and instruction regarding the resources and benefits of preventive medicine.[14] On an administrative level, the child health lobby targeted four domains: more intensive local health administration, the expenditure of more money on health work, better cooperation from the medical profession, and increased efforts in health education.[15] "Physiological needs," Frederick Minkler from the Ontario College of Education noted, "—health and happiness—are the first concern of the progressive school."[16]

Again, "progressive education demands a most comprehensive programme of health at all times. Indeed, the progressive programme was seen as necessarily including mental hygiene,"[17] emphasizing, above all, concern for prevention. The initial emphasis of the movement in regards to mental health was humanitarian care and treatment, but "the emphasis passed to questions of the prevention of mental disorders, and hence to the formulation of a conception of positive mental health and the provision of adequate mental health programmes in all phases of community work and service."[18] In terms of education and classroom practice, "early efforts of mental hygiene workers were directed towards analytical and critical surveys of educational practices"[19] including classroom organization, punishment, and rewards. By the last few years of the interwar period, it was commonly acknowledged that rather than motivate students by marks and rewards, intrinsic interest in the school work itself could be regarded as the key to preventative discipline. To disseminate the message that educationists needed to "regard the child as of greater importance than the subject matter"[20] in order to foster positive learning experiences, a number of initiatives were undertaken; these included the launching of a magazine for teachers, *Understanding the Child* under the sponsorship of the National Committees for Mental Hygiene in Canada and in the United States, as well as the publication of a manual for teachers and a bibliographic service to assist "teachers in understanding the nature of child development and the problems frequently encountered in the classroom."[21]

Certainly, the promotion of physical health, welfare, and prevention of disease affected school programming (health and physical education), school construction (open yards and playgrounds for exercise out of doors) and administration (school health and medical inspections).[22] In fact, Howard Ferguson, Minister of Education in 1929 boldly announced his "conviction that the year 1930 will take its place in the list of years marked by progressive measures in education on account of the change in inspection alone."[23] The increased concern for inspection and health examinations was a persistent theme throughout the interwar period, including campaigns by organizations like the Canadian Dental Hygiene Council, the Health League of Canada, and the Ontario Society for Crippled Children for healthy teeth and medical check-ups, and against such diseases as typhoid, diphtheria, and tuberculosis.[24]

The child study movement's supporters in Ontario, as in the United States, emphatically supported physical exercise, while extolling the virtues of nature. Often, like G. Stanley Hall, this writing was imbued with romantic or mystical qualities.[25] Nature mattered. Child study advocates argued that the health of individual children depended on being outdoors or on breathing fresh, clean air.[26] Advances in scheduling of timetables in the province's schools freed up more time for "so-called homework to be done in school," in part, so that children could get outside more for play and for exercise.[27] The "question of the physical well-being of the pupils in relation to their mental alertness is an important one, and teachers are wisely giving considerable attention to it," reported the province's High School Inspectors in 1932, while pointing to extra-curricular activities, auditoria, gymnasia, physical education classes, and the provision of "spacious and well-lighted rooms" as evidence of progress in the domains of environmental psychology and physical health.[28]

Health education was increasingly "regarded as a major concern of general education . . . of national importance."[29] The aim of physical and health education was intended to be the development of habits and attitudes that would form the basis of a healthy life. Bad habits left unchecked in children would be "repeated in the adult population, and the daily press carries discussions of items . . . based upon inadequacy of health knowledge."[30] The Deputy Minister of Health secured in 1930 from the Rockefeller Foundation traveling scholarship funds for the Director of Health Education, who would visit teacher training institutions and schools to lecture on health education. Further, a joint committee reporting by the Ministers of Health and Education was struck in 1936 in order to, among other tasks, develop a manual on health teaching, distribute health teaching aids to educators, and find ways to provide added instruction in secondary schools on health education.[31]

The child study lobby, in other words, provoked substantial changes in Ontario's schools, but what follows here shall be an examination of the child study movement's rhetoric regarding the three terrains contested by educational progressives: the relationship of schools to society, the emphasis on active learning construction, and the provisions for individual learners in the schools. While the rhetoric of the child study movement is infused in the progressive arguments throughout the various educational journals circulating in Ontario, in the Department of Education's Annual Reports, and in the reformed course of studies, particular emphasis will be given to the writing of William (Bill) E. Blatz. Blatz, developmental psychologist and pioneer of child study in Canada, was the founding director of the Institute of Child Study and the figurehead of the movement.[32]

His progressive vision for schooling in Ontario was not only particularly influential in the province, it demonstrates how hotly contested the educational progressive movement was. It has been said that he "guided the hands that rocked the cradles of a whole generation of Canadian children. From the mid-1920s to the mid-1950s Dr. Blatz was Canada's own world-renowned expert on raising children."[33] Despite all overlap and similarity with other interest groups, Blatz, a prolific writer and speaker, was intent on carving out a distinct terrain—institutionally, methodologically, and rhetorically—for child study. While he was the most renowned developmental psychologist in Ontario, organizations of teachers and parents, including the International Kindergarten Union, the "Association of Childhood Education, and the Toronto Kindergarten Union, further promoted the professional development of educators and the "progressive training and supervision of students" to meet the needs of both "the Canadian-born and the immigrant child."[34]

Yet, the child study movement was not contained to initiatives directed by the Institute of Child Study. By 1932, child study advocates had decided that there was strength in consolidation. "Mergers are the order of the day," announced the newly founded Association for Childhood Education through the *Educational Research Bulletin,* "even educational institutions are joining to form larger more powerful combines."[35] The International Kindergarten

Union disbanded in order to join the Association; the National Council of Primary Education also merged its identity with this larger entity in order to create a more formidable union that could join interests of the nursery school, the kindergarten, and the primary teacher. The first reason stated by the Conferring Committee made this last point emphatically: "The psychology of the child for the years from two to eight reveals common needs that indicate the necessity of the closest possible integration of the work of nursery school, kindergarten, and primary grades."[36] The organization explicitly stated that its greater size could make its attacks on educational policy more potent, "promoting progressive nursery school, kindergarten, and primary work throughout this country."[37] The progressive elements involved articulations of the importance of developmental psychology and child study in reforming school organization.

Schools and Society

The Institute of Child Study became a symbol for the child study lobby. It represented the potential of the *institute* to be a "co-ordinating and unifying force" within educational structures.[38] The Institute of Child Study was heralded as an experiment in higher education that concentrated on studying human development apart from any "rigid departmental or faculty pattern."[39] Whereas the increasing specialization of training and the demands for professional education had led to the isolation of subjects from each other and from actual life, the Institute represented a form of learning that was organic and whole. So, if education is to "preserve its real character, if it is to be an organism and not merely and organization, we must constantly be on our guard against the forces which tend to destroy its unity."[40] The progressive teacher "of the new school thinks in terms of pupil development and pupil growth. Further, she conceives of her task as the all-round development of her pupils."[41]

The child study advocates, then, were concerned with bridging studies of the normal development of children's physical, social, emotional, and intellectual capacities.[42] Similarly, they espoused belief that "theory and practice in child guidance must be continually dovetailed."[43] Its plan was to interrelate the laboratory study and investigation of developmental psychology with actual teaching and learning. The hypotheses and theory derived by the researchers would be applied to the Nursery School. From that teaching and learning context, questions would be derived to be reflected upon. The laboratory school became the "testing ground for theory and principle" and it translated "these into methods of practice,"[44] which were then passed on to the Parent Education Division for further discussion and distribution throughout the province.

Just as the school activities, as we shall see below, were correlated around learning experiences relating to actual life (rather than being taught as compartmentalized disciplines or subjects), the school and the home were seen as necessarily linked in the lives of children. The Home and School Movement, founded in Toronto in 1916 before becoming a provincial organization in 1919, was one of the primary advocates for the belief that "the home and the school are the two vital factors in the training of the child towards an adequate citizenship."[45] Its main interest centered on parent education and the child study movement, both of which shall be discussed in depth later. Both were particularly interested in the early, formative years of human life, when, according to one account, "the twig is bent, the sight is taken and the race of life has begun."[46]

What is important to note is that the bridging of education and society, for the child study advocates, meant bringing the home-house and the school-house into an actively cooperative arrangement, whereby the experiences of teachers and parents, as well as researchers and practitioners, could be shared and developed. The movement proclaimed itself an "essentially fundamental and progressive educational one," wherein teachers in schools and parents at home, representing "two great forces may work together harmoniously and in a spirit of intelligent co-operation."[47] Educational progress could only come with greater understanding of the development and nature of childhood. Such knowledge would help solve many educational problems as well as raise the standard of home and school life for learners. The Home and School Movement lobbyists stimulated change in how parents and teachers interacted throughout the province. The extent of social services offered in the school, along with the quick and steady rise of "parents' days [and] social meetings . . . increased the influence of the schools in the community."[48]

One main theme consistently espoused in the child study literature relates to the problem of *adjustment*. If individuals are "the centre of all intelligence, of initiative, of discovery, of creative thinking, and therefore the pivot of social progress," how were they to relate to others and to society?[49] The adjustment envisioned was a necessarily iterative one in which the child learned how to adjust behaviours in order to "fit into the existing social system. But even the arrival of the infant soon produces a considerable readjustment in any home."[50] Child study advocates saw adjustment as being both a social and individual requirement: "we seek to adjust both social institutions and individuals to ideals which are simultaneously reconstructed and reformed."[51] The integrity and security of that individual needed to be preserved. At the same time, each person had a responsibility to make the world a better place. Child study's concentration on the relationship between the individual and society

> Is progressive and democratic in that the evolution of methods of training is based not on a standard of mere adjustment to the world as it is but rather on the contribution an individual can make to a better world in which the welfare of the individual is fundamental.[52]

William E. Blatz's "concept of *security* has a solid foundation not only in knowledge of human nature but in a clear conception of what is good."[53] A *secure* child was one who could face the uncertainty and mutability of the world courageously and with self-reliance and confidence. Security theory, frequently referred to as "the gospel according to Blatz," gave primacy to the individual's right to make decisions. It contextualized those decisions in social and educational contexts that would dictate the consequences of those decisions (for which the individual was ultimately responsible).[54]

The security of a person throughout the lifespan of his or her development, argued developmental psychologists and child study advocates, following Blatz, sprung from the individual's "state of mind, not a state of economy nor the state of a nation nor the state of international affairs nor the state of any class in a country. Security rests with the individual."[55] In light of other progressive voices arguing that the individual's primary responsibility was the maintenance of democratic order or the preservation of industrial state of affairs, Blatz believed that the learner's natural and normal development was of prime importance and that other concerns were amongst the "great many factors, which interfere with his development."[56] "*Independent* security emerges" only when the child takes responsibility for his or her own behaviour and is not dependent of external demands or agencies for the inculcation of concepts or virtues.[57] Teachers were advised to give primacy to the individual without necessarily abdicating all responsibility for guidance: "lasting values in life come only from what people do of their own accord. You therefore leave everything you dare to the pupils' initiative."[58] A child must "emancipate himself, first from parental dependence" and then from social coercion in order to be truly responsible for his or her future actions and grow into an "adult who lives and thinks progressively."[59]

The concern for studying the child and the development of human drives or instincts was inseparable, in other words, from a concern for adjustment in and development of society. The child was seen as inseparable from life, which was organic, coordinated, inclusive, and yet changeable. This understanding is implicated in the child study advocates' stress on education being an active adjustment to the ever-changing conditions of life. "Education should be a training in not only how to make a living but a training in how to live," explained a medical doctor in regards to the health program in schools; each human, so "that he might live, has always been forced to adjust to his environment."[60] The school was regarded as "a community where the child dwells during his preparation for adult living."[61] Relating the needs of society "with respect to cleanliness, food, rest, and relaxation" to instruction in schools was a crucial part of recognizing "the importance of integrating the entire life of the school child in a programme of physical, mental, emotional, and moral health."[62]

Further, progress in the realm of understanding individual human development could facilitate social progress, as humans were the building blocks of society; knowledge of human development was also the promotion of social knowledge. This idea, still in its infancy, inspired much hope:

> It has been a fascinating experience to have participated in the beginning of a movement which is wholly constructive; in which the future has far more hope of fulfillment than the past. A good deal of the land has been cleared. There has been some rather erratic plowing; some seeds have fallen, *fortunately*, on barren ground; some few will survive to bring forth fruit. The next quarter century will be a period of consolidation for the great harvest of the succeeding centuries.[63]

Child study promised "to revolutionize existing ideas or to improve current practices."[64] Education that could coordinate its activities with knowledge of individual development would be "progressive" in the sense that it would be more in tune with the organic nature of life and the realities of existence in the "early decades of the twentieth century."[65]

These realities were intimately related to the social regeneration and reorientation following the First World War. Despite the fact that the first Child Study laboratory in the United States had been set up at the State University of Iowa in 1911, and that "private foundations that had long been concerned with the advancement of science in regard to human development, medicine, and education," the beginning of the interwar period also heralded the beginnings of child study in Ontario.[66] It began with social and educational programs for returning soldiers who had suffered physical and psychological traumas. The re-training, re-habilitation, and re-education of veterans for re-adjustment to society coordinated the efforts of medical doctors, social workers, educationists, and psychologists.

The postwar period in Canada, as in all countries involved in the Great War, was one of great disequilibrium and returning to "normalcy" was an explicit, if lofty, aim. More than 650,000 Canadians served in the armed forces and more than a tenth of these, about 68,000 lost their lives.[67] Approximately as many Canadians returned from the war with mental and physical traumas that made any seamless resumption of life difficult, if not impossible. These wounded survivors entered a vastly changed society. Many have been referred to as the "lost generation."[68] Although "more professional and 'scientific' than ever, medicine, psychology, and related social services were ill-prepared to ease their civilian readjustment."[69]

The work of these services "intensified the interest in psychological studies that dealt not only with war veterans but with the development of individuals longitudinally through the whole span of life;" it also demonstrated a need for personnel educated and trained in the concentration on needs of children whose home life had been disrupted by the war.[70] Having contributed to the rehabilitation programs for veterans at the University of Toronto in a medical capacity, William Blatz, future Founding Director of the Institute of Child Study—a union of the Windy Ridge and St. George School projects—saw the broader implications of education plans that were oriented towards the realities of social life. He "readily grasped the idea, first, that these same principles should apply in the dealing with persons through all stages of life, and second, that the early stages of this learning process should be the most basic period for study and application."[71]

Blatz completed his medical degree soon afterwards at the University of Toronto before pursuing his Ph.D. at the University of Chicago. "Thus my decision was strengthened," he reminisced in one of his last publications, "to find out exactly what psychology had to offer in the understanding of human beings."[72] At Chicago, Blatz encountered the pedagogy of John Dewey, who had ten years there establishing a laboratory school and developing "some of the progressive ideas that still influence today's education."[73] Psychologists at Chicago were reaching for functionalist explanations for what, how, and why people act as they do.[74] The functionalist concentration considered human adjustment to the social and physical environments as principal tasks.[75] The "interest in habit formation was a legacy from William James, passed through Dewey . . . to Carr and thence to Blatz, who applied it as the basis of his earliest ideas in child raising."[76] So it was that the seeds for Blatz's progressive pedagogical ideas were sown before he began his educational career in Ontario:

> Chicago had a profound influence on Blatz, an influence that showed in his work throughout his life. Apart from the obvious interest in progressive education based on an understanding of a child's needs and the emphasis on individual problem solving, Blatz was perfectly in tune with Dewey's pragmatic approach to testing ideas by their consequences.[77]

As Blatz would later explain concerning his emphasis on applied psychology and education, "the task here before us is neither new nor easy; in fact it is extremely complicated, but extremely practical."[78]

When he returned to Toronto, in 1925, private foundations and the university had coordinated their efforts to make child study a legitimate, institutionalized, field of research. The Canadian National Committee for Mental Hygiene, along with a grant from the Laura Spelman Rockefeller Memorial Fund, had secured a five-year commitment to the new discipline, setting up the St. George School for Child Study under Blatz. The school coordinated two very significant subdivisions, "each with a separate staff under the Director," a Nursery Laboratory School for the study and education of children, and a Parent Education Division.[79] This was in a context where, generally speaking, "postwar reformist discourses focused on potential: science, technology, and a sanctified motherhood would join forces to give life to a shiny new world."[80] "In the days of the little red schoolhouse," a teacher might have assumed to have knowledge of the classroom, whereas progressive and "modern ideas have given the teacher a less dominating role and have caused her to develop a philosophy that recognizes the personality" and natural development of children.[81]

Alongside the St. George's School, Blatz pursued a second educational project at Windy Ridge Day School, which had been "founded by a group of parents in 1926 as a co-operative kindergarten, and later they had added some grades and hired some teachers from the United States to make it into a progressive school."[82] These parents included many of Toronto's wealthiest, including the Gundys, Gooderhams, Burtons, and Eatons. In 1930, Blatz was named director of the school and renamed it "from the Progressive School to Windy Ridge."[83] This project established Blatz's reputation as a pioneering progressive educator, and he immediately "set to work with a will to advance the ideas of Dewey—ideas that he had admired from his Chicago days. He applied and adapted his experience with nursery education to the curriculum of older children. The ideas flowed."[84]

Parent education—beginning with the cooperation of parents at Windy Ridge and the Parent Education Division of the St. George School—was to become a major tool for correlating the study of children with society. It involved both sending out literature to parents across the province and bringing in parents to the Institute for discussion, instruction, and debate.[85] Between 1925 and 1940, 114 publications by the staff of the Institute of Child Study were recorded, including such titles as *Honesty* (1925), *The Importance of Failure* (1934), *How Children Learn* (1937), and *Social Work and Mr. Citizen* (1940).[86] Parent education was a relatively new, but flourishing field both in the United States and in Canada due to "an interest in learning formal parenting skills since before the turn of the century when groups of mothers first met to discuss the work of G. Stanley Hall."[87] The increased interest in child study amongst parents led to the establishment of Mothers' Clubs, Mothers' Congresses, Mothers' Reading Circles, Art Leagues, and Young Mother's groups all across the North American continent.[88]

The child study movement in Ontario tapped into the growing concern for parental education to support its cause; moreover, it advocated the creed that the study of human development in isolation from community participation was a hollow pursuit. "The chief aim of education," Blatz believed, "is the development of human values which will contribute to, rather than make demands upon, community life."[89] The emphasis upon coordination of society and schools was purposeful, and the work of the parent education department was, in a way, pioneering:

> There was no precedent to determine how it could best serve in its community; no public demand to be met; no niche in the professional world into which it fitted. The field of child study itself was relatively new when the Institute was organized; indeed it was one of the first four centres of child study on this continent. Thus the story of the Institute's growth is a single thread in the broader history of child study.[90]

Part of the mandate for parent education was consistent with an overarching of child study, the dovetailing of theory and practice; it involved balancing the "practical problems of child upbringing" with the more general theory of human development being developed at the laboratory school.[91] The attitude at the Institute to this balance was that "ideas lead to research study, thence to theories of child development followed by the formation of principles of child guidance, and finally result in suggested methods of care, education and management."[92] The problem-hypothesis-investigation-theory circuit was an ongoing one, which was to both inform and be informed by parents.

From the beginning, then, the child study movement saw that progress in terms of psychologists understanding of human development would be useless without tangible connections to social life outside of the laboratory. This social life involved the schools and, of course, the home. Therefore, as Frances Johnson noted: "from the beginning it has been assumed that only with intelligent parent co-operation can optimum results in child training be achieved."[93] This cooperation was particularly imperative because modernity and social progress had immensely complicated life. To keep apace and to deal with the complexity of social realities, schools and parents needed to work together. The child study would be an aid to parenthood, not a substitute for it:

> Most parents are resolved to do the best they can for their children. A conscientious parent, intent upon the task of rearing children, must be a moralist, psychologist, educator, philosopher, theologian, physician, nurse, and dietitian, in addition to being a father or mother. This has been for generations the task set for themselves by intelligent, well-intentioned parents. Unassisted, parents of today, knowing what he does about the possibilities of all these contributing factors to his child's future, would be undertaking an almost hopeless task.[94]

Teachers and parents, just like schools and homes, were of no use to each other if they operated under isolationist principles. In the *modern* and progressive world, "isolationism in the home," it was argued, was "as out of date as isolationism in world politics . . . to create a happy home is not enough."[95] Nor did it suffice to have progressive schools and unified theories of child development that did not affect social life or "lead parents to think objectively and adapt principles to the child's experience so that the child may emerge a responsible adult."[96] A new, dynamic, and progressive philosophy of education, required, also "a new philosophy of home a family life, set in this context of world affairs."[97] Social relationships are first learned within the home and in the context of family, which provide "an interesting field for the study of social interactions."[98]

According to Blatz, the normative question concerning the direction of progressive education is for society—the parents, in particular—to make. This question amounts to a responsibility and a duty for the physical and mental development of children. At the first meeting of Parent Education Classes, it was customary for Blatz to "ask the members . . . to write down 'what they wish their children to be.'"[99] "Since the dawn of history," Blatz continued, parents, "gazing upon their offspring . . . have projected their thoughts into the future."[100] The responsibility of pursuing these thoughts and facilitating both individual and social progress "may be delegated to teachers and to others for a time, but never given over wholly."[101] There were natural limits to the roles that schools could, or ought to, provide. Blatz argued: "The state, in a democracy, can never assume this prerogative" on its own.[102] Child study specialists, schools, and government "may *suggest* standards, may *arrange* safeguards, may *institute* plans, but these are only to assist the parents, never to replace them."[103] Parents, like children, needed to actively construct a vision of progress and pursue learning commensurate with that vision.

Individualized Instruction

Samuel Laycock argued that educationists aspire "to see their pupils *grow* . . . to see them develop wholesome personalities."[104] This necessitated abandonment of the no longer satisfactory attempts "to confine their efforts to the development of skills in "the three R's," or to cramming their children with facts."[105] A concern for the individual learner, the "whole child," necessitated acceptance of "the philosophy of modern progressive education that the task of the school is to develop persons" along physical, social, emotional, and intellectual terms.[106] The child was a whole person; he or she would with proper guidance develop into a healthy and well-adjusted qualitatively different kind of person—an adult.

In order to make provisions for the learning and development of individual learners, the child study advocates first concentrated on the "normal child." Like a statistical norm, this abstraction was a baseline that allowed the researchers and educationists to accommodate for and tend to the individual, who necessarily deviated from this norm and had a "unique, very distinct individuality."[107] Historians have observed that the "normalization" of children was predominately motivated by the "postwar desire to define and promote 'normalcy'" and was "infused with the spirit of industry, with its demands for regularity, repetition, scheduling, systematization, discipline, and productivity."[108] Yet, the ideal of scientific management was not an overarching principle; developmentalists, led by Blatz, made certain to differentiate their aims from the interests of social efficiency advocates and of industry:

> Today the nursery school must be looked upon neither as a charitable institution, nor as an expedient for increasing the number of mothers in industry, nor as a convenience for parents, but rather as a necessary adjunct to child care and training. . . . The nursery school if for neither the privileged nor the underprivileged, but for both. The nursery school is not a luxury, it is a necessity.[109]

Blatz, also and repeatedly, made clear that the modern and progressive child study movement in education was to be considered as distinct from the social meliorist interests.

This is because the first nursery schools, like the rehabilitation programs for traumatized First World War veterans, had been developed in line with social welfare initiatives. The nursery school in Ontario began as "a crèche for small children of working mothers; a place of instruction for very young retarded and feeble-minded children; a laboratory for research in child development; and an educational unit for children under kindergarten age."[110] But the modern and progressive nursery was neither a charitable institution, nor "an expedient for increasing the number of mothers in industry, nor as a convenience for parents, but rather as a necessary adjunct to child care and training."[111] This "training" was not dictated by industry or by charity, in other words, it was subject to individual will, inclination, and interest.

The search for the "normal" child, then (at least insofar as the child study interests were concerned), was rooted in the medical and scientific roots of the new discipline. It was the reaching for some standard of human development. As such, "child behaviour became a legitimate area of medical investigation just as child psychology was developing as a distinct field, and there was much inter-borrowing between medicine and psychology."[112] The developing child unfolded naturally in terms of stages that could be, at least in the abstract, studied and used to generate educational principles. These would involve three aspects:

> Therapeutics, prophylaxis, and promotion. There is undoubtedly some overlapping.
>
> *Therapeutics*, the curing of the sick, is an art.
>
> *Prophylaxis*, or the prevention of disease, is, however, an application of scientific discoveries to human welfare.
>
> *Promotion* of physical health is one of the latest interests in human welfare. To undertake a promotion program, a standard must be approved.[113]

Stages of human development spanned all of human life, each with its characteristic problems. Successful adjustment during each stage was regarded as the best way of guaranteeing successful adjustment in the next. Roughly, these demarcations included the pre-school period, the school age, adolescence, marriage, parenthood, middle life, and old age.[114]

Without such standards and without some understanding of how a "normal" child or person developed, educational progress would be, the developmentalists argued, impossible. There would be no criteria to use for achievement measurement or understanding development. It made little sense to measure progress in terms of day-to-day growth, because such increments were too small to detect growth. Instead, "*norms* of development, ascertained for different cross-section levels . . . are therefore a kind of shorthand for recording the differences observed at such levels . . . at the age of three months, of six months, a year, and so forth."[115]

Whereas "traditional methods of formal education" had proven both slow and inadequate, the study of human development and the application of psychology to schools demonstrated the promise of progress.[116] Child study better fulfill the province's obligation towards rearing children consistent with "modern ideas of pacifism and social rights."[117] This obligation was a particularly pressing one in "civilized countries" like Canada so that "all children should have an equal opportunity for the *best* education. There can be no justification for an educational program, which reserves special opportunities for special groups."[118] Blatz drew, as many school districts do today, a clear distinction between equality and equity. The principle of "'Equal opportunity for all,' should take into consideration the phenomenon of individual differences. This does not mean the 'same education for all,' as is frequently implied."[119] Blatz was appealing for what we now refer to as the aim of differentiated instruction—the need for schools to adapt the educational program to the skills and potentialities of the child. Progressive schools "in most progressive communities, there are special classes for the mentally deficient, the hard-of-hearing, the blind, and the physically handicapped, but these are not the only types under consideration here."[120]

What separates the developmentalist position of child study advocates like William Blatz from that of other progressive educationists at the time who were arguing for testing or streaming of children as a means of securing efficient employment in industry is the underlying reason for undertaking such initiatives. The developmentalists were not concerned with the efficient management and maintenance of the social and economic orders; they were interested in the happiness and psychological well-being of individuals in life. This is more than just semantics—and certainly a great number of social efficiency advocates couched their arguments for streaming children into industrial niche in the rhetoric of democracy—for it amounts to a fundamental difference in how the purposes of education were conceived.

According to one conception, the individual had a responsibility to maintain the order and proper functioning of society (particularly in economic and industrial terms). According to another, the individual had a primary responsibility to his or herself but was *also* to society. The Institute of Child Study prided itself on being the "first organization to achieve a truly child-centered philosophy—a philosophy which considers the child's experiences first and cultural expectations second."[121] This philosophy was, by no means, uncontroversial; media reports sometimes swirled with critiques of the Institute's faith in child study, as the following comment makes clear:

> For years the city teacup telegraph had been causing eyebrows to rise at the scandalous goings-on among the younger set at 98 St. George Street. The impression was abroad that those four-year-olds were really making the bric-a-brac fly in an orgy of self-activity. No one could safely

enter those premises, we thought, unless doubly protected in the armour of the spirit and a suit of medieval form.[122]

A fear of unfettered freedom was always in balance, was always the counterpoint to a resistance to give the impression that discipline and conformity were dominant notes in the school.

The issue of auxiliary, or special, education[123] is situated at this apparent nexus between the child study and social efficiency interests. The rhetoric surrounding the auxiliary classes was ripe with contradictions intermingling faith in and concern for the individual child's autonomy with eugenicist and industrial/utilitarian classifications. The recognition of some difference between a child's actual development and the *normal* learner's is one that has already been considered from the child study perspective. Particularly interesting to note is how that *normal* child is derived or understood. The students in auxiliary classes were identified by means of Intelligence Quotient (IQ) tests and their *mental* age was statistically demonstrated to be below the actual, or normal school age. Meanwhile, as we have seen, data collection at the progressive laboratory schools under the direction of William Blatz was largely a matter of observation and anecdotal reporting. Normal stages of development were general benchmarks for achievement that could guide instruction; there was no necessary discussion of age.

That is not to say that Blatz or any of the child study progressives were averse to intelligence testing. In fact, Blatz actually constructed an instrument for measuring parental intelligence, which addressed the "duties and responsibilities of *fathers* to their children."[124] Yet, the way that it was to be used and administered is indicative of the underlying difference in approach towards progressive testing and schooling. The test was "devised to stimulate thinking on the part of the fathers rather than to test their "knowledge about" children."[125] If it succeeded in stimulating discussion, Blatz believed, it would be justified. Parents would score the test themselves and the knowledge garnered from its results would help them develop as parents. No one was expected "to rate 100%, of course, for no one is a perfect parent."[126]

In other words, it was how an intelligence quotient score was used that mattered and not that it was actually administered. An IQ "reported by a trained psychologist is a far more reliable index to a child's educational needs than numerals marked on a written examination or the dictum of a single teacher's judgment," Blatz conceded.[127] Nevertheless, each of those three sources needed to be combined for a balanced view of the child's educational development. It was inconceivable for Blatz to suggest that intelligence quotients "should be the only criterion for later selection and educational opportunities."[128] Blatz saw the differentiated instruction and accommodations for struggling learners as progress. Schools had to be organized somehow, but "the arrangements for separating school children into groups should not make any early assignment irrevocable."[129] In an uncertain and mutable world, rigid or narrowly conceived testing methods and streaming of populations made little sense. However, for schools to be progressive, they would have to concentrate on individual learners' "accomplishments, interests, and capacities."[130]

The child study advocates' way of negotiating individual and the social needs led to very nuanced understandings of responsibility, compliance, and individualism. Blatz's security theory is a good example of the developmentalists' concentration on balancing societal norms and individual interests. Children needed to be given choice and allowed to pursue their own interests; they were responsible, however, for the choices that they made:

> At every moment of experience the individual must select a specific action pattern. From the beginning of his life there are situations in which a child may be *taught* to choose and accept the consequences of his choice
>
> Responsibility may be defined as the habit of choosing, and accepting the consequences of the choice of behavior.[131]

Further, no individual could function securely and confidently in an environment that was not suitable to his or her strengths and interests. While this has implications for industry and economy, the emphasis is on the individual within the broader network of structures. For this reason, Blatz argued: "A great deal of the unhappiness in the world is caused by the discrepancy—plus or minus—that may exist between the individual's potentialities and the requirements of his adult vocation."[132] Even in the high schools, argued D. S. Woods, Dean of the Faculty of Education at the University of Manitoba, educational programs ought to address "immediate, rather than the future needs of each individual."[133] Woods stated that a "new school outlook, conditioned by individual needs," was on the horizon.[134] In fact, this outlook was clearly "emerging and gradually winning sanction from public opinion and school teacher alike."[135]

Blatz noted that the focus on the individual student had to be tempered by or negotiated by the micro and macro social contexts in which students lived. There were, he noted "certain arbitrary and artificial rules of conduct" to which every person had to conform in order to "feel comfortable in the community."[136] Yet, at the same time, any plan of discipline or form of education needed to "provide an opportunity for non-conformity, also within approved limits."[137] Blind obedience to rules and dictates would ultimately lead to unhealthy resentment in the learner. Questioning regulations was necessary. In fact, the interest in promoting a progressive education was a necessary thing, for the members of any community, in this case the educational one, needed "opportunities . . . to alter the rules or laws to fit changing conditions and ideas."[138]

The child study movement and the increasing importance of developmental psychology had changed the dominant ideas on schooling and forced a progressive outlook on schools. This outlook was distinct from other ideas regarding progress because, in part, of its eschewing of the driving forces towards conformity. Progressive schools contested a "traditional" model, which Ontario teacher Fern Holland characterized as involved in promoting "the kind of education that consists in memorizing facts and dates and theories and delighting the teacher by showing that one has done the memorizing."[139] Such learning fostered too much compliance. Individuals needed to develop and retain their own "personalities and identities in spite of all the organized machinery of education could do to them, in an effort to make them conform to a general pattern."[140] Human development, whether industrial or ideological, was thus framed as a fundamental challenge for schools to consider.

Active Learning

The practical experience of the several early advocates for child study, such as William Blatz, was rooted in the rehabilitation programs for traumatized and wounded soldiers returning from the First World War. The principles of child study were, in large part:

> An outgrowth of the re-education methods and psychological principles that were developed for the muscle-function training of crippled veterans at the University of Toronto during 1916–1919, namely, that patient must not remain passive and psychologically dependent, but must become a participant learner, if he is to master his present limitations and thus be able to meet later situations with confidence.[141]

With respect to the study and education of children, the stage of the learner's development and the complexity of the tasks involved were simpler, yet the idea the emphasis on self-direction and on progressive achievement of small goals was the same. The educational motivation was a forward-looking one. In the case of the veteran, rehabilitation was slow progression towards some, often physical, objective. In the case of the child, the objective was the successful adjustment into the next *normal* stage of human development.

The nursery and laboratory schools that were integral parts of child study. Dorothy Millichamp and Margaret Fletcher described these as "outgrowths" of early work in developmental psychology, which "came into being at the same time when the human sciences were beginning to speculate upon the significance of childhood for human adjustment."[142] These allowed researchers to develop developmental hypotheses of real children as they actively engaged in pedagogically progressive activities with their peers. In constructing such environments, Blatz appealed to his experiences at Chicago and the model Laboratory School developed there by Dewey. According to Blatz's biographer, Jocelyn Motyer Raymond, the children "worked on a loom and baked bread. There were school trips to the harbour, to art galleries, and to the train station. A newspaper was launched, and Blatz hired a French teacher."[143] These ideas, commonplace today, were a far cry from the seatwork and rote learning characterizing the "traditional" classrooms in Toronto at the time.

Child study advocates promoted the idea that special techniques needed to be developed for dealing with each age as it continued to evolve through life. Each stage of development had its own pedagogical activities and challenges to tackle. Blatz wrote that regardless of age, children needed to enjoy at school "an atmosphere of freedom, self-dependence, regulated habits, adequate social contacts—and of serenity. The latter is the sine qua non of any well-conducted Nursery School."[144] The history of any child's learning needed to be a story of "increasing knowledge and deepening understanding . . . giving rise to growing wisdom in his management."[145] The basis and foundation of all learning, however, was experience.

Educational experiences were all about the active engagement with situations that promoted and provoked new knowledge. The child, in order to adjust to his or her stage of development and grow into the next phase, "has everything to learn."[146] The total personality of children developed only as he or she learned, which meant, of course, as they encountered developmentally appropriate experiences with which they could interact. Action was primary, whereas "the content of learning remained a matter of secondary consideration."[147] The best learning experiences were responsive to the developmental level of each child, which involved consideration of appropriate skills, interests, and habits.[148]

The goal of the teacher, then, is to understand the child's stage of development. With that knowledge in mind, an evolving educational plan needed to be constructed which could guide the learning experiences of children to ever-increasing stages of complexity. In this context, the learning situation "was defined simply but dynamically as the response whereby the child seeks to meet his needs within his environment."[149] Success in a learning situation requires effort and reflection on the part of the student. The teacher's role, on the other hand, is to provide situations for the learner to actively engage with and overcome.

The learning context, a laboratory school, was necessary a social environment. Studying child behaviour and human development in isolated individuals would be a meaningless enterprise because it would have no functional use in society. In fact, one of the main domains of study was the sociability and social activity of children. "Early observations of the social activity of young children yielded little helpful information about the process of social development," Blatz argued.[150] The observations did, however, verify the researchers' hypothesis that sociability, like other behaviours, is developmental and associated with experience.

Social development, the developmentalists concluded, was a matter of active learning and experience. The teacher, having set out an experiential program of learning for the students, then needed to observe these carefully and assume a supervisory role with a minimum of interference in the learner's free social play. The principle, first enunciated by Blatz, was to "let the children solve their own social problems."[151]

The experiential curriculum advocated for by developmentalists was largely directed towards the establishment and development of satisfactory social habits, which were accompanied by "experience in responsibility; of a pattern of "interested" activity; of a co-operative approach to other children; and of emotional stability through expression and control."[152] Successful experiences in solving problems, social or otherwise, would lead the child to develop confidence that solutions can be attained through the exercise of intelligent judgments. Further, children's active learning encouraged responsibility for their own behaviour and, in cooperative situations, practice working with peers to overcome obstacles.

Oftentimes, the solutions to problems required use of the "'art of nonconformity,' or so-called creative endeavour."[153] When children experienced working cooperatively, or how to "conform", they learned to believe in others; when children learned to be creative and independent, however, or to "nonconform," they learned to believe in themselves.[154] The teacher, as guide, had to develop both independence and dependence through a balance of cooperative and independent learning experiences. This demanded of the adult a dynamic rather than a purely passive role, involving, principally the discovery of ways to support and encourage the child to choose goals and to support various ways for their accomplishment.

For the child study movement, then, what was important was "not to instruct, but to provoke."[155] Blatz, a prolific public speaker and debater, was a provocative figure himself, who tried to engage his speakers in ways that would make them contradict him and express alternative views. In short, he "stimulated thought, while his listeners responded by silently but actively contradicting his statements, supporting his thesis by extending his examples, interpreting or misinterpreting his implications, rebutting his arguments, and appreciating or depreciating his wit."[156] His aim in public speaking was consistent with his goals in advocating an active curriculum, namely, the content of instruction is far less important than the action and reflection that it inspires. A student could be "irritated, challenged, baffled, enthralled, or inspired," but he or she should never "be bored."[157]

"School-age 'problems,'" Blatz explained, "arise from uninspiring teachers, unimaginative curricula, and rigid standards of progress. Superimposed on this quagmire is an astonishing intellectual snobbishness."[158] This perspective is one that he expressed frequently, particularly when espousing his functionalist doctrine: "All knowledge is useful only if it is used. How it is used is another matter. Unused knowledge does not lie fallow like a field resting; it just disappears."[159]

Without practical work and activity in the classroom, children would find learning what Gordon Young, one Ontario teacher, termed "meaningless, dull, and tiresome" schooling experiences.[160] Nothing "hinders progress," Young continued, more than boredom with school work.[161] Thus educators were charged with fostering enthusiasm and excitement for learning, which would allow students to explore ideas and experiment with tasks, leading them to test their abilities and interests. The outcome of such school work would be greater fulfillment in the lives of students, who could translate their efforts naturally into social and vocational life beyond, and after, schooling.[162] Ultimately, this emphasis on active learning was best expressed by Dr. C. M. Hincks, one of Blatz's first and strongest supporters at the University of Toronto, who (in actual reference to health) wrote that it "depends upon what you do—not upon what you know."[163]

According to Donalda Dickie " 'progressive' type" of school, then, was described as one that would develop the gifts and personality of each individual within a context acknowledging: "The individual cannot be isolated from the group."[164] The so-called "enterprise school," emphasizing learning activities to develop "co-operative achievement of a social purpose" was promoted as a progressive model of education with active learning at its core.[165] Enterprises, which were comprehensive learning situations akin to today's school projects, involved the analysis and identification of a social problem, guided discovery of some solution, and the cooperative application of that solution. The subject matter of a well-chosen enterprise was interesting to the particular developmental stage of any given group of learners, and provide "a good range of contacts, experiences, and activities" leading to future inquiry.[166] The activities correlated distinct subjects, blending the academic distinction between topics of study and related to the actual lives of students. In this regard, the topic and scope of scope of school work was intended to be intimately related to the actual development of learners' abilities and involve students in active inquiry.

Notes

1. William Blatz, *Understanding the Young Child* (New York: William Morrow and Company, 1944), pp. 16–17.
2. Herbert M. Kliebard, "Keeping Out of Nature's Way: The Rise and Fall of Child-Study as the Basis for the Curriculum, 1880–1905," in *Forging the American Curriculum: Essays in Curriculum History and Theory* (New York: Routledge, 1992), p. 51.
3. G. Stanley Hall, "Ideal School Based on Child Study," *Journal of Proceedings and Addresses of the National Education Association* (1901), pp. 474–488.
4. Kliebard, "Keeping Out of Nature's Way," p. 56.
5. G. Stanley Hall, *Adolescence* (New York: Appleton, 1904), p. 496.
6. Kliebard, "Keeping Out of Nature's Way," pp. 58–59.
7. David F. Labaree, "Progressivism, Schools and Schools of Education: An American Romance," *Paedagogica Historica* 41, nos. 1 and 2 (February, 2005), p. 276.
8. Ibid., p. 279.
9. Frank T. Sharpe, "What Would I Do If I Left School Under Present Conditions?" *The Canadian School Journal* (October, 1933), p. 355.
10. William E. Blatz and Helen MacMurchy Bott, *Parents and the Pre-School Child* (Toronto: J. M. Dent and Sons Ltd., 1928), p. v.
11. Sources for the history of the mental hygiene movement include Neil Sutherland, *Children in English-Canadian Society: Framing the Twentieth Century*

Consensus (Toronto: University of Toronto Press, 1976); Norman Dain, *Clifford W. Beers: Advocate for the Insane* (Pittsburgh: University of Pittsburgh Press, 1980); Wilbur Cross, *Twenty-Five Years After: Sidelights on the Mental Hygiene Movement and Its Founders* (New York: Doubleday, 1934); Nina Ridenour, *Mental Health in the United States: A Fifty Year History* (Cambridge: Harvard University Press, 1961).

12. J. T. Phair, "School Medical Inspection," *The Canadian School Journal* (September, 1932), p. 295.

13. Viola Henderson, "The School Child's Lunch," *The Canadian School Journal* (September, 1932), p. 296.

14. D. R. McClenahan, "Observations on Rural Public Health Work in Ontario," *The Canadian School Journal* (December, 1932), p. 314.

15. Ibid., pp. 313–314.

16. Frederick Minkler, "The Progressive Education Conferences in Hamilton and Windsor," *The School* (January, 1939), p. 379.

17. Ibid.

18. W. Line and J.D.M. Griffin, "Education and Mental Hygiene," *The School* (April, 1937), pp. 647–648.

19. Ibid., p. 648.

20. Ibid., p. 649.

21. Ibid.

22. Margaret S. Gould, "Education at the Expense of Health," *The Canadian School Journal* (October, 1934), p. 343.

23. Howard Ferguson, *Report of the Minister of Education, Province of Ontario for the Year 1929* (Toronto: The Legislative Assembly of Ontario), p. vii.

24. "Editorial Notes: Health Education," *The School* (March, 1936), pp. 550–551.

25. Kliebard, "Keeping Out of Nature's Way," p. 55.

26. Cynthia Commachio, *The Infinite Bonds of Family: Domesticity in Canada, 1850–1940* (Toronto: University of Toronto Press, 1999).

27. George S. Henry, *Report of the Minister of Education for the Year 1932* (Toronto: The Legislative Assembly of Ontario), p. vii.

28. R. W. Anglin, A. G. Hooper, A. G. Husband, W. A. Jennings, and I. M. Levan, "Report of the High School Inspectors," in *Report of the Minster of Education for the Year 1932* (Toronto: The Queen's Printer for Ontario, 1933), p. 16.

29. John T. Phair, Mary Power, and Robert H. Roberts, "An Experiment in Health Teaching in the Schools of Ontario," *The School* (September, 1936), p. 6.

30. Ibid.

31. Ibid., pp. 6–12.

32. The institute or centre idea was consistent with educationally progressive faith in correlation and integration. As an interdisciplinary centre for study, it was designed to bring different academic areas, including medicine, psychology, education, and sociology together for research on problems of mutual interest—in this case, children and human development.

33. Jocelyn Motyer Raymond, *The Nursery World of Dr. Blatz* (Toronto: University of Toronto Press, 1991), p. ix.

34. "Canadian Federation of Kindergarten, Nursery School, and Kindergarten-Primary Department," *The Canadian School Journal* (January, 1932), p. 97.

35. "Association for Childhood Education," *The Canadian School Journal* (January, 1932), p. 39.

36. Ibid.

37. Ibid.

38. Mary L. Northway, "Foreword," in Karl S. Bernhardt, Margaret I. Fletcher, Frances L. Johnson, Dorothy A. Millichamp and Mary L. Northway (Eds.), *Twenty-Five Years of Child Study: The Development of the Programme and*

Review of the Research at the Institute of Child Study, University of Toronto, 1926–1951 (Toronto: University of Toronto Press, 1951), p. viii.

39. Ibid., p. vii.
40. Ibid.
41. S. R. Laycock, "Extra-Curricular Activities in the Modern School," *The School* (October, 1941), p. 93.
42. Ibid., pp. 93–97.
43. Dorothy A. Millichamp, "The Organization of the Institute and Its Place in the Community," *Twenty-Five Years of Child Study: The Development of the Programme and Review of the Research at the Institute of Child Study, 1926–1951* (Toronto: University of Toronto Press, 1951), p. 19.
44. Ibid.
45. "The Home and School Movement," *The Canadian School Journal* (March, 1933), p. 85.
46. "The Editor's Page," *The Canadian School Journal* (January, 1935), p. 3.
47. "The Home and School Movement," p. 85.
48. Albert H. Leake, "Report of the Inspector of Manual Training and Household Science," *Annual Report of the Minister of Education, 1932*, p. 56.
49. W. C. Keirstead, "Indoctrination in Education," *The School* (May, 1940), p. 743.
50. Ibid., p. 744.
51. Ibid., p. 745.
52. K. S. Berhardt, "A Prophet Not Without Honour: The Contribution of William E. Blatz to Child Study," *Twenty-Five Years of Child Study*, p. 6.
53. Ibid., p. 7.
54. Blatz, *Human Security*, pp. 103–111.
55. W. E. Blatz, "Security," *The School* (February, 1941), p. 499.
56. Ibid.
57. Ibid., p. 501, italics in original text.
58. "Editorial: A Dilemma," *The School* (April, 1941), p. 683.
59. Blatz, "Security," p. 503.
60. Chas A. Alexander, "The Teacher's Place in the New Health Programme," *The Canadian School Journal* (January, 1935), p. 28.
61. R. H. Roberts, "Health Education," *The School* (October, 1935), p. 99.
62. Ibid., pp. 98–99.
63. William E. Blatz, *Bulletin of the Institute, No. 50* (Toronto: Institute of Child Study, 1951), cited in E. A. Bott, "Founding of the Institute of Child Study," *Twenty-Five Years of Child Study*, p. 13.
64. Bott, "Founding of the Institute of Child Study," p. 14.
65. Ibid.
66. Ibid., p. 15.
67. Commachio, *The Infinite Bonds of Family*, p. 70.
68. Ibid.
69. Ibid.
70. Bott, "Founding of the Institute of Child Study," p. 15.
71. Ibid., p. 16.
72. Blatz, *Human Security*, p. 3.
73. Raymond, *The Nursery World of Dr. Blatz*, p. 19.
74. Robert S. Woodworth and Mary R. Sheehan, *Contemporary Schools of Psychology* (New York: Ronald Press, 1964), p. 15.
75. "James Rowland Angell," in Carl Murchison (Ed.), *A History of Psychology in Autobiography* (Worcester, MA: Clark University Press, 1936), p. 23.
76. Raymond, *The Nursery World of Dr. Blatz*, p. 20.
77. Ibid., p. 22.

78. Blatz and Bott, *Parents and the Pre-School Child*, p. v.
79. Bott, "Founding of the Institute of Child Study," p. 15.
80. Commachio, *The Infinite Bonds of Family*, p. 92.
81. Rae Chittick, "The Place of the Teacher in a Mental Hygiene Programme," *The School* (March, 1940), p. 568.
82. Raymond, *The Nursery World of Dr. Blatz*, p. 89.
83. Ibid., p. 90.
84. Ibid.
85. Blatz published articles in a number of popular magazines for parents and mothers, in particular *Chatelaine, Childhood Education, Progressive Education, Child Welfare, Child Study Magazine*. Government agencies were also involved in literature distribution, most notably the "Little Blue Books" Mothers' Series written by Dr. Helen MacMurchy and published by the Dominion of Canada's Department of Health in 1923. Titles included *The Canadian Mother's Book, How to Take Care of the Children* and *How to Take Care of the Mother*.
86. "List of Publications by the Staff of the Institute of Child Study," *William E. Blatz Fonds*, Thomas Fisher Rare Book Library, Box 28, Number 1.
87. Raymond, *The Nursery World of Dr. Blatz*, p. 28.
88. William Scott, "What Child Study Has Done for the Teaching World, Dominion Educational Association Proceedings (1901)," in Douglas Lawr and Robert Gidney (Eds.), *Educating Canadians: A Documentary History of Public Education* (Toronto: Van Nostrand Reinhold, 1973), p. 185.
89. W. E. Blatz, *Hostages to Peace: Parents and the Children of Democracy* (New York: William Morrow and Company, 1940), p. 169.
90. Millichamp, "The Organization of the Institute and Its Place in the Community," p. 18.
91. Ibid., p. 19.
92. Ibid., pp. 19–20.
93. Frances L. Johnson, "Activities and Aims of Parent Education," *Twenty-Five Years of Child Study*, p. 39.
94. W. E. Blatz, *Understanding the Young Child* (New York: William Morrow and Company, 1944), p. 255.
95. Johnson, "Activities and Aims of Parent Education," p. 44.
96. Ibid., pp. 43–44.
97. Ibid., p. 44.
98. Helen Bott, *Bulletin of the Institute*, No. 50 (Toronto: Institute of Child Study, 1951), cited in Johnson, "Activities and Aims of Parent Education," p. 44.
99. Blatz, *Understanding the Young Child*, p. 2.
100. Ibid., p. 1.
101. Ibid., p. 8.
102. Ibid., p. 9.
103. Ibid.
104. S. R. Laycock, "The Diagnostic Approach to Problems of Pupil Adjustment," *The School* (February, 1939), p. 461, italics in original.
105. Ibid.
106. Ibid.
107. Minkler, "The Progressive Education Conferences at Hamilton and Windsor," p. 378.
108. Commacchio, *The Infinite Bonds of Family*, pp. 96–97.
109. Blatz, *Understanding the Young Child*, p. 240.
110. Ibid.
111. Ibid.
112. Commacchio, *The Infinite Bonds of Family*, p. 134.

113. Ibid., p. 256.
114. Blatz and MacMurchy Bott, *Parents and the Pre-School Child*, p. 15.
115. Ibid., p. 16.
116. Ibid., p. 258.
117. Ibid., p. 134.
118. Ibid., p. 233, italics in original text.
119. Ibid.
120. Ibid., p. 234.
121. Dorothy A. Millichamp and Margaret I. Fletcher, "Goals and Growth of Nursery Education," *Twenty-Five Years of Child Study*, p. 27.
122. "The Institute of Child Study: The School Reporter Takes a Chance," *The School* (April, 1941), p. 692.
123. Today, we would refer to "auxiliary education" as "special education."
124. William E. Blatz and Helen MacMurchy Bott, "An Intelligence Test for Fathers," *William E. Blatz Fonds*, Thomas Fisher Rare Book Library, Box 1, Number 43, p. 1, emphasis in original.
125. "William E. Blatz to G. J. Hecht, Personal Correspondence, April 2, 1930," *William E. Blatz Fonds*, Thomas Fisher Rare Book Library, Box 1, Number 43.
126. Blatz and MacMurchy Bott, "An Intelligence Test for Fathers," p. 1.
127. Blatz, *Understanding the Young Child*, p. 234.
128. Ibid.
129. Ibid.
130. Ibid.
131. Ibid., p. 187, italics in original text.
132. Ibid., p. 234.
133. D. S. Woods, "Trends in the High School Curriculum: General Courses and University Requirements," *The School* (April, 1940), p. 658.
134. Ibid.
135. Ibid.
136. Blatz, *Understanding the Young Child*, p. 57.
137. Ibid.
138. Ibid.
139. Fern Holland, "To-morrow," *The Canadian School Journal* (September, 1934), p. 316.
140. Ibid.
141. Bott, "Founding of the Institute of Child Study," pp. 15–16.
142. Millichamp and Fletcher, "Goals and Growth of Nursery Education," *Twenty-Five Years of Child Study*, p. 26.
143. Raymond, *The Nursery World of Dr. Blatz*, p. 90.
144. W. E. Blatz, *University of Toronto Monthly: June* (Toronto: University of Toronto, 1926).
145. Millichamp and Fletcher, "Goals and Growth of Nursery Education," p. 28.
146. Ibid., p. 29.
147. Ibid.
148. T. A. Brough, "Revising the Curriculum in British Columbia," *The School* (October, 1936), pp. 101–105.
149. Ibid., p. 30.
150. Ibid., p. 31.
151. Ibid., p. 32.
152. Ibid., p. 33.
153. Ibid., p. 35.
154. Ibid.
155. Northway, "Preface," in Blatz, *Human Security*, p. ix.
156. Ibid.

157. Ibid., p. x.
158. Blatz, *Human Security*, p. 6.
159. Ibid., p. 8.
160. Gordon Young, "Optional Subjects," *The Canadian School Journal* (December, 1933), p. 427.
161. Ibid.
162. See, for instance, J. D. Griffin, "News and Comments," *The Canadian School Journal* (December, 1933), p. 446.
163. C. M. Hincks, "Do You Know? Do You Believe?" *The Canadian School Journal* (February, 1934), p. 55.
164. Donalda Dickie, "Education Via the Enterprise: The Task of Education," *The School* (September, 1940), p. 4.
165. Ibid.
166. Ibid.

3 Social Efficiency and Social Change

Schools, Workplaces, and the Alignment With the World to Come

> It is the school's task to discover—and to encourage—those natural powers and tendencies of the child which have proven to be useful to society, and are therefore approved by society . . . The psycho-analysis of the individual is seldom the starting point in a modern guidance scheme; the provision of trustworthy information about employment opportunities is usually the start.[1]

Advocates for social efficiency as a driving force for progressive education pulled no punches:

> Idealists, humanists, radicals, and labour unions have been one in the spending of the taxpayers' money, the result being our huge overhead of today. Appraisal of our position calls for action. The advice of trained business economists should be obtained and followed before our educational costs get out of hand.[2]

Elimination of educational waste, whether defined as individual student strengths, educational costs, or curricular congestion, could be facilitated by the principles of efficient management promoted by and perfected by industry. "Education should be considered a business," and its costs could be reduced without impairing its standards.[3] Such progress, particularly when involving a close correlation between schooling and business or industry, was imperative. The diagnosing and management of individual intelligence, aptitudes, and abilities would benefit individual learner's adjustment to life and would further economic stability. "So-called idealists, humanists, radicals, and labour unions were one in spending difficulty paid taxes they might be aroused . . . today the child is everything but a legalized ward of the state."[4] This ward, a "pupil product," needed to be found and trained for "useful employment."[5]

Society's needs and structures had altered. Planning and management of schools was as required in educational matters as it was in industry, where progress was largely controlled, directed, and efficient. In educational contexts, it was important to help "pupils whose characters are developing, not only to make it possible for each student to discover his proper place in the educational scheme, but to direct him into it as soon as his aptitudes and capacities are known with reasonable accuracy (and that is surprisingly early)."[6] Efficiency, the hallmark of success in industrial and business contexts, could be promoted in schools. Progress in education required such efficiency and demanded such management. It was, from this viewpoint, evident that Canada had entered

> the scientific age. In government, industry, and even retail business, experimentation, study, and planning are the order of the day. The merchant who relies solely on his own 'intuition' faces extinction. So in education—the day of haphazard idiosyncrasies in the little red schoolhouse is gone.[7]

By the end of the interwar period, the efficiency movement as a progressive interest and lobby had achieved significant gains. From the 11 reports submitted by Departments of Education to provincial governments across Canada, including Newfoundland, in 1940, marked tendencies were clear. According to the editors of *The School*, "educational progress" was most predominately marked by two domains: "vocational and practical subjects [and] trades schools."[8] "Gaining ground" were the issues of larger administrative units and educational and vocational guidance.[9] The war effort accounted for much of the concern for practicality and industrial need.

"Of the varied and sometimes frenetic responses to industrialism and to the consequent transformation of American social institutions," Herbert Kliebard has noted, "there was one that emerged clearly dominant both as a social ideal and as an educational doctrine. It was social efficiency."[10] The Canadian context was unique, but in the face of massive social and industrial change, the doctrine was consistently maintained on the promise of social stability and control. During the interwar years, at least four economic recessions—not to mention the crippling and humbling years of the Depression—made the economic and social circumstances of life unstable, to say the least. In such a context, "when the influence of certain social institutions such as family and church were believed to be in a state of dangerous decline, the functions of schooling had to be restructured radically in order to take up the slack."[11]

Apart from the direct and precise social management advocated for by social philosophers and sociologists such as Edward A. Ross, efficiency itself was central.[12] Here, the principal figure was Frederick Winslow Taylor, the so-called father of scientific management," who promoted the scientific management of factories for the promotion of increased production at decreased cost, as well as for better regulation and order.[13] At the core of his model of scientific management, explained in his hallmark 1911 text, *Principles of Scientific Management*, was a five-step process or specifying and sequencing the tasks required for the completion of a goal These included identification of a model or aim, breaking down and categorizing operations, assessing the time required to reach objectives, eliminating wasteful or useful movements, and ordering the processes to promote speed and efficiency.[14]

Taylor's language and conceptual apparatus for the promotion of progress and the commitment to reform was readily applied to education in the twentieth century across the North American context, targeting the seeming inefficiency of schools and the disconnect between industrial order and educational disarray. Schools could be approached, managed, and controlled scientifically, as industry was. By 1934, the dominant note of progressivism espoused at the Ontario Educational Association annual convention hearkened heavily to the scientific management principles of Taylorism:

> The school is a great industrial institution, turning out a natural product the value of which is determined by the usefulness and service of the finished product. To achieve a well graded product, each grade functioning in its proper sphere, is a responsibility which must be borne by the employer and employee.[15]

Scientific management of schools promoted, at the core level, what the *Canadian School Journal* described as a "more orderly and less contentious society. It was a reform that political conservatives could easily embrace."[16] Progressive and efficient schools would reform education and improve social order but, as others have demonstrated, the elimination of waste has heavily eugenicist elements in educational contexts where the raw material was, principally, children.[17] The principles of evolution and Social Darwinism—often envisioning progress as Herbert Spencer might have, as the survival of the fittest in a laissez-faire environment—were implicated in the debates surrounding social efficiency and scientific management of schools.[18] Elimination of educational waste, concern for productivity and maintenance of the industrial order, and streaming of children according to the results of mental testing have been criticized as means of sorting society and maintaining unjust social or class divisions.[19] These criticisms aside, the social efficiency movement, a progressive force in the reform rhetoric of interwar Ontario, shall be considered as the other progressives were, in light of their commitment to relating school and society, to individualizing instruction, and to building active learning experiences.

The Schools and Society

Schools, under the influence of the efficiency advocates and the pressures of industry had ceased during the interwar period to be "merely educational institutions . . . The teaching of the 'three R's' has now been extended to embrace the specialized training of boys and girls for every sphere of commercial, industrial, and professional activity."[20] The schools were to be the foundations of future society and progress, particularly its industrial and economic development. The cultivation of skills, habits, and character conducive to such gains were the responsibility of a progressive educational system.

Diagnosing the demands of industry and the fulfilling the interests of the business community were, for the social efficiency advocates, the foundations of such sound and forward-looking systems. Making society a "better place in which to make a living," explained Alberta's Supervisor of Schools, G. Fred McNally, "means that education should be required to justify itself by the return of definitely recognizable dividends."[21] The meanings of terms such as "democracy" and the construction of "peaceful and successful" communities were infused with an overriding concern for industry. "Community needs," noted an article in *The School*, were "based to a large extent upon the business principles that supply food, clothing, shelter and other essentials to all those who live within the community."[22]

The schools needed to play an important role in the commercial, technical, and industrial progress of society. As such, they needed, within the framework of business courses and in the general curriculum, to reinforce such ideas as business ethics, transportation, retail practice, banking, savings bank accounts, contracts, buying a house, furnishing a house, thrift and investments, public utilities, taxation, travel information, communication, remittances, and the duties of a club treasurer."[23] This is all implicated in the trend towards increased specialization and streaming in education, which was justified in the *Canadian School Journal* on the grounds that "every large business institution demands highly trained and educated men, each an expert or specialist in his own particular field."[24]

Progressive schools helped students, through training in such practical activities and subjects relating to financial and industrial well-being, to "make a place for themselves in the community."[25] Educational institutions could then offer practical and, consequently, meaningful views of community life to students and facilitate their adjustment to and progress in normal life. In the words of one secondary school teacher: "business has had a most pronounced relation to Secondary schools."[26] The author implied that a business model of specialization and financial stringency was required in education to promote progress and increased efficiency. This entailed cutting of costs and streamlining of educational programs; it would require that "frills of education must be done away with at once and the curriculum adjusted so that the education received in our secondary schools will be such that a boy or girl will be properly fitted" to a position in business, industry, and, more generally, life.[27] The more practical and the more efficient, the less wasteful—and the more progressive—subjects were considered to be.

The question that this section, like the entire study, undertakes is not a normative one, which is to say that it does not ask if there is anything morally or ethically wrong with a province's schools considering progress in terms of the efficient training for, orienting towards, and bridging of work environments for citizens. A more prudent question in this context would ask what makes the social efficiency viewpoint different from that called, earlier, developmentalist. Certainly, no one would argue—in present-day Ontario, as in its past—that employability and employment are insignificant things. However, the role that schools and society should take in the guidance and preparation of individual learners was certainly up for debate. Guidance programs, commonplace today in Ontario's secondary schools, were important progressive developments in the province's schooling during the interwar period, whose role in brokering between the students and the industrial order cannot be understated. Certainly, from the perspective of efficient social management, they denoted progress in the movement to align individual ability with society's need.

The "educational objectives, so far as business is concerned, should be set with a view of preparing those who will enter the ranks of industry and business enterprise for their future work," explained the President of the Robert Simpson Company Limited to trustees, ratepayers, parents, and teachers.[28] A modern society efficiently manipulated every "convenience or utensil for every occasion and to suit every condition of life."[29] Just as the "earth's resources were progressively tapped to the world of trading" and led to the great industrial age, the resources of society—namely, children— could be marshaled to efficiently manage future progress and evolution.[30]

"At a time when Canadian education is in the throes of a revolution," exclaimed Dalhousie University Professor of Education B. A. Fletcher at a meeting of the Canada and Newfoundland Education Association, "it is important to reaffirm the *fundamental principles* upon which all education should rest."[31] This revolution, as we have seen, was a challenge to the so-called old regime, which was portrayed as subjugating individual ability to the demands of content and curriculum. The social efficiency interests, at one extreme, interpreted intelligence and mental testing in ways that set ceilings on the perceived potential of each learner. These ceilings justified classification of students, which imposed limits upon their perceived abilities and future career paths. There were, in other words, very clear "limitations to the mind of a child."[32] At another end of the spectrum was a moderate approach to vocational guidance and mental testing that was informed by developmental psychology. As discussed earlier in relation to William Blatz, emphases were placed on mental hygiene and the promotion of mental health.[33]

Vocational guidance was not the exclusive domain of efficiency advocates and subject to only the results of intelligence testing. Perspectives that were more moderate emerged largely in response to the over-use and consequent misuse of single measures such as I.Q. for the classification of students into curricular programs and into career paths. Such views made explicit arguments in the teacher journals to counter the (well-founded) notion that mental testing was a dominant diagnostic tool for the cultivation of social efficiency:

> The best practices in vocational guidance are of value, and that some tests are sufficiently reliable to be very valuable aids in analyzing the

individual, but that vocational guidance based on test scores alone or school marks alone, or on a combination of these, is decidedly unsound.[34]

School psychologists, new entities in the schools, whose perspectives on educational progress had much more in common with the child study advocates than with the efficiency interests, were promoters of a more balanced view of assessment to inform school guidance.

"A school psychologist," explained Florence Dunlop, Psychologist for the public schools in Ottawa, "is not merely a 'mental tester', but a fully qualified person who aims to apply the findings of psychological research to school and classroom situations."[35] The I.Q., from the developmentalist perspective was considered a very important factor, but not the penultimate one. It had to be supplemented, she continued, by "pertinent data on health, developmental history, physical condition, personality, mental age, rate of mental maturation, school progress, special abilities and disabilities, interests, desires, home and community conditions."[36]

The point worth stressing here is that vocational guidance programs, whether at their core informed by holistic assessment strategies or by strictly mental testing were, at their core, concerned with the efficient progress of students through the educational system and into a seemingly appropriate employment. Expressed differently, the idea of efficient progress through school into industry and work was, at its core, built on belief that there was a niche for each person; informed guidance from trained experts facilitated this progress to a fitting and successful economic life. As such, the underlying principle in progressive education

> is training in the principles of citizenship, enabling the boy or girl to find his or her proper groove in order that they may make a worth-while contribution to the day and generation in which they are privileged to live.[37]

In 1932, Ontario's Minister of Public Welfare, William Martin, noted that the "discovery of special abilities dictates the need for manual and mental training to go hand in hand."[38] Such was the dependence on *objective* mental testing examinations and the extent of collaboration envisaged for school systems and industrial niches. Increasingly organized, centralized, and tied to the College for Technical Teachers, vocational guidance in Ontario expanded steadily.

This was particularly evident after the formation of an Ontario Vocational Guidance Association in 1934, which organized in order to study the principles, problems, and techniques of guidance.[39] The increasing emphasis on vocational guidance in the early and mid-1930s as the meeting point for educationists makes great sense in the context of the Depression, where employment was not only difficult to earn and maintain, it was often unhappy and insufficient. In the words of Agnus Macrae, quoted in

The School, the place "in which a man spends one-half of his waking hours should, if possible, be given as he can perform successfully and happily is a proposition which receives the very ready assent of persons of sane mind."[40]

In other words, a progressive society could by no means expect its citizens to spend their days toiling away at work that is both unsatisfactory and unfitting to their natures. "Work which interests" noted Charles Burton, "is the greatest elixir which can be found for good health and happiness."[41] Guidance, and an understanding of the intellectual limits of individual natural ability, could not only help promote efficient transitions, they could lessen the mental stress caused by the displeasure of some work-personality mismatch.[42]

"Yet in Ontario," argued educationist Marion Goode in advocating for the expansion of guidance programs throughout the province:

> Guidance of young people into vocations to which they well be well and happily suited is, like the much-talked-of development of personality, still in the vague realms of experimentation, and is left largely to chance. We concentrate on mass production, and leave the individual to develop as best he may, and drift into whatever field comes along at the moment.[43]

Therefore, there should be efficient management and control of employment. People are, the argument followed, suited to particular tasks. It is important enough to fit people where they belong than to let things just happen. The same kinds of energies that we use in industry and in the mass-production at factories needs to be concentrated on individual job placement.

"An unwise choice of work may be dangerous, not only to mental health but also to moral character," argued Cyril Burt in his rather widely-cited and voluminous tome on the role youth and delinquency.[44] Marion Goode used Burt's study to contend that "there is, a very definite relationship between uncongenial employment and juvenile delinquency."[45] Such delinquency, she argued requires the resources of the state and constitutes a waste of human potential. "The maladjusted worker," she continued, "must often fail to achieve material prosperity; and such failure, in addition to aggravating his mental discontent, may affect his physical well-being and that of his dependents, who, indeed, may suffer in more ways than one."[46] Such aggravation comes at a cost. The language employed is clearly appropriated from business and industry.

The inefficiency of schools, also, then, was framed with respect to its relationship to teacher education and hiring practices. Parents, alone, were deemed unable to provide the necessary guidance. They lacked expertise and were, consequently too ignorant; professionals in social science and in guidance, however, marshalling information garnered from intelligence tests and from other data sources, were better qualified to serve as guides and advisors. The methods of scientific analysis and careful study of industrial needs were prerequisites for the guidance of youth:

> As for the great mass of working-class parents, it is obvious that limitations of knowledge, experience and ability must often make it impossible for them to offer wise counsel. In many cases they accept chance opportunities without regard to their suitability; and in many cases they allow children who deserve a better fate to drift into blind-alley occupations, more heedful of immediate gain than of future advancement.[47]

In the past, industry, economy, and society were different, it was argued. The world had changed and matters of society, industry, and education were deemed infinitely more complex and, consequently, requiring scientific management, control, and management. Industry was perceived as the leader and exemplar of this increased complication. It was constantly evolving and increasing in efficiency, and education needed to follow suit. "We are in the midst of an industrial revolution," proclaimed George Rogers, Chief Director of Education under both George S. Henry and Duncan McArthur,

> the tendency toward rapid production is so great that an industrial plan is good for only a few years. New machines are coming out every day and old ones being scrapped . . . what is true of machinery may also be true for courses.[48]

As the economic and industrial order of life grew more complicated, and as urbanization had fostered a distance between vocation and individual, past models of apprenticeship and training no longer held sway. So-called "modern high school students," Rogers proclaimed, were members of a more progressive and, consequently, "different society than were the students of several decades ago. With the shift of population to urban centres, there has arisen a variety of problems in the areas of health, safety, leisure-time activities, and other aspects of group living."[49]

Within this increasingly complex and complicated social structure, "boys and girls should be taught to view the prospect of work with greater care, and with the hope of developing in themselves the capacity to choose wisely their most suitable employment" so that they would not "drift carelessly into unsuitable work."[50] This sentiment was not one limited to the Ontario context; a circular sent out by the Office of Education of the U.S. Department of the Interior, for example, aimed to draw readers attention to "the fact that as a civilization increases in complexity, schooling is more necessary than ever before . . . To-day we live in a complex civilization which it is necessary to understand in order to be adjust to it. Schools are the means by which"[51] that adjustment happens. Employment choices were not easy to make in complex environments; specialization, study, and guidance were, in this context, necessary.

Further, "small industries are being absorbed by large scale industries so that there are no longer abundant opportunities for young people to get their vocational education as apprentices on the job itself. Change in industry"[52] had wrought considerable changes on family life and organization. Fewer people worked and spent the majority of their day in the home. Parents, consequently, had less time with their children. The influence of religious institutions and the church also lessened. Because of these changes,

> the education and stability which youth formerly received form industry, the home, and the church, must now be supplied by some other institution if young people are to make successful adjustments to our present complex society. Much of this responsibility rests on the school.[53]

These ideas are not new ones in the realm of progressive education. In fact, they are at the core of John Dewey's educational philosophy and are indicative of the tendency to provide very shallow readings and narrow interpretations of Dewey's writings. *The School and Society*, in particular, an extremely influential text that was required reading for teacher candidates in Ontario, was interpreted in ways that reinforced the ideas of efficiency and scientific management. Interpretations of Dewey's ideas, explicitly or implicitly stated, abounded throughout the interwar period and continued through to the end of the context studied. Even during the Second World War, the trend continued:

> It is evident from the position taken by Dewey and many others that the responsibility of the school extends beyond the classroom, that an effective secondary school must not only know the child and his individual needs, interests, and abilities, but that the school must also know and utilize all the factors and influences of the environment in which the child lives. 'Not only is the totality of the pupil to be considered in each learning situation, but the totality of the environment enters as an important element.'[54]

Here, at the point where the integration of the individual into the total environment of society as understood in industrial or economic terms, was where the need for vocational guidance was rooted.[55]

"Much failure," explained Marion Goode, who was a frequent contributor to *The School*, "it is found, could be averted by preparing the pupil for both present and future adjustment."[56] Goode's argument equivocated the adjustment of the individual to the surrounding circumstances with success. This adjustment involved fitting into an established place, which was conducive to the individual. The primacy of the established order, from this viewpoint, is apparent. Goode cited Gertrude Hildreth, the author of a text on psychological services for school-aged children to elaborate on her argument:

> As far as present adjustment is concerned, we should expect at least nine results: (1) Fewer pupils dropping out of school. (2) Increase in standard of scholarship because more people will be working to their full capacity. (3) Increase in pupil successes; fewer subject failures and withdrawals. (4) Better morale in the student body, as the pupils realize the friendly interest of the school in their present and future progress. (5) Reduction in the amount of retardation and probably an increase in percentage of acceleration. (6) Fewer misfits because of unwise selection of courses of study. (7) Better all-round school life. (8) Fewer personality or social maladjustments. (9) Pupils who are better able to guide themselves. As far as future adjustment is concerned, we may look for: (1) Fewer misfits in higher institutions of learning. (2) Less waste in getting and keeping a permanent job. (3) Fewer occupation misfits. (4) Better citizenship in the community."[57]

The rhetoric of industrial and economic efficiency barely needs noting. The individual, in their adjustments to work, needed to develop a positive attitude, if not submissive, attitude. In opposition to what the child study progressives would deem most important—namely, the tailoring of studies to the individual interests and stages of development of students—it was professed by the school in an editorial on the subject of "work" that: "of all the annoying, worse than impertinent, discouraging, baffling, and infuriating words to the human ear, there are none to compare with 'I doan wanna.' "[58] It continued:

> capacity for liking is such that if you want always to do what you like, you soon won't like anything that you want . . . who started this idea that people have to do only what they like to do?[59]

The need for cultivating efficiency and industry superseded that of individual interest. The editorial persisted that "no one should be taught even indirectly that he has a right to do only what he likes, he has a right to be obliged to do only what is needed."[60]

Efficient schools were depicted as requiring students to think about their vocational opportunities and their potential fit within the larger structure. "Modern industrial and progressive conditions have made vocational guidance imperative," announced an editorial feature in *The Canadian School Journal*, and "without proper guidance both the individual and the state may suffer loss."[61] The most efficient means of building a relationship between individual students' strengths and the economic or industrial needs of society would involve industrial and civic leaders to guide children through the school system and into a proper place in industry and in society. The article conjures images of business owners and corporate leaders serving as mentors to children—boys, in particular—and steering their course of studies towards meaningful and productive employment.[62]

Placement services began in Ontario's secondary schools in the 1930s working in close collaboration with school guidance programs.[63] According to the description offered by a teacher at Scarborough Collegiate Institute, students were assigned to vocational centres, spending "several entire school days there, being excused from regular classes."[64] In these centres, they would receive "demonstrations of different office machines such as the Dictaphone, Multigraph, Comptometer, etc."[65] Part of the goal here involved showing students various occupations that existed nationally and internationally and promoting study of economy and of industry. Placement officers taught students—the "prospective employee"—how to prepare for and conduct himself during an interview.[66] This was detailed work that even involved learning how to fill out applications forms neatly and correctly.[67] Because transference of skills was not deemed always easy or possible, comprehensive lists of questions actually used by large corporate firms of different types were provided so that students could practice interview and application skills.[68] Placement officers in the school supervised and interpreted the data collection, facilitating and, often, arranging for interviews in industry.

Very few students, relative to the overall population, were destined to university or to normal school studies. The idea that Ontario's public education should have its methods and curricula dictated to by post-secondary institutions was irreconcilable with social reality and need: "To meet the situation, the vocational school has endeavoured to provide courses which are helpful to the larger group who seek employment in industry, trade or commerce," explained W.H.H. Green, "and at the same time to give all possible assistance to those who hope to go to university for engineering, household science, or commerce."[69] Green's 1941 manuscript, *The Development of the Vocational School to Meet Community Needs*, was a further elaboration on the idea that Ontario's schools could only be progressive if they were reorganized in order to correlate more efficiently to the modern industrial order.

By 1942, a supplement on "Educational Progress in Canada" proudly proclaimed, "the vocational schools have become the training ground for a vast industrial army."[70] The militaristic rhetoric is, of course, common throughout the educational progressive rhetoric during the Second World War, but the particular interpretation of progress is more interesting for this chapter. The vocational schools were deemed instruments of social progress because they increased the efficiency with which schools could turn students into functioning parts of the industrial order. Increased funding to the schools was predicated upon this objective. Much "progress is reflected in the upward tendency in the amount of the annual legislative grants which are payable on efficient work done."[71] The more efficient the schools were at correlating the strengths of individual learners with society's economic and industrial needs, the more progressive they were.

In order to ensure this correlation, principals and administrators kept in close personal touch with the occupations of the community: "By visits to various offices and industries, and by first-hand observation and discussion, the principal and staff endeavour to discover the needs of the community and to co-ordinate the work of the school with those needs."[72] Occupational surveys of cities were undertaken in most urban cities during the interwar period. Surveyors of Guelph, funded by the Ontario Training College for Technical Teachers, noted two aims that they had to keep in mind: "The first was to learn something definite about the industries, commerce, and major occupations in the city. The second was to analyze this information in its relation to secondary education and the kinds of courses required."[73]

The industrial and occupational needs of the community were primary; the progressive school's responsibility was to bring educational matters in line with these needs as efficiently as possible. As a review of an occupational survey noted, business interests were not merely observed; they were involved in the school process and practice:

> From time to time business men visit the school, and go through all departments with the principal, discussing with him and the staff, as well as the pupils, the requirements for certain occupations. A high standard of achievement is required before the school will graduate a pupil in any department. Business men know this and take recommendations from the school at their face value. For convenience in organization, the school is divided into three departments—industrial, home economics, and commercial.[74]

Socially efficient and progressive schools were, in other words, the lynchpin between industry and individuals. Progressive educational guidance would be built on models developed in the United States, where great headway had already been made towards the aim of adjusting individual learners towards their future vocational positions. In terms of the development and training of personnel, and in the analysis of jobs and the social needs of industry, the guidance movement, unsurprisingly, targeted secondary schools.[75] Ontario's advocates for guidance programs looked to the United States for exemplars, as these programs, particularly in states such as Rhode Island, were well advanced and exemplified progressivist ideas. "Compared with the work being done in guidance in the United States and in Europe, our progress here is meager," explained Marion Goode, arguing that steps needed to be taken included business practice, shop work, and summer training courses for teachers.[76] Overall, the vocational programs were not seen merely as means of utilizing data on mental intelligence. Beyond the domain of measuring and marshalling student's abilities, was an interrelated concern for training students to behave appropriately in industry. The cultivation of business habits grew in significance. These included:

Personal habits (grooming of person and clothes, neatness of persona and work, general appearance) . . . courtesy and co-operation (politeness and consideration, willingness and promptness to work with teacher and class) . . . alertness (ability to do necessary work on own initiative, leadership, ability to interpret and carry out instructions) . . . dependability and stability (thoroughness, integrity) . . . general employability.[77]

The programs, then, essentially, normalize students into the ideal kinds of workers desired by industrial and business types. This entire progressive enterprise was facilitated by the constant interaction that the schools needed to maintain with industry, and vice versa. Schools were encouraged to be perpetually in touch with various and sundry corporate firms and employment sites, considering the potential placement of students within these spaces.[78]

In the years preceding the Second World War and throughout the war, progressivist voices imposed on schools a particularly daunting responsibility, corresponding to the general interest in correlating education with social needs. An editorial article in *The School* implicated vocational schools, in particular, in the "war of machines."[79] Schools were part of the war effort. They were "of direct service in winning the war."[80] Mental testing would distinguish prospective officers from different classes of trained personnel. The abilities of each individual needed to be placed in the appropriate position and, in this enterprise. "Marks still count," noted a 1942 editorial in *The School*, which argued that gains were made through intelligence testing that could help Canadians garner objective information about each citizen's mental ability and potential role. "We are learning," the article stated, "slowly that control by intelligence is necessary to win the war."[81] It continued to pursue the argument that careful diagnosis, management, and control of individual intellects and abilities, "provided that all the people are educated to recognize intelligence and to distinguish it from emotional force masquerading as intelligence to serve the interest of some particular group."[82]

The war effort was persistently used to justify the expansion and funding of vocational and technical programs. The more specific the training of individuals could be, the more efficiently their transition to the battlefield and war room would be, it was argued. This management of human potential and strength was a vigorously progressive measure, in the minds of efficiency advocates, for neither the infrastructure nor will to sustain such projects had existed in the Great War. Progress in scientific management gave the opportunity for teachers and for school administrators to directly play a role in winning the war. Particularly, the technical schools, which had been established in 1914 within the Ontarian context, would produce graduates who had the technological, manual, and intellectual training that were essential in a modern, progressive age.[83]

Despite the increase of production and of industry in the years before the war, efficiency advocates were still not satisfied with the progress being made in preparing people for essential jobs.[84] A heavy recruitment program was undertaken in Ontario, which employed posters, press, and radio talks to advertise "War Emergency Classes" that were intended to "turn out semi-skilled workers—mostly machine operators, bench workers, and some gas and arc welders."[85] In many cases, the schools were operating 24 hours a day, and attendance was quickly increased to 5,000 pupils.[86] Interestingly, these classes did not explicitly attempt to train students—again, boys, in particular—who would be mechanics in a general sense. They would train students to perform particular skills and tasks that were preparatory in nature and directed at particular needs gleaned from relationships established with industry.[87] Schools were thus sites that developed programs to find students work. This work was specific in nature and, in turn, the school work was also tailored and directly transferable.

The circumstances of the war were extenuating. But there is not the slightest pretense that schools, in the context, were intended to do anything but be of immediate relevance to the needs identified by the leaders of industry. Developing a progressive sense of social responsibility, in this particular sphere and from this particular perspective, meant that public schools could take the child as a raw product and refine it to a fully functional and useful adult. In the words of Electa Bissell, take the student "from his baby ways, teach him to walk by himself, and make him realize that he is an important cog in the machinery of a smoothly-running world."[88] Teachers, like pupils, had important roles to play for the integration of schools and industrial life. Teachers were depicted as loyal and industrious workers, committed to the public—or, at least economic and industrial—good.[89] Their well-being was necessary considering their important role in studying society and turning out students who manifested a progressive and "socially efficient personality."[90]

Individualized Instruction

The rhetoric of efficiency advocates with regards to individual instruction is couched—as is the case with all progressive discourse—in the lofty language of democracy and equality of opportunity. As it remains today, democracy was a notion subject to great interpretation. Most frequently, the testing of individual children's mental intelligence and the use of that data for the classification of exceptional children was justified as necessary in an equitable and democratic state.[91] Progressive education ought to provide equality of opportunity, which "means that every child, dull, average, and bright, shall have the chance to develop in accordance with his own particular abilities and needs."[92] These needs and abilities needed first to be measured, classified, and categorized so that efficient programs of study could be constructed. Thus, in 1942, it is declared within *The School* that "the ultimate end of education is the production of efficient citizens."[93]

Classifying children, particularly those who were below-average pupils and those who were of superior intelligence was framed as a democratizing effort that would help schools align their work to the real world through scientific methods.[94] This effort was commensurate to providing them what one teacher called "the right to an opportunity to develop their talents, no less than other children, to the greatest extent commensurate with the good society."[95] Children deemed "exceptional" often hated school, and this was a direct consequence of traditional schooling, which degraded the experience of learning in a classroom with learners of different, or normal, intelligence.[96] Special programs designed for special children would provide exceptional children with the "attention they deserve and require; average classes will cease to be clogged with ill-adjusted trouble-makers."[97] The study of individual intelligence could thus make public schools more efficient, and learners would "get fuller value" for the time spent in school and save on expenses associated with reformatories, delinquency, and academic struggles, allowing children of higher and lower intelligence to be engaged citizens inside and outside of the classroom.[98] Concentrating on I.Q. as a means of understanding the individual was of prime interest to the efficient, well-run society. Schools were compelled to teach traits that were not disruptive of the social order, including discipline, knowledge that related to contemporary industrial life, and training in character that was associated with "proper conduct".[99] In the final sum, "the prevention of crime is far more important" than most other factors. Key was proper adjustment and placement in a vocational sense, as seen above in relation to vocational guidance and placement program development.[100] Identification of exceptional learners through objective, standard measures, it was argued, would allow structures for schools and society to train these individuals "in habits of work in such a way that they will be self-supporting in later life, and to develop in them such desirable social qualities as honesty, self-control, reliability, truthfulness, and the ability to live and work contentedly."[101]

Of course, there was a different, if less popular model for dealing with exceptional individual learners in an efficient system. This entailed concentrating instruction on the gifted pupils who would return society's investment of time and effort by developing into the leaders of society. The analogy of farming is a recurring one, as this anecdote should make clear:

> He said: "Fertilize that hillside field? Heck, I've wasted enough good manure and seed on it to cover the country. Every rain there's a run-off that washes everything away except the fences. A man can't do a thing with that field. It ain't fit to plant pig-weed in, let alone wheat!" Then he added, thoughtfully: "Son, put your effort where it'll net you some profit. Every hour spent on this field is money in my pocket. But the other one—last time I worked it, I seeded it four times, and never got a crop.[102]

The moral of this parable for efficiency is transparent in the context of schooling and intelligence testing. It also bears frightening implications of social evolution, eugenics, and a laissez-faire disregard for all that is not most strong and fit. Individual strength, fitness, and potential were to be identified and the individuals employed for social ends. The enthronement of efficiency as tantamount to progressivism and the related paranoia concerning wastefulness as the greatest enemy to progress were implicated in the movement to stream, classify, and identify children's intelligence quotients and intellectual abilities:

> Instead of wasting time and energy in trying to hold a mentally slow or defective child up to the level of progress which is normal to the average child, it would be wiser t give this child an intelligence test and grade him according to his mental ability so that he will progress at the rate which is normal to him, whether the rate be slow or whether the rate be fast. All children cannot be held at the same standards of school age.[103]

Thus, the intelligence tests were means of garnering objective understanding of the child, enabling the teacher to grade students according to their mental ability. A progressive school could then divide children into groups according to their intelligence and they could be taught more efficiently.

Somehow, the rewards of developing intelligence would trickle down and benefit individuals with lower I.Q. In this way, the entire social system would progress most efficiently. Such *progressivism* depended on the identification of strengths and weaknesses of individual components (students) and the management of these parts within an efficient and organized structure. The question, from an efficiency perspective, then, was: "The farmer knew by experience what would, and what would not, pay dividends. Should formal education fail to recognize what is obvious to practical economists?"[104] Practical economy was the linchpin model for efficient and progressive school systems.

Yet, it is worth repeating that the predominant rhetorical justifications for and explanations of a socially efficient system of schooling were dripping with democratic overtones. Sometimes, the concern for identifying and classifying individual learners was not only classified as a democratic duty, it was a religious one. Both "Democracy and Christianity" explained S. R. Laycock from the University of Saskatchewan's College of Education, were "founded on a recognition of the worth of each individual and on reverence for personality."[105] Even "the moron, the borderline, the dull-normal child" and the "handicap" deserved the full benefits of citizenship, including the right to vote, to "affect community practices and standards as to public health, civic co-operation, the quality of education, and the nature of our recreational facilities."[106]

While it was incongruous with democratic and Christian principles to eliminate children of low intelligence from society, it was perfectly acceptable to give such children fitter and happier lives. "Dull" and "less able" children required the full attention of teachers and a school curriculum that presented "material and activates which are not too complex for the child."[107] The tailoring of curricula to intelligence and the establishment of auxiliary classes was not only the democratic and Christian thing to do, it was argued, it was the best way of promoting social progress and efficiency. This rhetoric is particularly dominant in the years dominated by the threats of Stalinism, Fascism, and Social Democracy:

> Unless we adopt the Nazi plan of doing away with below-average individuals, we have no alternative but to guide them to the fullest life which they are capable of living and into channels of work and play where they can best serve their fellows.[108]

It did not seem apparent, from the efficiency perspective, that the ideas of a full life and one of servitude were, perhaps, incommensurate. Philosophically, this matter constitutes the most fundamental difference between the progressive orientation considered in this chapter and the one examining the social meliorist orientation to educational progress.

From within the social efficiency perspective, then, progress meant eliminating wasteful practice. With respect to the individual student, "diagnostic and remedial school programs" were ways for superintendents, inspectors, principals, and classroom teachers to become "aware of the problem" so that they might plan for its "correction."[109] Since the problem was primarily deemed one of children's sub-normal intelligence and ability, the correction necessarily entailed auxiliary and "remedial school programs."[110] These programs represented new and progressive ways of dealing with difference of individual ability, and they required a dramatic break from the traditional ways of evaluating and organizing school systems. Across the country, David Russell of the University of British Columbia's Department of Education told Ontario's educators, education required a reorientation in priorities:

> Teachers and administrators are content to have classes conducted in the same old way, thinking nothing of the human waste involved. With a few exceptions, Canadian schools generally have been slow to adopt the diagnostic and remedial point of view, which has done much for retarded children in other systems.[111]

The diagnostic perspective, then, emphasizing the garnering of information about students for needs assessments and for the tailoring of instruction for efficient progress in society, was predicated on the collection of reliable and objective data on individuals: "Intelligence tests, mechanical aptitude tests, art ability tests, stenographic ability tests, the school nurse reports, and personal interviews, play an important part in helping pupils to find their right places."[112] It amounts to the thesis that there is a suitable place for every person in the economic and social structures. A niche for each person exists, and guidance/vocational programs' goal is to tailor the individual to that niche.

Marion Goode, writing on guidance as a method, noted:

> The collecting of educational and vocational information is a major activity. Every home-room teacher needs to know something about vocations and vocational opportunities, just as every home room teacher should know something about the areas of health, of social relationships, and of mental hygiene in order that he may assist all students.[113]

Every teacher, she continued, takes charge of pupils under his or her direction and is, consequently, responsible for their growth towards a vocational orientation or goal. Goode highlighted seven aspects of vocational guidance, which require consideration: personnel records, research, intelligence, tests, interviews, try-out experiences, placement, and follow-up.[114] Collectively, these were framed as means of gathering objective and subjective data concerning the pupil's aptitudes, interests, strengths, and weaknesses.[115]

Further, on the subject of intelligence testing, Goode argued that these should be thought of as a system, which should be administered several times in the pupils' career, including achievement tests at the beginning of each term. Surveys of study habits, autobiographical sketches, and anecdotal records should also be made. Interviews would concern the choice of electives, educational and vocational plans, periodical check-up on the progress made, and follow-up reports of the efficiency in transition that might inform "possible changes in the school curriculum and programme."[116]

The progressive and "new-type or objective examinations" took hold of the field of educational measurement and, in this context, each teacher was asked to become familiar with their use.[117] The strength of so-called objective testing to measure students' intelligence and mental ability was seen as residing "mainly in the fact that *they tend to excel in reliability or consistency*; that is, repeated testing of the same candidates tend to give closely parallel results."[118] A person's intelligence quotient and ability was seen as something operating with limited parameters. Any student could be trained to learn more about particular subjects, but their ability to think about matters intelligently was a fixed and relatively rigid thing. Intelligence tests would typically garner consistent results.

Traditional examinations and tests were regarded as very different from any progressive reaching for objectivity:

> Behind the unreliability of the conventional essay-type examination lie two principal causes—limited sampling and subjective scoring. In history, for example, there will be time for only five or six questions to be answered in an examination period, a woefully limited sampling of questions selected by the examiner from the hundreds of different questions at his disposal. The candidate obviously is not able to handle all

questions equally well, so that his fate is rather largely determined by chance: if certain questions appear on his paper he will do well; if certain other appear he will do poorly.[119]

Conventional examinations were woefully behind progressive testing tools, which had a larger stress on quantitative concerns. During the time that a student would spend responding to merely "six essay-type questions a candidate could answer two or three hundred objective items, and with such numbers chance is a negligible factor."[120]

Subjective measures were merely too unreliable to be *progressive*. Intelligence tests, on the other hand "eliminate this cause of unreliability entirely. The answers are definite and the test is scored by the use of a key."[121] In terms of increasing efficiency in testing and examination means, there were further benefits to eliminating questions requiring interpretation or subjective analysis: "The objective examination offers some guarantee that the attention of the examinee will be directed as intended. We are all acquainted with the student who skillfully writes around a topic without ever coming at it directly."[122] What is more, the "new type test gets rid of these difficulties: it holds the candidate to his point."[123] Intelligence tests allowed for no bluffing or wavering, for the answer was correct or incorrect, known or unknown.

Further, objective examinations promoted progressive efficiency in terms of each student's mental work and concentration. Whereas, "in the essay-type examination the candidate is so slowed up by the mere mechanics of writing, that he manages to express surprisingly few ideas in a two- or three-hour period."[124] This emphasis on quantity of information to be memorized and then recalled for the purposes of examinations is a relatively surprising one for a progressive interest group that primarily criticized the *traditional* methods of schooling for emphasizing rote memorization and regurgitation of facts. It would appear that these progressives were, in principle, not as concerned with the careful expression of ideas as they were with the efficient recall of information. From an administrative perspective, also, "objective examinations are *easily and quickly scored*."[125]

Less evident in the progressive rhetoric of efficiency advocates are acknowledgments of the weaknesses inherent in intelligence testing and other supposed objective examination. Probably the most serious of these is the limitations imposed on them by their piecemeal nature. They tended to measure isolated elements of information and could be adapted only with difficulty to the measurement of large or intricately organized units of study. This fundamentally undermines much of what we might think is a progressive connection between schools and society, as well as the correlation of activity and school life. Further, and more significantly,

It has been urged by critics of new-type tests that they *measure mere facts*. Usually this criticism comes from men of a philosophic turn of mind, for to the matter-of-fact scientist there is no such thing as a "mere fact": facts are to him the only basis for sure knowledge and are always matters of first importance. This criticism is frequently advanced by teachers of history, who argue that new-type devices give the examinee no scope to show his originality or to show his ability to organize his knowledge in a logical matter. For the most part the argument is well founded, but often when new-type tests are singled out for this particular criticism, it is merely a matter of the pot calling the kettle black. If one examines our matriculation papers in history he will find little to show that the candidate is expected to do more than record legibly and grammatically certain facts which he is expected to have acquired from his teacher and his textbook.[126]

So, in essence, the efficiency progressives' advocacy for intelligence testing and objective examinations seemed to do little more than make the same testing of facts more efficient, if less "legible and grammatic." In addition, despite the critique that essays allowed students to write "around" the issue and feign knowledge that they do not have, the author admitted, "new-type tests encouraged guessing. This is a weakness which must be admitted."[127]

Ontario had the largest number of special education classes for students considered sub-normal in intelligence by the start of the Second World War. A survey of the education of exceptional children in Canada, sponsored by the University of British Columbia, reported that 310 classes in the public system and 13 in the separate schools had been established just in Toronto, with enrollments of 6029 and 236 children, respectively.[128] Entire schools were set up for "dull boys and dull girls in Toronto, Ottawa, and Hamilton."[129] In Ontario, London, East York, York Township, Kitchener, and North Bay all had more than five special education classes, while "approximately fifty other centres have opportunity classes or handicraft and special industrial classes."[130]

The particular bases of selection of so-called exceptional children varied across Canada, but every system reported the results of individual intelligence examinations and the recommendation of teachers as dominant factors. The appeal of seemingly objective exams such as intelligence tests has already been considered with regards to efficient diagnoses of mental strength, but "practically all the school systems report more boys than girls in their classes for the dull, a possible indication that the factor of behaviour problems is more important than some schools indicate."[131] The subjective qualities of placement point to an increasing concern for the cultivation of work habits deemed conducive to industrial or office work, such as cleanliness, promptness, and obedience.

Certainly, the promotion and inculcation of character traits conducive to industrial efficiency emerged as dominant themes in the final years of the Great Depression. In 1934, for example, the National Education Association (NEA) of the United States distributed, through its *Bulletin*

(Vol. XII, No. 3) a study conducted by its Research Division on the various meanings of "Education for character."[132] First amongst these was "good character as conformity."[133] The second and third were "a composite of desirable traits and ideals" and "specific habits and attitudes needed in life," respectively.[134] The contents of the NEA report make evident that character-building programs were important for future vocational success, and that efficient progress would entail integration of the curriculum, guidance, and administration.

The fact that "in Ontario, the number of special classes in urban centres almost doubled in the ten-year period from 1929–1939, and rural classes were established in 1934"[135] can be seen under the purview of the increasing influence of the idea that social efficiency constituted progress. Expanding the means by which children could efficiently be trained for industry, find work, and maintain the proper functioning of the economic-industrial orders had brought into Ontario a period of "definite progress."[136] In the words of a school psychologist: "We are fortunate in having a progressive school board which has made ample provision for all children requiring special attention."[137]

In short, specialization and the problems of training transfer had, from an efficiency perspective, forced considerations of progress to models of focused differentiation, rather than integration. "Mental defectives should be separated,"[138] was the most common argument, in this regard, "not only should the mentally unfit be weeded out, but the mentally alert and those showing special promise along various lines should be encouraged to proceed further than the average along the lines of special abilities."[139] This was not only because "slow" children impeded the progress of more "able" ones, but also because of "a high percentage of low grade mentality in those who become delinquent and finally a charge on the community."[140] Special abilities needed to be identified, harnessed, and directed to their appropriate niche in life. The "crowded curriculum" provoked a need for "specialization" and the elimination of unnecessary subjects, most typically regarded as those that do not have immediate and practical relevance.

"In mathematics, as in all other subjects, a problem is created by the existence of three main groups of students: the exceptionally bright, the exceptionally otherwise, and the great middle class between."[141] Essentially, here, we see the construction of classes, like those that exist outside of schools and relating to socio-economic status. The intelligence of a student was equated in a discursive way, at least, with capital and earning potential. While it is was deemed "desirable to give the extreme groups specialized attention, the teacher should remember that the average pupils must also be taught. A few suggestions are offered for the adaptation of class-teaching procedure to meet the needs of exceptional groups."[142] Social efficiency advocates that were not unilaterally in support of the over-concentration of resources on above- or the below-average students argued that it was important not to neglect the average child who remained the majority of school populations.

A progressive system needed to train all individual learners according to their ability, regardless of intelligence or exceptionality.

In spite of that, it was a common complaint that there was too much stress on the identification and placement of exceptional children at the expense of the so-called gifted learners: "So often the so-called 'brilliant' students have turned out in later life to be utter failures or to achieve only mediocre success, while the steady plodders with only average ability have scaled the heights to fame and fortune."[143] The public school system, from this perspective "has left the gifted children in the regular grades, with a great deal of spare time on their hands, and with very little outlet for their abundant energies and creative abilities."[144] This trend was very commonly described in terms of socio-economic classes. Fully integrated classrooms, then, were the educational equivalent to forcing the rich to stay with the poor and middle classes, where they have no way to take advantage of and spend their fortunes. As a result, they end up squandering potential and living average or mediocre lives. In a progressive environment, however, where their assets could be put to full and efficient use, vaster fortunes could be made and benefits would trickle down to all others in society.

Such environments, initially titled "advancement classes," corollaries to the Auxiliary and Special Education classes, were created, first in the city of London, drawing, "for each class some three dozen children . . . from practically every school of the city."[145] Throughout the interwar years, critiques of general or *liberal* education often hinged, as already noted, on the notion that transfer of training was impossible. Learning of one particular skill in a particular context, in other words, was not transferable to another, where different learning and training was required. From the efficiency standpoint, the solution to this issue was clear: students and teachers, particularly those deemed exceptional, needed very particular, practical, and specialized preparation for life.

"We are no longer satisfied with a system of general education," explained Ontario's Minister of Public Welfare, before the Trustees' and Ratepayers' Department of the Ontario Educational Association at the 1932 annual convention, so "the work of training the boy of to-day must follow along some particular line instead of fashioning our youth in a common group."[146] From the standpoint of increasing efficiency in educational practice, progress required a social will to "take the boy of school age and seek to fit and equip him for some special and definite avocation or calling."[147] In this perceived "age of specialization," the only way to give each student a fair and equal chance in life while promoting the efficient progress of students through the stages of life was through specialized, distinct, and practical learning contexts.[148]

This "new solution which allows these children to progress" at a rate commensurate with their individual ability was enforced despite "many difficulties in the way—public opinion (the man in the street was sure a race of prigs would be engendered), expense, location, transportation, and others."[149] This type of class was seen as essential for the provision of adequate individualized instruction and stimulation for intelligent pupils through interaction with gifted learners. Such interaction would help them see the importance of fulfilling their potential and working to the fullest capacity of their abilities: "They need this inspiration to bring them to their highest achievement. Gaining success at trifling tasks that were beneath their ability did not give them that genuine sense of self-respect that is so necessary to their mental health."[150]

They were also "noticeably generous in helping their classmates."[151] This goes to show the desire to develop a class consciousness. These identified students could not fit into the regular grades because, intellectually, they were superior. They needed to support each other, to develop as individuals and as a common group. "To be free from the teasing of 'normals' who called them 'a bookworm, a sissy, or a teacher's pet."[152]

"Undoubtedly these pupils will, in later life, be called upon to take responsible places in the publicize of the community. Therefore a course in public speaking is made an important part of the programme."[153] This would be the ruling class, in other words: the ones to be responsible for social progress, having been developed and progressed themselves. They could command, control, and manage others who were less intelligent and able.

Such children would constitute the skilled tradesmen, the factory workers, and the labourers. For certain, despite all their strengths, the intelligent pupils were not fitted to tasks requiring physical strength and dexterity, and "as a general rule, manual dexterity in these pupils is not as highly developed as the mental . . . usually their handwork is less satisfactory than that of the average child."[154] The children who were intelligently gifted were, from this perspective, seen as being excellent thinkers but bad doers. Clearly, the factory jobs, which required physical strength and manual dexterity, were not for these gifted children.

Active Learning

An activity curriculum was necessarily one that allowed for direct, specialized, and hands-on training of knowledge and skills that could correlate to the state of life, including vocational preparation and effective citizenship. Efficiency advocates spearheaded a movement to revolutionize "the field of pedagogy as far-reaching as any revolution ever affected in the political affairs of mankind, or in the industrial world."[155] This revolution aimed to posit "a new viewpoint in the minds of educators, a new objective for the schools, a new test of the school's efficiency."[156] The viewpoint of efficiency in educational institutions in Ontario was a very conservative one, in relation to life. Even if so-called traditional schools were the straw man against which progressives framed their reformist agendas, the model of humanistic schooling offered, at the very least, a different orientation to living and learning, than that propagated by industrial and economic reality.

The revolution demanded by social efficiency educationists, on the other hand, was essentially a means of supporting, maintaining, and progressing the extant social, economic, and industrial structures.

In *Toronto Saturday Night*, C. C. Goldring, a recognized progressive tour de force within the Toronto Board of Education, stated the conservative aspects of social efficiency quite clearly:

> Since it is certain that all the mature members of a society will die, it is obvious that the conservation of a society depends upon raring the new-born members in such a way that they will appropriate its functions and sustain its values.[157]

"School graduates will look for positions in business," Goldring continued, arguing that "it is important for the school people to have some knowledge of the viewpoint and requirements of the employers in industry."[158] The active seeking out and contacting of people in industry for the surveying of traits required in young students has already been noted with reference to vocational schools. The number of surveys conducted over the 30-year interwar period is astounding, each resulting in sundry lists of characteristics or traits desired of progressive young citizens entering the workforce, several of which have already been noted above. Reforms to report cards by 1935 in Toronto schools normalized desirable personality characteristics, making

> provision for a record of progress in school subjects and for a record of progress in some of the qualities of a good citizen. The development of personal qualities is as important as a good standing in the subject of study.[159]

Active citizenship for a progressive society, for example, required direct training of students by the schools of all those characteristics that would foster conservative obedience to the state order, including:

1. Respect for authority—(a) Parental; (b) Positional.
2. Industry—(a) Thoroughness in work done; (b) Time not wasted.
3. Thrift—(a) Regular savings; (b) Avoidance of waste.
4. Courtesy—(a) Recognition of the rights of others; (b) Politeness, good manners.
5. Integrity—(a) Honesty, Truthfulness; (b) Trustworthiness.
6. Care for property—(a) Private; (b) Public.
7. Tidiness—(a) Personal; (b) Environment.
8. Contribution to the public good—(a) Cooperation; (b) Initiative, suggestiveness.
9. Self-control—(a) Actions; (b) Feelings.
10. Courage—(a) Physical; (b) Moral.[160]

Certainly, the spirit of these ideal traits is admirable and very difficult to disagree with in many respects. Equally certainly, if these are the founding principles of a revolution, it is difficult to see the revolutionary qualities within it in a broad and social sense, unless initiative and suggestiveness are taken to mean something more radical than their common usage might suggest. What is progressive about the social efficiency viewpoint in this case is its interest in doing away with the so-called traditional curriculum and replacing it with one that actively upheld and furthered the aims of an industrial and economic order in society. From an evolutionary perspective, educational progressivism from the standpoint of efficiency and scientific management would promote further economic and industrial progress.

It is essentially this kind of pre-specification of pedagogical objectives based on "the notion of activity analysis" that in the United States characterized the new "science" of curriculum making.[161] Leading the thrust of curriculum theorists seeking an educational ideology appropriate for the *modern* and progressive world and applying the "same success as science applied to business in the form of scientific management," were Franklin Bobbitt and W. W. Charters.[162] Bobbitt had drawn heavily on business techniques while encouraging maximum utilization of school resources, development of technical expertise, and business language for the improvement of education.[163] Charters, similarly, approached educational reform from a scientific management perspective; his main concern was with the method of activity analysis, which essentially involved a careful analysis of "the particular activities that defined the role and then placed these in relationship to the ideals that would control these activities. The training involved in performing the activities well would then become the curriculum."[164]

Charters's concern for tailoring the curriculum, ideals, aims, and methods of schooling to the realities of industry and business bear direct relevance to the personality characteristics noted immediately above, as well as to the main thrust of vocational guidance and training schools in Ontario.[165] The key matter to note here is that the principles of job analysis, scientific management, and social efficiency were in no way particular to the Ontario context; indeed American progressives such as Bobbitt and Charters provided Canadian reformers "in the twentieth century with the concepts and metaphors—indeed, the very language—that were needed to create an aura of technical expertise without which the hegemony of professional educators could not be established."[166] Educational programs that followed precepts outlined by the social efficiency progressives needed to be based specifically and precisely upon the development of skills and experiences necessary for life.

Several such progressive programs were established in Ontario's schools in order to train students actively and specifically in the habits of mind consistent with a social efficiency viewpoint. Besides Manual Training, Domestic Science, and Technical Education being introduced into the province's curriculum, the Penny Bank program was one specifically designed for teaching children the value of regular savings, thrift habits, and business practice. Under the terms of the Penny Bank Act of 1904 that was passed by the federal Minister of Finance and with the cooperation of local chartered banks, the Penny Bank of Toronto was organized in 1905. It began taking deposits of May 1, 1905, and by the end of that school year had enrolled 42 schools in the provincial capital, with a combined balance of $50,400.[167] By the start of the First World War, 187 schools in 48 different cities with a total balance of an astounding $395,000 were involved with Penny Banking.[168] The progressive program for active learning that correlated to real life was maintained throughout the Depression, actually expanding during that period to 470 schools and 124 cities, serving as custodian for $1,200,000 belonging to the children of the province.[169] Active learning was necessarily progressive because it broke with the traditional model of passive, rote learning, memorization, and recall that characterized the stereotypical and old-fashioned school. Teaching knowledge unrelated to life, efficiency advocates argued, was both wasteful and not sufficiently utilitarian. As Reverend C. R. Durrant said in his address at the 1934 Ontario Educational Association Convention, a new and progressive school system would "train for living. Many things we have regarded as fads, frills and fancies, will be looked upon as necessities in the new day approaching."[170]

One educationist, Charles Deeley, wrote an article for *The School*, debating the use of projects in school. "The new curriculum," he argued, "has given a very marked impetus to individual or class projects in both the public school and lower school grades."[171] These projects, Deeley continued, could facilitate

> more purposeful activities in the classroom. Teachers, let us evaluate our project before the activity is begun by two criteria: first, the knowledge which such an undertaking will convey to our pupils; second its value in the light of the time and labour which the work will entail.[172]

In other words, the content itself should be meaningful, in the sense of being practical and purposeful. But the project itself should be constructed to concentrate activity as efficiently as possible, in terms of time and effort on the parts of teacher and student. The activity curriculum could thus develop skills that could be transferable to vocational or social life.

Pupils were considered to be disinterested in regular routines geared solely around the inculcation of academic knowledge and habits. In the past, when high schools were for the elite in Ontario society, such attitudes could be excused. An editorial article in *The School* noted that "high schools enroll upwards of three-fourths of the young people of high school age."[173] More problematically, it postulated, "a fair proportion of those who enjoy no outstanding ability are included."[174] These students deserved the right to actively pursue studies that would prepare them for "vocational life," as efficiently and as adequately as possible.[175] Active learning involved relevant, hands-on, and immediately practical training of skills projected as necessary and requisite for work. Strictly academic work "might better be abandoned."[176]

The principle of educational efficiency was largely an administrative issue, relating to the management and control of testing systems, school organization, and finance. Yet, in the microcosm of the classroom, the public school teachers were the ultimate interpreter of any policy or edict. For this reason, S. B. Sinclair, Principal of the Hamilton Model Training School argued: "the first step in the wise selection of a teacher is to determine, in a general way, the special kind of teacher required."[177] Hiring of teachers, Sinclair believed, required prudence, and a number of factors were crucial to the development and cultivation of useful, efficient citizens.

There was no reason to hire or, even, retain teachers who G. F. Rogers, Chief Director of Ontario's Department of Education termed "poor disciplinarians."[178] "If we are serious in our desire for economy," Rogers noted, "we may have to change the organization of many of our schools. Teachers will have to perfect a technique for handling" their students, particularly in large classes, more efficiently.[179] The distilment of proper habits of work and mind, and the teaching of skills required efficient teaching methods. Particularly in the case of vocational schools and technical training institutions, Rogers argued "there are a number of large boys who are behavior problems, a teacher who is known to be a good disciplinarian is better than one who has no experience."[180]

Since the very possibility of transfer of training happening was debatable, the efficient teacher would have to be efficiently trained. Particularly in the domains of technical and vocational schooling, courses were set up during the summer, in the evenings, and in the Normal Schools for the specific preparation of teachers in different domains of training. In terms of academic and professional training, Rogers stated:

> the candidate who holds a first class certificate and certificates for successful courses in Agriculture, Household Science, Music, Drawing, Physical Culture, Auxiliary Class work, two years Normal School training etc. is sure to do better work as the result of superior preparation.[181]

More training and increased specialization in preparation, were imperative for the promotion of progressive teachers who could take input from school inspectors, school principals, administrators, and peers in order to improve the efficiency with which they were able to fulfill their responsibilities with respect to the cultivation of reliable citizens.

The Ontario School Trustees' and Ratepayers' Association (OSTRA) was a key organizer and distributor of educational ideas regarding efficient schools, both with regards to financing, and to school organization. As the official organ of the Ontario Educational Association and publisher of *The Canadian School Journal*, the Association argued, throughout the interwar period, for a number of alterations to the schooling system in Ontario. Many of these reforms drew on developmental psychology and on social meliorism or democratic rhetoric to support claims, but an overriding concern is quite clear: progress is efficiency. Of course, the debates about what directions or orientations should guide progressive reforms were not ignored. But the sense that the terrain of *progressivism* was contested territory was neither guarded nor masked.

Despite the relative absence of a combative spirit in progressivist rhetoric, instances of a missionary ethos are noticeable. An editorial in the *Canadian School Journal*, for instance, preached:

> Too many of us forget that we must win those who do not see eye to eye with us. In fact all our convention and association effort is really directed to winning the active co-operation of those who are either opposed to certain ideas which we consider progressive; or are indifferent upon the matter.[182]

Active engagement with educational progressivism seemingly required active cooperation, debate, and conference. "The greatest need of the world today is conference," began the argument, but "we hesitate to confer about our problems. We are too sure that our ideas are the only ones that are right."[183] From the matter of larger and more efficient districts of administration to the issues of training or vocational schools and educational financing, "there was much debate—some enthusiastic support, and a great deal of very active opposition."[184] The greatest test of any progressive reform, from the efficiency perspective, was "the test of its value."[185]

Such investigations were commonplace throughout the interwar period, sponsored by government, university professors, and even the teachers' federations. Rogers argued that surveys were investigations of the educational field were essential if Ontarians could "discover, if possible, where we are wasting effort and money."[186] As an administrator, fiscal concerns certainly preoccupied Rogers' mind.

Yet, even the teachers' unions equated progress with efficiency, particularly during the Depression years. The Ontario Secondary School Teachers Federation, in 1932, sought to investigate Ontario's schools to discover "where eliminations, combinations, and reconstructions can be made, that will at the same time relieve the burden and increase the effectiveness."[187] The Depression, as an editorial in *The Canadian School Journal* noted, "accentuated the movement for reducing educational costs."[188] Notably, the publication was published by the province's ratepayers' association.

Even as the Depression accentuated the efficiency advocate's pleas for increased financial and institutional revision and refinement, this rhetoric was not limited to 1929–34. As society, industry, and the economic order were always changing, evolving, and *progressing*, school reformers needed to be actively engaged in the refinement of Ontario's educational orders:

In the transition from the more cultural period of our system to the intensely practical, the system has, through the enthusiastic efforts and appeals of the many idealists, become so cumbersome as to be a burden to both the teacher and pupil and correspondingly ineffective.[189]

Progress sustained itself on ongoing study of the practical, industrial, and economic realities of life and active critique, refinement, and reform.

Time and again, efficiency advocates drew on the seminal aspect of progressivist rhetoric: society had change, but schools have not adequately reformed to keep pace. Another editorial in the ratepayers' journal exemplifies the sentiment: "The same administrative machine we set up sixty years ago, some of it nearly one hundred years ago."[190] This machine, the article concluded, "works badly."[191] Efficiency, as an aspect of progressivist education, required vigilance and perpetual alignment between schools and society. As Ebel Snider, First World War veteran and Inspector of Schools for Durham and Northumberland, would note from the pulpit of *The Canadian School Journal*, wherever "increased efficiency is obtained without increased costs, or even with increased costs due to new buildings, etc., that is good economy."[192]

Notes

1. J. G. Althouse, "Some Troublesome Questions About Our Schools: Address to the Zonta Club, Toronto, February 1938," in *Addresses By J. G. Althouse: A Selection of Addresses By the Late Chief Director of Education for Ontario, Covering the Years 1936–1956* (Toronto: W. J. Gage Limited, 1958), pp. 5–6.
2. H. M. Cooke, "Secondary Education," *The Canadian School Journal* (November, 1932), p. 381.
3. Ibid.
4. Ibid.
5. G. F. Rogers, "Present Day Problems in Education," *The Canadian School Journal* (May, 1933), p. 173.
6. "Secondary School Costs," *The Canadian School Journal* (January, 1933), p. 15.
7. "Educational Experiments, Research, and Progress in Canada," *The School* (December, 1940), p. 278.
8. "Supplement: Reports on Educational Progress in Canada and Newfoundland, 1940–1941," *The School* (June, 1941), p. 907.
9. Ibid.
10. Herbert M. Kliebard, *The Struggle for the American Curriculum, 1893–1958* (New York and London: RoutledgeFalmer, 2004), p. 76.
11. Ibid.
12. Ross was a prolific writer on the subject. For his most explicit expression and most celebrated book on the subject, consult Edward A. Ross, *Social Control: A Survey of the Foundations of Order* (New York: Macmillan, 1901).
13. Ibid., p. 80.
14. Frederick W. Taylor, *The Principles of Scientific Management* (New York: Harper & Brothers, 1911), pp. 117–118.
15. "The 1934 Convention," *The Canadian School Journal* (March, 1934), p. 85.
16. Ibid., p. 82.

17. Cynthia Commachio, *The Infinite Bonds of Family: Domesticity in Canada, 1850–1940* (Toronto: University of Toronto Press, 1999); Mona Gleason, *Normalizing the Ideal: Psychology, Schooling, and Family in Postwar Canada* (Toronto: University of Toronto Press, 1999.

18. Kliebard, *The Struggle for the American Curriculum*, pp. 21–24.

19. For further reading, see Bruce Curtis, D. W. Livingston, and Harry Smaller, *Stacking the Deck: The Streaming of Working-Class Kids in Ontario Schools* (Toronto: Our Schools/Our Selves Education Foundation, 1992).

20. "Editorial Notes: The School and Society," *The School* (November, 1934), p. 185.

21. G. Fred McNally, "Curricula for Canadian High Schools, *The School* (January, 1935), p. 377.

22. J. L. Jose, "Is Business Practice Meeting the Community Needs?" *The School* (January, 1941), p. 389.

23. Ibid., pp. 389–391.

24. J. Ferris David, "Secondary Schools and their Relation to Business," *The Canadian School Journal* (April, 1933), p. 128.

25. Jose, "Is Business Practice Meeting the Community Needs?" p. 391.

26. Ferris David, "Secondary Schools and their Relation to Business," p. 128.

27. Ibid.

28. C. L. Burton, "Business as an Objective," *The Canadian School Journal* (October, 1932), p. 340.

29. Ibid.

30. Ibid.

31. B. A. Fletcher, "Some General Principles of Education," *The School* (January, 1939), p. 371.

32. J. E. Robertson, "An Educational Survey," *The Canadian School Journal* (March, 1932), p. 120.

33. Florence S. Dunlop, "The School Psychologist," *The School* (May, 1940), p. 753.

34. Olive Russell, "Is Vocational Guidance Feasible?" *The School* (March, 1939), p. 565.

35. Dunlop, "The School Psychologist," p. 753.

36. Ibid.

37. W. G. Martin, "Education for Citizenship," *The Canadian School Journal* (May, 1932), p. 194.

38. Burton, "Business as an Objective," p. 342.

39. "Notes and News: Ontario," *The School* (May, 1935), p. 811.

40. Angus Macrae, *Talents and Temperaments* (London: Nisbet & Co.), cited in Marion E. Goode, "The Need of Guidance," *The School* (October, 1940), p. 108.

41. Burton, "Business as an Objective," p. 342.

42. Goode, "The Need of Guidance," p. 108.

43. Ibid.

44. Cyril Burt, *The Young Delinquent* (London: The University of London Press, 1925), p. 286.

45. Goode, "The Need of Guidance," p. 109.

46. Ibid. Goode continues: "The employer, if through ignorance or leniency he retains the service of the incompetent muddler, suffers on account of the inferiority, in quantity or quality, of the work done. If, on the other hand, he discharges him, he is involved in the expense of training a substitute who may prove up to be no better than his predecessor."

47. Ibid. Goode is emphatic: ""How many school teachers have chosen their particular profession because of the long holidays and the salary attached to it!"

48. G. F. Rogers, "Present Day Problems in Education," *The Canadian School Journal* (May, 1933), p. 174.
49. Ibid., pp. 110–111.
50. Burton, "Business as an Objective," p. 342.
51. William John Cooper, "Educational News," *The Canadian School Journal* (November, 1933), p. 403.
52. Goode, "The Need of Guidance," p. 111.
53. Ibid.
54. John Dewey, *Democracy and Education* (New York: Free Press, 1997).
55. Goode, "The Need of Guidance," p. 109.
56. Marion E. Goode, "The Function of Guidance," *The School* (November, 1940), p. 192.
57. Gertrude Hildreth, *Psychological Service for School Problems* (World Book Co.), cited in Goode, "The Function of Guidance," p. 193.
58. "Editorial: Work," *The School* (November, 1940), p. 185.
59. Ibid.
60. Ibid.
61. "Vocational Training and Vocational Guidance," *The Canadian School Journal* (November, 1932), p. 371.
62. Ibid.
63. E. E. Kidd, "The Guidance Programme at Scarborough Collegiate Institute," *The School* (May, 1941), p. 835.
64. Ibid.
65. Ibid.
66. Burton, "Business as an Objective," p. 342.
67. Kidd, "The Guidance Programme at Scarborough Collegiate Institute," p. 835.
68. Ibid.
69. W.H.H. Green, "The Vocational School and the Community," *The School* (November, 1940), p. 211.
70. "Educational Progress in Canada: Vocational Education," *The School* (June, 1942), p. 871.
71. Ibid.
72. Ibid.
73. A. M. Laird and J. E. Durrant, "An Occupational Survey of a Small City," *The School* (April, 1939), p. 655.
74. Ibid., p. 212.
75. Marion E. Goode, "The Methods of Guidance," *The School* (December, 1940). Goode noted: "its special field, although considerable headway has also been made in higher institutions. As we are only beginning our journey on the road of vocational guidance here in Canada, we might do well to note the sign posts which they have placed along the way," p. 288.
76. Ibid., p. 290.
77. Ibid., pp. 290–291.
78. Ibid., p. 291.
79. "The Schools and the War of Machines: A Report of the Work of the Vocational Schools of Ontario," *The School* (February, 1941), p. 504.
80. "Ibid.
81. "Editorial: High Marks Still Count," *The School* (March, 1942), p. 557.
82. Ibid.
83. "The Schools and the War of Machines," p. 504.
84. Ibid.
85. Ibid., p. 505.
86. Ibid.
87. Ibid.

88. Electa Bissell, "Developing a Sense of Responsibility in the Grade II Child," *The School* (November, 1929), p. 224.

89. E. J. Transom, "Time Off for Thinking," *The School* (February, 1941), p. 507.

90. Ibid.

91. Donald Peat, "Two Sides to a Question: If Teachers Are to Devote More Time to Exceptional Children, to What Intelligence Group Should Most of the Additional Attention Be Given? To Below-Average Pupils," *The School* (February, 1942), p. 464.

92. S. R. Laycock, "Helping the Bright Pupil," *The School* (March, 1942), p. 561.

93. Marion Goode Hodgins, "Permanent Values in Education," *The School* (May, 1942), p. 760.

94. C. W. Greer, "Two Sides to a Question: If Teachers Are to Devote More Time to Exceptional Children, to What Intelligence Group Should Most of the Additional Attention Be Given? To Pupils of Superior Intelligence," *The School* (February, 1942), p. 465.

95. Peat, "Two Sides to a Question," p. 464.

96. Ibid.

97. Ibid.

98. Ibid.

99. Alfred E. Lavell, "Abstract of an Address on 'Home, School, and the Prevention of Crime," *The Canadian School Journal* (April, 1932), p. 148.

100. Ibid.

101. Peat, "Two Sides to a Question," p. 464.

102. Greer, "Two Sides to a Question," p. 465.

103. R. S. Murray, "The Problem of Teaching," *The Canadian School Journal* (December, 1934), p. 415.

104. Greer, "Two Sides to a Question," p. 465.

105. S. R. Laycock, "Helping the Below-Average Pupil," *The School* (February, 1942), p. 467.

106. Ibid.

107. Ibid., p. 468.

108. Ibid., pp. 467–468.

109. David H. Russell, "Subject Matter Disabilities," *The School* (February, 1942), p. 471.

110. Ibid.

111. Ibid.

112. W.H.H. Green, "The Vocational School and the Community," *The School* (November, 1940), p. 212.

113. Goode, "The Methods of Guidance," p. 288.

114. Ibid.

115. Ibid.

116. Ibid.

117. John A. Long, "The Construction and Use of New-Type Tests," *The School* (October, 1940), p. 95.

118. Ibid.

119. Ibid.

120. Ibid., pp. 95–96.

121. Ibid.

122. Ibid.

123. Ibid.

124. Ibid.

125. Ibid., italics in original text.

126. Ibid., pp. 97–98.

127. Ibid., p. 98.

128. David H. Russell and Fred T. Tyler, "Special Education in Canada," *The School* (June, 1942), pp. 882–889.
129. Ibid., p. 883.
130. Ibid.
131. Ibid.
132. "Education for Character," *The School* (October, 1934), p. 95.
133. Ibid.
134. Ibid.
135. Ibid., p. 887.
136. Ibid., p. 888.
137. Dunlop, "The School Psychologist," p. 754.
138. Burton, "Business as an Objective," p. 341.
139. Ibid.
140. Ibid.
141. Harold W. Hill, "Above-Average and Below-Average Students," *The School* (December, 1940), p. 327.
142. Ibid.
143. H. Ruth Hooper and Edna Lancaster, "Classes for More Intelligent Pupils," *The School* (December, 1940), p. 352.
144. Ibid.
145. Ibid, p. 353.
146. W. G. Martin, "Education and Citizenship," *The Canadian School Journal* (May, 1932), p. 194.
147. Ibid.
148. Ibid.
149. Ibid., p. 353.
150. Ibid.
151. Ibid.
152. Ibid.
153. Ibid., p. 354.
154. Ibid., p. 355.
155. J. R. Littleproud, "School Savings: A Project in Citizenship," *The Canadian School Journal* (January, 1934), p. 9.
156. Ibid.
157. C. C. Goldring, "The School and Business," *The Canadian School Journal* (January, 1935), p. 10.
158. Ibid.
159. C. C. Goldring, "Educational News," *The Canadian School Journal* (November, 1935), p. 325.
160. Goldring, "The School and Business," pp. 9–10.
161. Herbert M. Kliebard, "Rise of Scientific Curriculum-Making," in *Forging the American Curriculum: Essays in Curriculum History and Theory* (New York: Routledge), pp. 83–84.
162. Ibid., p. 84.
163. For two notable texts by Bobbitt paralleling educational and business efficiency, consult Franklin Bobbitt, *The Curriculum* (Boston: Houghton Mifflin, 1918) and *How to Make a Curriculum* (Boston: Houghton Mifflin, 1913).
164. Kliebard, "Rise of Scientific Curriculum-Making," p. 85.
165. For further reading on Charters's activity analysis method and the principles of scientific management, consult Werrett W. Charters, *Methods of Teaching: Developed From a Functional Standpoint* (Chicago: Row, Peterson & Co., 1909); *Curriculum Construction* (New York: Macmillan, 1923); and *Teaching the Common Branches* (Boston: Houghton Mifflin, 1913).
166. Ibid., p. 84.

167. Ibid., p. 10.
168. Ibid.
169. Ibid.
170. C. R. Durrant, "The Search for an Educational Ideal," *The Canadian School Journal* (April, 1934), p. 123.
171. Charles F. Deeley, "Two Thoughts on Projects," *The School* (January, 1941), p. 405.
172. Ibid.
173. "Standards in the Middle School: A Discussion of Methods in Measurements in Matriculation Subjects," *The School* (March, 1941), p. 621.
174. Ibid.
175. Ibid.
176. Ibid., p. 622.
177. S. B. Sinclair, "How Rural School Trustees Can Select an Efficient Teacher," *The Canadian School Journal* (March, 1932), p. 94.
178. G. F. Rogers, "Present Day Problems in Education," *The Canadian School Journal* (May, 1933), p. 176.
179. Ibid.
180. Ibid.
181. Ibid.
182. "Conference vs. Debate," *The Canadian School Journal* (March, 1932), p. 93.
183. Ibid.
184. Ibid.
185. Ibid.
186. Rogers, "Present Day Problems in Education," 175.
187. Robertson, "An Educational Survey," p. 120.
188. Editorial, "Control of Expenditures for Education," *The Canadian School Journal* (October, 1932), p. 339.
189. Ibid.
190. "School Administration and School Finance in Ontario: Can They Be Improved?" *The Canadian School Journal* (May, 1932) p. 190.
191. Ibid.
192. Colonel E. E. Snider, "How Shall We Achieve Greater Efficiency in our Schools," *The Canadian School Journal* (September, 1935), p. 253.

4 Social Meliorism and Educational Progress
Making the World a Better Place Through Schooling

> It is, then, the responsibility of educators of every grade and rank, from the primary school to the university, to acquaint themselves with the facts of the present day world, and if possible, to determine a philosophy adequate for the construction of that new society which may emerge from the present chaos.[1]

Ameliorating the conditions of school and society was not the exclusive domain of the interest group examined in this chapter, which considers social meliorsm. There is no exclusive trademark on meliorism. At the most basic ideological and conceptual level, however, meliorist progressives were interested in reforming Ontario's society through the schools, with the ultimate aim of promoting social justice.

This is a fundamentally different goal than that upheld by social efficiency advocates who promoted refinement and management of schools so that they correlate more closely to extant societal conditions, whether they be industrial, economic, or material. This is also quite dissimilar from the developmentalist orientation, which promoted a closer correlation of schooling to the development, interests, and psychological welfare of children. In this case, the reformist thrust of social meliorist progressives was far more radical, for it envisioned a reconstruction of society in ways that would promote critical citizenship, foster debate, and target the inequalities in standard of life and opportunity entrenched in interwar Ontario societal structures. Social meliorism confronted, then, through the rhetoric of progressive school reforms, what Dewey called "the continuation of that hypocritical religion of 'prosperity' which is . . . the greatest force that exists at present in maintaining the unrealities of our social tone and temper."[2]

Herbert Kliebard's examination of the social meliorist progressives in the United States suggests that the concern for confronting social injustice in society through educational reforms reached its zenith during the Great Depression.[3] Dissatisfaction with social inequities, Kliebard noted, "had been gathering momentum among a small group of literati for some time and had expressed itself in the novels of Sinclair Lewis and the muckraking of Upton Sinclair. The Russian Revolution had attracted the admiration of a number of" intellectuals who were no longer with the direction that laissez-faire capitalism was taking.[4] George Counts, a disciple of John Dewey's and a faculty member at Columbia University's Teachers College, tore into the social efficiency agenda, critiquing the "standardization of life" and "the principle of social conformity" that had found its way into progressive education.[5]

Attacking other progressives, Counts challenged educational reformers to abandon the principles of scientific management and what he called an "efficiency without purpose, an efficiency of motion" because these ideas inevitable led to a state where "the school will become an instrument for the perpetuation of the existing social order rather than a creative force in society."[6] Counts even countered the "orgy of testing that swept through the entire country" that had led to

> the feverish and uncritical fashioning of tests in terms of the existing curriculum and in the name of efficiency has undoubtedly served to fasten upon the schools an archaic program of instruction and a false theory of the nature of learning.[7]

The matter of so-called objective testing and mental intelligence measures has already been examined in the chapter considering social efficiency progressives.

Counts, to reiterate, was not after the so-called traditional or humanistic curriculum. His shots were fired at other progressives, some of them, such as Edward Thorndike, were his colleagues at Teachers College. What had been seen as progressivism was a veneer of conservativism, perpetuating the same defects and drift that had spawned educational *progressivism* in the first place. The divides between progressive interests become very clear at this point of intersection. Not only were the social efficiency progressives a target of the meliorists, the developmentalists were also, although to a lesser extent, under attack. The seminal voice here, as is often the case with progressive education, is that of John Dewey.

According to Dewey, school was not progressive only because it advocated "a certain atmosphere of informality" or because it upheld individual, psychological development as being paramount.[8] Just as the social efficiency progressive lobby could only be embraced by educationists who were "satisfied upon the whole with the aims of the process of existing society," the child study progressives could be deemed correct only if individual freedom and interest were of prime significance.[9] Unfortunately, Dewey continued, "freedom is no end in itself."[10] In other words, neither the individual nor the industrial interests were penultimate factors in being progressive about schooling. The rejection of supposed traditional schooling was not tantamount to a fully realized progressivist educational ideology. A commitment to the ideals of social reform and social justice was prerequisite for any progressive educator, the meliorist fervently argued.

Counts had a knack for the dramatic. In 1932, at the annual meeting of the Progressive Education Association, his address titled *Dare Progressive Education Be Progressive* chastised the entire field of educational progressives to stop seeing themselves as "a superior breed" whose allegiance to "capitalism, with its deification of the principle of selfishness, its reliance upon the force of competition, its placing of property above human rights, and its exaltation of the property motive" was misguided.[11] Progressives, Counts argued, were in the whole weak in their convictions, and they had "elaborated no theory of social welfare, unless it be that of anarchy or extreme individualism."[12] Herbert Kliebard has highlighted the fact that, following Counts' speech, "the rest of the program for the day was virtually abandoned, and the board of directors felt it necessary to call a special meeting in order to discuss Counts' challenge."[13]

Counts would publish a revised reiteration of his speech under the title *Dare the School Build a New Social Order* later in 1932, which continued the attack upon laissez-faire individualism and capitalism.[14] Counts was not alone in his advocacy for social justice and meliorism. Boyd H. Bode had, a half decade earlier, emphasized "the relationship between education and the vision of renewed society, and for him, an improved social order was not synonymous with efficiency or even with the creation of law-abiding citizens."[15] Bode presented critiques of the social efficiency doctrines espoused by such prominent progressives as Bobbitt and Charters, as well as the extremist developmentalist orientations towards uninhibited interest and activity. He denied that there was any possibility that educationists could be progressive insofar as their agendas were derived from activity analyses and unbridled enthusiasm for the scientific method.[16] Bode also attacked the "mystic faith in a process of 'inner development'" that saw no role for the orientation of children towards social responsibility and welfare.[17] Progressive education required that schools emphasize what the New Education Fellowship, writing in *The School*, described as "training in reading, in observation, in discussion, and in thinking for themselves . . . not by indoctrination."[18]

Harold Rugg, like Counts and Bode, had a profound impact on the terrain of social reconstructionism and meliorism in the domain of progressive education. Rugg not only represented the Progressive Education Association on the New Education Fellowship, an important progressive force for schooling in Ontario with roots in British schooling reforms, he developed the first social studies textbooks in the Unites States, titled *Man and His Changing Society*. These texts, despite the economic collapse and financial cutbacks affiliated with the Depression, sold an astounding figure of 1,317,960 copies and 2,687,000 workbooks between 1929 and 1939.[19] Rugg's textbooks, before being slandered and burned as subversive and socialist texts in the build-up to the Cold War, targeted social inequities, disparities between the rich and the poor, racial stereotypes, and changing gender roles in society.[20] The social meliorist movement in educational progressivism was clearly a distinct and very controversial entity in the domain of school reform rhetoric.

Rugg wanted to change the future of the world by changing the world as it functioned every day, parochially. He expressed this relentlessly in his prose and his texts, but even in verse:

Tomorrow Is Today

There are moments in history when Tomorrow is Today,
When the mammoth glacier of social trend
   taking movement down the Valley of History
   can be diverted by men
Into pathways towards Tomorrow.

There are moments in history when Today is merely
   Today . . .
   inert, unchanging . . .
When no mustering of energies
Can prod man out of his inertia.

Then comes the moment when Tomorrow is Today,
When the flux is at free flow.
Then Man is Captain of his Soul
And the principle of the effective human act
   Works in a world at social crisis.

I'll say it in this way, then—

There is a favored moment . . . a place . . .
and a mustering of energies
   Which, in unison, will produce and effective
   human act.[21]

He spoke in Ontario upon a number of occasions, most notably at the first Canadian conference of the New Education Fellowship at the King Edward Hotel on April 23 and 24, 1937. Rugg represented the Progressive Education Association in the Fellowship and became an important mediator between the European and U.S. versions of the "new education."[22] Attendance at the conference exceeded organizers expectations, most likely because Ontario was in the midst of a revision of their school curricula under the leadership of Duncan McArthur and Leo Sampson. The general theme of the conference was "Tradition and Freedom in Education," and Rugg's two speeches emphasized the importance of social settings, the activity approach to learning, social cooperation, and knowledge of the changing nature of culture. Most notably, media coverage of the event in the teacher journals isolated the term "progressive education" by placing it within quotation marks, emphasizing Ontario educator's "desire to learn what the 'new education' really is."[23]

As would be expected, there was a lag between what Kliebard called the "heyday of social meliorism" in the United States and in Ontario.[24] In the build-up to the Second World War, where social cohesiveness and the principles of democracy, including critical thinking and debate, were emphasized, an onrush of meliorist rhetoric flooded educationally progressive texts. That is not to say that there were no persistent expressions of dissatisfaction concerning social injustices and laissez-faire capitalism throughout the interwar context. The discussion that follows, which examines social meliorist progressive interests in Ontario in light of their positions on the relationship between schools and society, individualized instruction, and active learning, should make the more sustained quality of reconstructionist reform concerns more evident.

The Schools and Society

Social meliorists readily admitted that the circumstances of life had changed. An editorial article in *The School* summarized this sentiment aptly: "A new world is in the making, or so they tell us. Civilization has struck its tents, and is on the march."[25] Like during the Renaissance and during the Industrial Revolution, argued Joseph McCulley, Headmaster of Pickering College, society was "passing through another such period of change."[26] The "progress of civilization has been a series of protests, of struggles against the mass inertia of large groups," he continued, and "vested interests and pressure groups of one kind and another did not give way to the new conceptions of life without struggle."[27]

Furthermore, in terms of the context of progressive schooling, the struggle for a more socially just world was enabled by the industrial, social, and economic fluxes that characterized the interwar period. In the words of William George Martin, Minister of Public Welfare, "if there was ever a time in history when there was a need for a great crusade of youth and older men for the betterment of the lot of humanity that hour is to-day."[28] A progressive society was one built on the principle of cooperation within the parameters of meliorist principles. Educationist John Cook used the *Canadian School Journal* as a medium for arguing that the public ought to attend to "several practical ways that co-operation of individuals has aided them to build up our great civilization faster and more satisfactorily and so to live more successfully than individuals could possibly do by living alone and individualistically."[29]

A persistent debate, in Ontario and across Canada, centered on the meaningfulness of the term indoctrination. "Is indoctrination just another name for education?" W. C. Keirstead, a faculty member of the University of New Brunswick asked Ontario educators, "or may indoctrination be used in education?"[30] Could anyone or any institution claim "superconsciousness over that of individuals and no good other than the good of persons."[31] Individuals in a democratic society, Kierstead argued, were akin to active cells of a living body, which have independent and yet cooperative functions. Each part of the body depended upon the health of other parts, and no society could be a healthy one without tending to the well being of all its elements.

Mixing metaphors, Kierstead argued that wealth could only be measured by "increased richness for all."[32]

When George Counts of Columbia University spoke at a meeting of the Toronto Branch of the New Education Fellowship, he concentrated on the subject of indoctrination and its threat to democracy. This talk spawned discussion on the matter of a teacher's role in protecting personal freedom through democratic institutions:

> What can teachers do? They must not attempt to merely indoctrinate their pupils, first, because education is futile, and secondly, because a certain section of the public will not allow us to indoctrinate their children or their young people. Teachers can, however, do much. In general they must educate their pupils to gather information, to weigh evidence, to analyze propaganda, and to come to their own conclusions.[33]

Democracy was most notably the tool and instrument for progressive reforms to social institutions and structures because it was mutable and permissive of rational debate and dissent. "One of the chief arguments for the development of public education was its influence in effecting social reform," explained an editorial article in *The School*; progress in educational terms would "lessen poverty and vice. It was essential to democracy."[34]

Reformism and the spirit of cooperation were, at times, however, far more socialistic than democratic. The debates between left- and right-wing factions of educationists were, at least as far as their coverage in popular press and teachers' journals is concerned, far less strained in Ontario than they were in the United States. In 1935, for example at the National Education Association annual convention in Denver, "as was no doubt anticipated, much of the convention's energy was spent in a struggle between [these] factions."[35] Almost one-fifth of the one million public school instructors in the United States were members of the Association, and the stakes were inevitably high. "Leftists" in the debate were led by professors John K. Norton and Jesse H. Newlon from Teachers College, Columbia University, who passionately argued that "united with other progressive elements . . . the school cannot, should not, and will not be neutral in the struggle of social forces now going on."[36]

Social meliorists within the academy identified academic freedom as a critical part of social reconstruction. As an editorial article in *The School* argued, "administrators and schools should have full opportunity to present differing points of view on all controversial questions, in order to aid students" with their adjustments and reflections upon the changing conditions to social life.[37] On July 6, 1935, following the National Education Association conference, a front-page article in The Times Educational Supplement written by an unnamed author addressed the matter of teachers organizing in order to assert greater political influence and affect the terrain of social improvement:

The leaders of the movement, in their fervour for social reconstruction, appear to close their eyes to a large number of factors which sand in the way of their programme. They fail to realize that teacher and schools cannot move any faster than society is willing to approve. They assume that all teachers are ready to accept the same political, social, or economic programme . . .

It is doubtful whether such opposition would have been aroused, if the campaign had not concentrated on making teachers class-conscious, militant propagandists. A less vociferously conducted movement for a programme of educational enlightenment on crucial issues of the day, for a genuine training in intelligent citizenship, would have met with greater success.[38]

Certainly, insofar as Ontario's media coverage of teacher militancy or revolutionary approaches to social reform are concerned, the note upon which the anonymous author cited above ends the article is the most reasonable one. Schools and society were not perfect, and many educationists could readily point to a number of injustices worth changing; a more moderate mission for change, however, would not alienate the more conservative elements amongst meliorist advocates for educational reform.

Within the National Education Association camps, moderate notes of social meliorism were more tenable. Late in 1935, the Board of Directors of the Association asked their President to "propose desirable social-economic goals, and to indicate the materials and methods which the schools should use to attain these ends."[39] The ensuing report, published in the Research Bulletin of the National Education Association, provided a bibliography of books and articles published over the previous decade in social-economic education in schools that was recommended to Ontario teachers involved in newly designed Civics classes in the province.[40] Experiments in civic education and in the pursuit of social justice were, thus, an important part of progressive schooling between 1925 and 1935.

By December 1935 in Ontario, the movement for compulsory or automatic membership in teachers' federations, which had been active for years in the western provinces and in Nova Scotia, was well under way.[41] While the federations gained strength, they pushed for increasing work stability and professionalization for Ontario's teachers. Teachers' federations considered associating with the Trades and Labour Congress of Canada in order to facilitate campaigns pushing for more adequate organization in 11 domains: better enforcement of educational laws, wider uses of the school organization, reduction in class sizes, upward revision of teacher's salaries, increase of school revenues to develop school facilities, cooperation between school boards and teachers in cases of controversy, tenure of position, sound pension laws, protection of schools from propaganda or exploitation, labour representation on school boards, and, finally, compulsory school attendance.[42] Ultimately, the association between the teachers and the Trades and

Labour Congress was not made official, because the initiative had emerged from groups of teachers independent of the administrative officials, and many considered affiliation to be unprofessional. This is despite the fact that Patrick Drape included intellectuals such as teachers and actors amongst the same ranks.[43]

The most aggressive social meliorist arguments that were published in the popular press and educational periodicals were critiques of the economic order and the laissez-faire selfishness inherent in market capitalism. Cooperation and individualism were deemed antithetical within "our so-called capitalistic system" in the words of John Cook.[44] Could democracy accommodate capitalism and an increased emphasis on the personal? Progress in this regard, meant something akin to moving beyond capitalism and embracing an economic order that was more conducive to social justice and social cooperation:

> Capitalism as long as there was a scarcity of the necessities of comfortable living, and as long as the employment of every individual who was able to work was required to produce sufficient goods to keep people living satisfactorily, was a great success. It maybe as good an economic system as could be evolved to meet a situation where there was a scarcity of the necessities of life. However, when the time came that the machinery set up by the system was easily able, without the assistance of the whole working population, to produce more than could easily be consumed by the whole population, difficulties became apparent. Unemployment became general.[45]

Misdistribution of wealth, poverty, and unemployment in the midst of plenty was blamed on inherent flaws within capitalistic theory. Capitalism had proven incapable of dealing with the inequities and injustices that it promoted, particularly during the Depression. Progressive education could not possibly prepare students vocationally and socially for the world of the future and still maintain a belief that it served as a foundation for a world that was socially just.

An editorial in *The School* argued that the public good suffered as a result of social and economic changes to Ontarian society:

> In all industrial sections of Canada the problem of looking after children whose mothers are working in industry is becoming more acute. Many school-age children are subsisting on a very ill-balanced diet— some leaving home in the morning after a breakfast of bread, returning at noon to an empty and cheerless house for an inadequate or injudicious lunch, and ending the day with a dinner prepared by one already tired from other employment.[46]

Inequality of opportunity in education, as in society, had, as a prime cause, the "poverty of some parents" and social-economic inequities.[47] Schools could not promote equality within a progressive educational system without consideration of the inequalities that were ripe without.

The editors of *The School* were at the forefront of meliorist critiques of public schooling. They equated human flourishing with democracy and tyranny with economic manipulation and self-interest. Thus, the "coming triumph of humanity" could only be realized through "the securing of a fuller life by all mankind" for all its citizens.[48] "Tyrant, gangster, murderer, persecutor—ruthless trade monopolists, exponents of racial superiority, nation gobblers, and one-party advocates—these and their ilk" were depicted as opponents to social progress, freedom, and social justice.[49] The editorial marked a progressivist spirit as encompassing:

> A wider distribution of material benefits, fundamentally by a wider distribution of three related abilities: the ability to recognize the universal good, the ability to recognize the good in others, and the ability to assume responsibility in co-operation with others to achieve the common good.

"Materialism is the chief curse of civilization," explained the Director of the Citizen's Research Institute of Canada, Horace Brittain.[50] "Education," he continued, "has not escaped its deadly influence."[51] Schools were implored do their utmost not to preserve and maintain a system of classes and advantages emerging from an economic order promoting individualism and competition. As such, it was "the duty of the Province so to control the funds it distributes as to provide equality of financial ability in relation to local needs"[52] through a system of centralization that could ensure some areas were not at a greater advantage than others throughout Ontario.

Laissez-faire sentimentality was depicted as an historical relic with respect to public schooling. At the 1935 High School Boards' Annual Convention Joseph McCulley called for a "revolution" in schooling.[53] "A wider socialized viewpoint on the part of teachers and trustees is necessary," McCulley continued, noting that social reform was seminal to progressivist educational ideas.[54] Charles Minkler, perhaps inadvertently, summed up the beliefs that distinguished social meliorists. Some progressivists, he noted, believed that progressivists ought, "not to attempt to change the social order directly, but to so develop the emergent generation that it will formulate a better and better democratic society," while others were concerned with "attempts to fit the child into a pre-determined mould, to train him [sic] to fit into the social order to which he belongs."[55] Neither route, Minkler insinuated, was sufficiently progressivist. C. C. Goldring noted: "Man [sic] is essentially adaptable and is capable of doing a wide variety of things equally well."[56] "If the *new education* is to succeed," Goldring stated, it needed to envision a unique way forward that did not seek to define one way forward for any individual student to succeed.[57]

Social meliorists equated progressive education with civic engagement. Bereft of social activism, *The School* argued in a typically activist editorial article, progressivism "might lead to unprogressive conservativism rather than progress."[58] Another editorial in the same journal concentrated on the development of "Education Weeks" by teachers' federations. Federations ought to engage with the public and with the media, the article noted, whether teachers were prone to "like it or not."[59] In the modern age, it was vital for teachers to "put up a persistent sales campaign for education."[60]

When democratic rhetoric was at its apex during the start of the Second World War, the theme for Education Week was, not surprisingly, "In Defence of Democracy."[61] Since education was a matter of significant expense to the public purse, meliorists, like other progressives, felt a need to "sell" ideas like social justice, equality, and democracy to Ontario's citizens. Admittedly, they recognized that:

> Selling is not an activity congenial to teachers. To those who live in the academic calm, salesmanship connotes a glib and shameless sophistry with enthusiastic intent to deceive. Nevertheless we teach in a world where commodities survive on their publicized merits, in years when the demands on the public purse are heavy beyond precedent, and under conditions which will make people question the value of everything they paid for on trust before.[62]

Good salesmanship entailed making clear statements about the necessity of certain reforms for progress. In terms of social meliorism, publishing articles and inviting parents and children to contemplate the welfare of all Ontarians was seen, to a certain degree, as a mission of communitarian enlightenment. Also, since all citizens contributed financially to the educational enterprise, the direction of educational progress should not be in the interests or under the influence of "private control."[63] Departments of Education across Canada were realizing that "education, like any other commodity, has to be sold to the people, and that a certain amount of showmanship is always necessary in promoting a program . . . in other words, the pill has to be sugar-coated."[64]

The scope of cooperative citizenship was seen as one extending beyond the provincial domain and into the international arena. Joseph McCulley from Pickering College, for example, was elected chairman of publicity and promotion for the conference of the West New York branch of the Progressive Educational Association, which included teachers in private and public schools, parents, and educationists interested in working on basic ideas of international cooperation and understanding.[65] The idea that citizenship education was a global matter and that Ontario's population needed to know about world citizenship grew in prominence following the First World War and the creation of the League of Nations.[66]

Democratic citizenship and education were promoted as counterparts to Kaiserism. Even as the League failed to rise up to counter Mussolini's attacks on Ethiopia and the Nazi threat appeared to go untamed, the League was not seen to have failed in its purposes insofar as it was "moving in the direction indicated in the preamble to the covenant . . . international co-operation and world peace."[67] A progressive, socially just, and "proper education is the key to world peace."[68] It was at times related to the British Commonwealth and Empire, and, during the build-up to the Second World War, was a progressive response to Stalinism, Nazism, and Fascism. As "the possibility of war hovers continually over the world,"[69] international cooperation and the promotion of progressive meliorist ideas would be key in preventing a repetition of the tragedies of the Great War.

The meliorist mission for reforms in schools and society was thus expressed as part of a larger conflict, namely the "struggle between two ways of life, 'Hitlerism' and 'Democracy.' "[70] The cultivation of critical thinking, democratic debate, intellectual curiosity, and equality of opportunity were what could separate a progressive Ontario from the kinds of oppressive contexts represented by totalitarian regimes. While no one in Ontario, for example, would agree that a progressive educational system would train "teachers to be Liberals or Conservatives," in 1936, it was with great horror that educational journals noted that "in Germany schools are being established by the government with the avowed purpose of training National-Socialist leaders."[71] A circular by the International Bureau of Education communicated the program and aims of the Nazi National-Political Educational Institutes aimed at developing strong leaders; it provided evidence for meliorist educationists in Ontario to reinforce the importance of democratic freedom and progressive education for a more just world.

"Democratic education," explained an editorial in *The School* during the Second World War, when the expressions of democratic freedom seem most fervent and pressing, "challenging the rigid procedures of tradition, showed disdain for any emphasis on efficiency—at least in theory. It was considered enough that the teacher should strike from the child the shackles of arbitrary authority."[72] Any citizen "who is participating in the democratic way of life has an inquiring and critical mind," argued Dr. David H. Russell of the University of British Columbia, for "democracy must be free from the atrophy of the critical faculty that is imposed by the modern-style dictatorship."[73] Yet, no struggle for freedom from coercion or indoctrination could be progressive from the meliorist viewpoint if it were purely individualistic or exclusive.

At the same time, a softer strain of meliorism saw the preservation of democratic principles and debate as evolving from peaceful negotiation and not war. If progress were to be made in Ontario in terms of ameliorating social and economic conditions of life for all, cooperation and not competition were required. "The truth is," an editorial article in *The School* noted, "democracy and war are mutually exclusive. They cannot exist together."[74] It continued to argue that "good world citizenship begins with good Canadian citizenship."[75] Concentric circles of loyalty, beginning with the provinces and extending to the country, Empire, and the entire world, would promote international cooperation and eliminate the competition that provokes so much harm in the globe.[76] The basis of any just and progressive system of schooling must arise from "a knowledge and understanding of the people of Canada—all of them, by all of them."[77] Just as war and competition within the province was regressive, war between nation states was antithetical to the spirits of cooperation, world citizenship, and global progress.

Still, the principles of a strong and progressive Canadian citizenship were the foundations of any equitable and socially just international structure. These principles were, at the most basic level, committed to the preservation of "the dignity of man and . . . human happiness"[78] for all. The definition of democracy offered by James G. Gardiner, former Minister of National War Services further elucidates this perspective: "freedom to live, freedom to think, freedom to learn, freedom to agree or disagree, freedom to choose one's calling, freedom to change one's mind, leavened by a healthy community spirit, which permits us to bear one another's burdens."[79] Liberty, equality, and fraternity, the triumvirate of freedoms upon which the French Revolution were based, seemed endangered by the over-obedience to industry, efficiency, and tradition.[80]

Democracy was necessarily critical. It required debate, but it beseeched each citizen to participate in the discussion. It was, in part, for this reason that the meliorist reforms were deemed progressive with respect to the established methods of schooling in Ontario. Education was more than making students literate or developing standardization and efficiency, it involved helping students to "learn to think independently and live co-operatively."[81] A progressive "school must spring from the life of the people. Freed from the encumbrances of traditional subjects and no longer pre-occupied with remote and meaningless abstractions, it must adapt itself to the needs of the community it serves" and ameliorate conditions for all.[82] Walter Lipmann, in 1919, broadcast the following statement, which was cited by numerous Ontarian progressivists:

> Democracy cannot be made to work by people who think it is enlightened to be cynical, grasping, concerned with the expediency of the moment, and contemptuous of all standards which transcend it. There is not enough intelligence or character in this way of life to govern a nation successfully. For democracy was founded by men who had the conviction that there is truth and that there is good and evil; it was never meant for men who reject this view of life and insofar—and it is now very far—as democracies have fallen into disbelief and untruth, they are in a desperately dangerous muddle about everything that matters most and to their children.[83]

What "mattered most" for meliorist progressivists was a healthy and critical communitarianism that rejected the compulsions of dictators, as well as that of industrial leaders.

Individualized Instruction

"Individualism," Dalhousie University Professor B. A. Fletcher told Ontario's teachers, "is the quality that more than any other sharply distinguishes the democratic from the totalitarian idea . . . It is the concept that is finding expression in all the recent efforts to provide equality of opportunity."[84] This individualism, in a progressive and educational context, posits the individual as more than "the functionary of an imposed regime" and more than the expression of a selfish and "disturbing egoism."[85] The individual student had an obligation and a privilege to "help his fellow man who, in the fell clutch of circumstance, finds himself"[86] in turmoil or trouble. This social aim is one that lasts a lifetime, whereas specialized training could be made "obsolete at any time. His particular trade may disappear almost over night."[87] A progressive individual, then, was not one who was taught to be skillful in terms of a particular niche; it is a person who was "adaptable to new conditions, able to meet emergencies as they arise."[88]

In other words, because life is contingent, fluid, and ever changing, schools had a responsibility to encourage critical thought and adaptability. Students were "living in an environment of mystifying change," noted John Long from the Ontario College of Education at the start of 1936.[89] The pervasive sense of change, he continued, "marks all phases of contemporary life."[90] An individualized instruction plan that concentrated on a very particular and limited set of skills was insufficient, for "changing conditions require adaptable minds, and conditions are changing most rapidly."[91] Critical thought was the antidote to a narrow, specialized, and skills-based education, which would only promote conformity and subjugation to the dominant industrial and social orders. These orders leave individuals "driven to ruthlessness by forces" that subjugate "initiative and self reliance."[92] In "a progressive, industrial world, nothing is taken for granted."[93]

Education was both "broader than" and "longer than" school.[94] The home, the church, agencies such as the Girls Guides, Boy Scouts, Junior Red Cross, Y.M.C.A., and Y.W.C.A, along with adult education initiatives, all contributed to the progressive visions of social justice and welfare outside the school house. Greater cooperation with these missions, and a broader sense of education that could contribute to the reformation and regeneration of society along equitable terms could support the progressive aims of social meliorists. "Voluntary agencies play a prominent part in education," explained a 1933 editorial on the work community organizations in London, where efforts were made to "secure the best possible educational opportunity for each child" regardless of socioeconomic status.[95] Cooperation between schools, families, and community groups could best facilitate a progressive vision for a socially just world.

Fragments of two notable addresses, "Some Problems of Government" and "The Endless War," by President Nicholas Murray Butler of Columbia University commemorating the 183rd year of his school were reproduced in Ontario's educational journals in October 1936.[96] Butler argued that education of adults and children needed "genuine co-operation" to conduct "the war for righteousness, for justice, and for moral standards of thought and feeling."[97] In a healthy democracy, critical intelligence was necessary and social justice was required. Respect for democratic institutions emerged from its practicality and, in a sense, to its empowerment of individuals to change the order of society, when necessary, to meet the changing needs of a progressive world.

This points to a very interesting reversal of how the idea of a practical education could be interpreted. The most practical knowledge any learner could have when living in a cooperative "community in this rapidly changing world," was that which promoted critical thought and adaptability.[98] The efficiency rhetoric, rooted in transfer of training language justifying apparent need to train students to complete very particular and specific tasks, was entirely too narrow and lacking in pragmatism. "We live in a world of change," admitted George S. Henry, Premier of Ontario and Minister of Education for the province, at the Ontario Educational Association 1933 convention: "Nothing is perfect. What satisfies us to-day will not satisfy us to-morrow."[99] The course of studies in progressive schools, in other words, needed to prepare students for a world of change, not for a changing world.

The individual, as part of a community, needed to be considerate of the welfare and well being of all others. More than that, schools had a responsibility to "teach the young folks the absolute necessity of co-operative action and a spirit of self-sacrifice; or the whole fabric of our civilization will be in danger of destruction."[100] This spirit of self-sacrifice differed in a very grand way from the social efficiency mindset, which saw the individual as an important cog in an established order. The efficient management and control of society required, from that perspective, the individual to find a place where they could most effectively contribute to the maintenance of that order in a relatively isolated way. Competition and laissez-faire capitalism were not dramatically interrogated or asked to be replaced. Here, however, the social meliorists rebelled against the notion that individuals were intended to be unquestioning and uncritical components of an ultimately competitive and self-motivated context. The child should not be made to "fit" the extant society, just as "we cannot make the pupil fit the school. But it should be quite possible to make the school fit the pupil," who will, in turn, reshape society. [101]

A progressive and democratic system of schooling would never "think of the state as a machine in which the citizen is a mere cog."[102] There was nothing to be gained from burying children's heads "ostrich-like, in the sand and ignore . . . Controversial subjects in the classroom."[103] Human kind, it was argued, is both social by nature and "has shown in the past remarkable powers of adaptation . . . the new education that will teach men how to best live with one another in the closer social and political contacts that seem inevitable will do most to help the new generation to adapt itself" to change.[104] A social education that brings people to each other will help society progress together without benefiting the few at the expense of the many. A "socially-minded citizenship will be the strong defense of the democracy of the future."[105]

Progress as integration and cooperation, then, was of great importance to social meliorists. Individualized mental testing schemes isolated learners from the community in which they lived and to which they contributed. Streaming of children into classes, likewise, created imbalances in the ways learners were treated and labeling them crudely in accordance to supposedly objective measures:

> 'Below average' is the least offensive term of several synonyms to describe them, but it does suggest beings of a generally inferior sort. It should not. The fact is that achievement marks are a much too facile instrument in education and are too often interpreted as indicating much more than they do.[106]

Vocational classes, such as manual training for boys and domestic science classes for girls divided gender roles and reinforced traditional stereotypes. C. C. Goldring, Superintendent of Schools for Toronto, provided a view of manual training that was both very Deweyan in orientation and startlingly different from that espoused by social efficiency advocates. The subject "should be taught," he believed, "essentially as a cultural subject, and as a means for the boy [sic] to express himself . . . He should find satisfaction and happiness in this work."[107] The work of manual training, Goldring explained, could be transposed to a general shop class, which would enable students to work cooperatively and to explore "a wide range of interests" that could contribute to an emotionally and physically pleasant leisure time through life.[108] Individuals in a cooperative learning environment needed to work together to complete shared tasks and to realize common goals. Consequently, "the developing in the pupil of the spirit of co-operation is one of the teacher's most vital responsibilities."[109]

Active Learning

Progress in society and in education was considered to be prompted by circumstances and events that "arise which cause a general unsettling in the intellectual atmosphere; in this environment creative thinkers find a more satisfactory opportunity to achieve their purpose and change comes about much more rapidly than at other times."[110] New conceptions of life could never supplant established dogmas and doctrines without struggle, advocacy, and the active support of citizens. In life, as in education *progressivism*, or, for that matter, "any 'ism' or 'ology' which is sufficiently critical of present conditions or which claims itself as a panacea for the ills of our body politic will find at least its quota of adherents."[111] Moreover, these adherents needed to be sufficiently critically minded to debate viewpoints without blind adherence to any doctrine.

Active involvement in terms of promoting social welfare and justice involved more than reading and reflection.

> Don't stand aside and leave it to others, [implore the social meliorists,] for the opportunities are at your threshold, in every town and village where you happen to live. The tasks are there and every one of us can play a part, for the race is not necessarily to the swift nor the battle to the strong.[112]

Concern for the common good invokes each meliorist to do their best for each other in society. Each person was considered equally capable of this task, and neither intelligence testing nor auxiliary classes could replace a commitment to active involvement in the reconstruction of society. The alternative, a strict and narrow efficiency view of progress, was a fundamentally immoral one: "for the application of this method to human beings see *Mein Kampf* by A. Hitler, who bases his social and educational philosophy on Darwinian theory."[113] A truly progressive vision for schooling would promote a model of schooling wherein each child would "assume responsibility for his own welfare and the welfare of all."[114]

Accordingly, if progressive schools were to develop in children an understanding of the benefits of cooperative living and social welfare, they should be engaged in classroom activities that build relevant experiences. The pupil, "having been shown the particular value of this principle in the world around him, should be placed in a position where he may take part in the actual demonstration of it."[115] Cooperative activities and purposes with a social purpose—everything from the construction of benches for needy organizations to choirs that could tour the community and promote good will—were frequently cited as the principal way of gaining active experience with the benefits of mutual care and sharing. The beginnings of concern for social justice were seen in cooperative work habits, which grounded and contextualized a progressive spirit of sympathetic interest in the welfare of the entire community. This spirit "emphasized the outward movement from the classroom" to all society of a meliorist concern for remedying social injustices.[116]

A democratic and progressive province required active and committed citizenship. There was nothing self-perpetuating about democratic states, meliorists argued repeatedly, and "unfeeling, apathetic citizenship of people is proving fatal to democracy."[117] A progressive school was one that fostered and promoted active, critical reflection and promoted cooperative, responsible, and associative living centering on the question: "Who is my neighbour?"[118] In resounding Deweyan tones, F. J. McDonald, Inspector of Separate Schools for Ottawa, argued that if active citizenship, debate, adaptability, and "the improvement of social order" were to be promoted, "The

Progressive school" would have to promote "learning by doing."[119] Active citizenship entailed far more than memorization of facts relating to government, civics, or morality, it involved a habit of living democratically. In part, this had several implications for progressive education:

1. that civilization is a co-operative task
2. that living is a joint responsibility
3. that the success of the social enterprise depends upon individual effort, Sociability and dependability

> These aims are to be constantly held in mind in training our citizens. And the greatest of these is participation,—activity.[120]

Children learn to be good citizens by living a life of good citizenship. Likewise, "if the society is to be successful in revealing democracy, it should train each member in a democratic way."[121] The formative place for this life was at school, where the lessons of communal work and play were first learned. The elementary school teachers' federations, accordingly, sent out to their members a memorandum "supporting attitudes and teaching methods which will foster democracy as a way of life. Democratic teaching rather than teaching democracy is approved as desirable practice in elementary school."[122]

Civics courses were one way that active and experiential training for citizenship was enabled. While the school curriculum had been overextended and overloaded with courses that were either entirely academic or vocational, the most practical necessity of all, learning about being a critical and reflective citizen of the province had been neglected. "It is not possible for all to become carpenters, or dressmakers, or milliners," explained James Keillor from North Toronto Collegiate Institute, but "all are called upon to assume the duties of citizenship."[123] In the "progressive educational journals and in the columns of our daily newspapers," Keillor argued, "we read much regarding efforts to adapt the curricula of our public and high schools to the needs of the average Canadian citizen."[124] A truly progressive school system would concentrate on the study of society, and understand that "the pupil can learn citizenship only by being an active citizen during his school life."[125] Most importantly, in terms of active learning,

> a text-book, if any is used, will be valuable chiefly for reference in seeking more information after class discussion . . . the chief value of such action lies in the development of habits of right social thought and action.[126]

The idea of "social studies" was being widely adopted in the rhetoric and curricula of schools across Ontario in the 1930s intimately with the social meliorist orientation towards progressive schooling.[127] Previously, the term had "been used rather loosely to include history, civics, geography, and economics. Some effort has been made to correlate these subjects, but up to the present they have generally remained quite separate."[128] Other models of classes typically referred to as "fusion courses" were essayed, to the dismay of meliorists because they frequently consisted of fragments of different subjects without a theme centering on actual social circumstances of life. The Ontario government issued the *Report of the Commission on the Social Studies* in 1936, which was prepared by L. C. Marshall and R. M. Goetz on the subject; Part XIII, titled *Curriculum Making in the Social Studies* argued that the "essential task" that schools faced was "to aid youth to the fullest practicable understanding of our social order; to a meaningful realization of the ways in which the individual, both pupil and adult, may participate effectively in that order; and to motivate for effective participation."[129]

A unity of the studies could best be achieved through thematic study of various social problems and injustices, which the newly-introduced social studies facilitated. Not only did this subject enable the student be able to draw upon personal experience and a range of different subjects, including socio-economic and political factors leading to inequities in public health and housing, it created a playing field that enabled active participation in the improvement of community life for all. Social studies were seen as potential domains for the study and improvement of social life in a systematic and cooperative way; they resembled "laboratory study of social living. In some substantial sense, this approach means a laboratory study of social living. Every pupil provides his own singularly complete laboratories; and his laboratories are not artificial—they are real life."[130] Social studies was represented as a dynamic way of taking independent subjects away from a teaching trajectory concentrating on "collections of insignificant facts" and focusing them on "the scientific study of the development of the society in which we live."[131] The progressive teacher could use the subject as a means of developing methods of instruction that would focus school work on the social work that individuals were beholden to undertake in their communities.

The social meliorist platform extended beyond the realm of public schools. The Canadian Association for Adult Education actively lobbied for and promoted opportunities for adults, not merely the student population, particularly in rural areas. The Association stood, primarily, for the following purposes: "(1) to serve as a clearing-house and maintain a working library; (2) to develop interest by means of publications, radio, and conferences; (3) to suggest methods and to improve the work in adult education;" and to cooperate with existing agencies or organizations.[132]

Extensions of educational opportunities were pursued on a vigorous scale throughout the interwar period, even during the Depression when construction and expansion of infrastructure were typically halted. Innovative measures included the development of railway school cars that visited children whose families had settled in northern Ontario, where the forestry and mining industries boomed. Many of these families were new Canadians, who immigrated to Ontario within a single generation. Correspondence classes, which provided a course of studies to individuals unable to attend school because of physical distance or physical disability represent another extension of the educational franchise in Ontario.[133] Radio broadcasts, slide lectures, agricultural talks, and moving motion picture machines were all part of the "increasing effort . . . to reach the most remote parts" of progressive provinces in Canada, particularly Ontario and Alberta, following the First World War.[134]

Progress in schools entailed, in part, equality of opportunity. The lobby to actively extend access to education for Ontarians who had been disadvantaged in the past, including not only adult, but also rural populations, then, was affected by the meliorist concern for equality of opportunity. "Adult education is indeed closely bound up with democracy itself," explained R. S. Lambert of the Canadian Association for Adult Education.[135] Ideally, it is:

> Based on the very principles which make democracy flourish—the development of individual personality, the encouragement of the creative instinct, the rational approach to social and international problems, and a sound balance of duties and responsibilities in citizenship.[136]

Adult education was thus envisaged as a "powerful antidote to the evils of propaganda."[137] In an ever-changing world, the development of critical skills and democratic principles in the adult population would further the cause of educational and social progress.

Notes

1. Joseph McCulley, "Education in a Changing Society," *The Canadian School Journal* (February, 1932), p. 60.
2. John Dewey, "Why I Am for Smith," *New Republic* 56 (1928), p. 321.
3. Herbert Kliebard, *The Struggle for the American Curriculum, 1893–1958* (New York and London: RoutledgeFalmer, 2004), pp. 151–174.
4. Ibid., p. 154.
5. George S. Counts, *The American Road to Culture: A Social Interpretation of Education in the United States* (New York: John Day, 1930), p. 121 and p. 123.
6. Ibid., p. 126 and p. 137.
7. Ibid., pp. 147–148.
8. John Dewey, "Progressive Education and the Science of Education," *Progressive Education* 5 (1928), p. 198.
9. Ibid., p. 200.
10. Ibid.
11. George S. Counts, "Dare Progressive Education be Progressive?" *Progressive Education* 4, no. 9 (1932), p. 258 and p. 261.
12. Ibid., p. 258.
13. Kliebard, *The Struggle for the American Curriculum*, p. 163.
14. George S. Counts, *Dare the School Build a New Social Order* (New York: John Day, 1932).

15. Kliebard, *The Struggle for the American Curriculum*, p. 146.
16. Boyd H. Bode, *Modern Educational Theories* (New York: Macmillan, 1927).
17. Ibid., p. 163.
18. "The N.E.F. Conference," *The School* (May, 1937), p. 742.
19. E. A. Winters, *Harold Rugg and Education for Social Reconstruction.* Unpublished Ph.D. manuscript (University of Wisconsin, Madison, 1968), p. 91.
20. Kliebard, *The Struggle for the American Curriculum*, pp. 170–173.
21. Harold Rugg, *Now Is the Moment* (New York: Duell, Sloan and Pearce, 1943), xiii.
22. "The N.E.F. Conference," p. 741.
23. Ibid.
24. Kliebard, *The Struggle for the American Curriculum*, p. 151.
25. "Editorial Notes: The School and Society," *The School* (May, 1933), p. 737.
26. Joseph McCulley, "Education in a Changing Society," *The Canadian School Journal* (January, 1932), p. 58.
27. Ibid.
28. William G. Martin, "Education and Citizenship," *The Canadian School Journal* (May, 1932): 194–199.
29. John A. Cook, "Co-operation in Education," *The Canadian School Journal* (November, 1933), p. 406.
30. W. C. Keirstead, "Indoctrination in Education," *The School* (May, 1940), p. 743.
31. Ibid.
32. Ibid.
33. "Editorial: Schools and Democracy," *The School* (February, 1939), p. 459.
34. "Editorial Notes: The School and Society," p. 737.
35. "Academic Freedom," *The School* (September, 1935), p. 2.
36. Ibid.
37. Ibid.
38. Ibid.
39. Editorial, "Survey of Experiments in Social-Economic Education," *The School* (November, 1935), p. 181.
40. "Survey of Experiments in Social-Economic Education," p. 182. See, also, National Education Association, *Bulletin* XII, no. 3 (May, 1935).
41. "Compulsory Membership in Federations," *The School* (December, 1935), p. 271.
42. "Teachers and the Trades and Labour Congress," *The School* (December, 1935), p. 272.
43. Ibid., 273.
44. Cook, "Co-operation in Education," p. 406.
45. Ibid.
46. "Educational News: Ontario," *The School* (April, 1942), p. 723.
47. Horace L. Brittain, "Some Views of Administration of Public Education," *The Canadian School Journal* (December, 1934), p. 406.
48. "Editorial: The Coming Triumph of Humanity," *The School* (December, 1941), p. 275.
49. Ibid.
50. Horace L. Brittain, "Some Views of Administration of Public Education," *The Canadian School Journal* (December, 1934), p. 406.
51. Ibid., p. 407.
52. Ibid.
53. Joseph McCulley, "Press Extracts From Addresses," *The Canadian School Journal* (March, 1935), p. 87.
54. Ibid.

55. Ibid.
56. C. C. Goldring, "Some Possible Phases of Vocational Guidance in Canadian Schools," *The School* (June, 1933), p. 842.
57. Ibid., p. 379, italics in original text.
58. Editorial, "Editorial Notes: Canadian Educational Association," *The School* (October, 1936), p. 93.
59. Editorial, "Editorial: Education Week," *The School* (November, 1941), p. 181.
60. Ibid.
61. Ibid.
62. Ibid.
63. Editorial, "There Is a Tomorrow," *The School* (May, 1942), p. 741.
64. E. A. Corbett, "Can the Radio Be Used Effectively in University Extension Work?," *The School* (October, 1935), p. 94.
65. "News From Home and Abroad," *The Canadian School Journal* (June, 1935), p. 196.
66. George E. Foster, "The League of Nations," *The School* (March, 1928), pp. 645–651.
67. "The Canadian Education Association," *The School* (December, 1936), p. 283.
68. Ibid.
69. Lawrence J. Burpee, "The Work of the International Joint Commission," *The School* (February, 1937), p. 467.
70. A.S.H. Hill, "Is Democracy Worth Fighting For?," *The School* (May, 1940), p. 750.
71. "Editorial Notes: Indoctrination," *The School* (April, 1936), p. 641.
72. "Editorial: School and Society," *The School* (September, 1941), p. 1.
73. David H. Russell, "Education for Critical Thinking," *The School* (November, 1941), p. 188.
74. "Editorial Notes: Democracy at War," *The School* (October, 1939), p. 95.
75. H. P. Plumptre, "Education for World Citizenship," *The Canadian School Journal* (September, 1935), p. 247.
76. Ibid., pp. 247–250.
77. "Editorial: This Is Our Country," *The School* (June, 1942), p. 833.
78. Angela A. Hannan, "Canadian Leaders Deserve Respect," *The School* (September, 1941), p. 11.
79. Ibid.
80. Ibid., pp. 12–13.
81. C. C. Goldring, "Manual Training or the General Shop?" *The School* (February, 1935), p. 470.
82. "Editorial: Two Sides to a Question," p. 91.
83. Ibid., p. 12.
84. B. A. Fletcher, "Some Principles of Education," *The School* (January, 1939), p. 372.
85. Ibid., pp. 372–373.
86. Martin, "Education and Citizenship," p. 194.
87. "Vocational Training and Vocational Guidance," *The Canadian School Journal* (November, 1932), p. 372.
88. Ibid.
89. John Long, "A Review of the Year, 1935," *The School* (February, 1936), p. 467.
90. Ibid.
91. "Changing the Educational Emphasis," *The Canadian School Journal* (March, 1933), p. 84.
92. "Editorial: As a Man Thinks," *The School* (December, 1939), pp. 283–284.
93. Ibid.
94. Ibid., p. 249.

95. "The Work of Voluntary Agencies," *The School* (November, 1933), p. 188.
96. See, for example, "President Butler and Democracy," *The School* (October, 1936), p. 95.
97. Ibid.
98. "The Convention of 1933," *The Canadian School Journal* (May, 1933), p. 163.
99. Ibid.
100. "Despair or Courage," *The Canadian School Journal* (January, 1933), p. 5.
101. Henry Conn, "Measuring Aptitude for School Work," *The School* (April, 1931), p. 717.
102. Watson Kirkonnell, "Democracy for Canadians," *The School* (June, 1941), p. 881.
103. Joseph McCulley, "Education and the War," *The School* (February, 1940), p. 473.
104. Editorial, "Education for a Changing World," *The School* (January, 1935), p. 370.
105. G. Fred McNally, "Curricula for Canadian High Schools," *The School* (January, 1935), p. 379.
106. "Editorial: Below Average," *The School* (February, 1942), p. 463.
107. Goldring, "Manual Training or the General Shop?" p. 470.
108. Ibid., pp. 470–471.
109. Cook, "Co-operation in Education," p. 406.
110. McCulley, "Education in a Changing Society," p. 58.
111. Ibid.
112. Martin, "Education and Citizenship," p. 194.
113. Editorial, "Working Together," *The School* (February, 1941), p. 407.
114. Ibid.
115. Cook, "Co-operation in Education," p. 406.
116. R. H. Macklem, "The Community School," *The School* (April, 1942), p. 656.
117. F. J. McDonald, "Character Training and Citizenship," *The Canadian School Journal* (June, 1934), p. 238.
118. Ibid.
119. Ibid.
120. Ibid., pp. 239–240.
121. B. C. Taylor, "The Latin Society—I," *The School* (September, 1941), p. 41.
122. Editorial, "Educational News: Democracy," *The School* (November, 1941), p. 260.
123. James Keillor, "High School Civics," *The School* (September, 1926), p. 59.
124. Ibid.
125. Ibid.
126. James Keillor, "High School Civics," *The School* (January, 1927), p. 492.
127. "Editorial Notes: New Approaches to the Social Studies," *The School* (April, 1937), p. 645.
128. Ibid.
129. Ibid.
130. Ibid.
131. Editorial, "The Social Sciences," *The School* (January, 1936), p. 363.
132. E. A. Corbett, "Adult Education and the School," *The School* (September, 1938), p. 18.
133. Editorial, "Extension of Correspondence Courses," *The School* (November, 1935), p. 250.
134. E. A. Corbett, "Can the Radio be Used Effectively in University Extension Work?" p. 93.
135. R. S. Lambert, "Adult Education," *The School* (June, 1941), p. 883.
136. Ibid.
137. Ibid.

5   A Case Study in Educational Reform

Duncan McArthur, Progressivist

> We have turned out an elaborate educational machine which has turned out pupils fashioned in the same mould; the time has come when we should realize that children are more important than systems and that human personality cannot be confined within the bounds of tidy compartments.[1]

Duncan McArthur embodied many of the complexities inherent in progressivism during the period considered by this manuscript.[2] The tides of different progressive currents wash over one another and the divisions separating different orientations become extremely difficult to discern. This is particularly true in a historical project, where the classification of pedagogical viewpoints threatens to not only be inorganic and desiccate, but false. I use McArthur as an example of an educational leader who endeavoured to negotiate competing definitions and positions of progressivism.

The tensions and seeming contradictions embedded within McArthur's educational perspectives shall be considered in the contexts of the educational, intellectual, and political climates during the interwar period and extending slightly into 1942, which marked the Minister of Education's passing. McArthur's educationally *progressivism*, as well as his social scientific approach to reform in Ontario, seems absolutely commonplace in these contexts, where modern, industrial, and progressive orientations were eroding the prominence of the established Victorian orders. This examination of Duncan McArthur, whose *progressivism* bears signs of a comprehensive attempt to reconcile a wide range of ideological influences, is a necessary conclusion to this manuscript. Having endeavoured to disentangle the rhetoric of educational *progressivisms*, I now aim to reconcile these by considering a single, educationally progressive figure in the province whose approach to educational matters, inevitably, weaved together many rhetorical threads. There were no *pure* progressives in the sense that no individual was purely and exclusively limited to the child study, efficiency, or meliorist orientation throughout his/her lifetime. No wave of reforms is separable or distinct from the values or orientations that follow it, or from those that it overtakes. The complicated qualities of McArthur's educational writings make this point clearly.

These writings were, surprisingly, difficult to uncover. At the Archives of Ontario, not a single file or folder is devoted to the man who spent eight years engineering substantive changes in the province's system of schooling. One single picture exists in the online descriptions database[3] but to find it, one must misspell the former education Minister's name (MacArthur).[4] The Queen's University archives prove a slightly better source of information, but only if the researcher is more concerned with McArthur the historian rather than with McArthur the educationist. Manuscripts and essays, not directly related to pedagogy, form the substantive portion of his files at the university where he studied and worked for most of his life. Following a contextualization of biographical and intellectual influences upon McArthur's life, I shall proceed to examine the late Minister's particular educational beliefs with regard to the different *progressivisms* discussed over the previous three chapters.

Biographical Overview

Before entering the Department of Education as Deputy Minister and Chief Director of Education on July 11, 1934, Duncan McArthur was professor of history at Queen's University. He was born in 1884 in the township of Dunwich, located in Elgin County not far from Kingston, Ontario. His family descended from the United Empire Loyalists and had settled the area during the American War for Independence. After attending elementary and high school in the rural village of Dunnon, Ontario, he began undergraduate studies at Queen's University in 1904.

Following his graduation from Queen's with a Bachelor of Arts, in 1907, McArthur began graduate studies working in political science and history with celebrated social scientist Adam Shortt. McArthur won gold medals at Queen's for his studies in three subjects: political science, history, and philosophy. Following his graduate work, he began working at the Canadian Archives with his mentor, Dr. Shortt. In this capacity, he collaborated with Drs. Doughty and Shortt to write and publish a number of constitutional documents on the Canadian political context.

In 1912, McArthur began to study law at Osgoode Hall, University of Toronto, and graduated three years later. He began practicing law immediately afterwards, and continued to do so until 1917, when he was named manager of estates for the London, Ontario-based Canada Trust Company. Two years later he became assistant general manager of the London and Western Trusts Company. Three years afterwards, in 1922, the chair of Queen's University's history department, J. L. Morrison retired and McArthur was offered and accepted his position.

Over the next 12 years, Duncan McArthur was involved in educational matters at Queen's, where he helped begin the summer program for archival and historical study, in the city of Kingston. During this time, he was a member of the Board of Education, and at the Department of Education, where he participated on several special committees. In the early 1930s, McArthur helped the Education Department to develop and implement midsummer examinations for high school students. His experiences in this regard would provide him with sound experience upon which he based his educationally progressive philosophy. [5]

Duncan McArthur's *progressivism* in educational matters is one that historians have acknowledged but not examined. His writings, speeches, and actions on education typified him as a reformer. To examine these reforms in light of the disentangling of *progressivisms* that has been undertaken in the previous four chapters, this section shall concentrate on the way that one individual reformer reconciled and integrated different progressive orientations—developmentalism, meliorism, and efficiency—into one comprehensive vision for Ontario's schools.

I am also inclined to approach McArthur broadly and eclectically; in so doing, I refuse to denote him either, strictly speaking, as a developmentalist, efficiency advocate, or social meliorist. None of this is to say that different pedagogical or political ideologies were competing on equal terms and with equal footing in interwar Ontario, but it would be inconsistent with my approach so far to identify any individual with one singular, thoroughly consistent, and particular ideological orientation towards progress. The eclectic reading of progressivism is also supported by Herbert Kliebard's definition of progressives as engaged in shifting coalitions of interests around particular topics.[6] What is more, it cannot be understood without consideration for the intellectual and spiritual environment of Queen's University between the end of the nineteenth century and the beginning of the twentieth, which was infused with elements of idealism, civic humanism, and new liberalism. Many of the ideas that characterized McArthur's educational *progressivism* were consistent, also, with the rise of a social scientific approach within academic study. Important figures in this context that were associated with Duncan McArthur's education at Queen's include George Grant, John Watson, Adam Shortt, and John Harold Putman. McArthur's *progressivism* in education matters, then, needs to be contextualized—even briefly—in light of the different intellectual and ideological influences with which he interacted, more generally throughout his life, but more specifically at Queen's University where he spent a great portion of his academic life, as both a student and a professor.

Contextual and Intellectual Influences

The university was a sea rich with many intellectual currents. It would not be correct to argue that each of these currents was as strong or as influential as all the others. Nor is it possible here, in this chapter, to engage in a protracted explanation and categorization of all the philosophical and ideological movements making waves throughout the interwar period at Queen's. What it is possible—in fact necessary—to do in order to contextualize

McArthur's particularly progressive attitude towards educational reform, is to discuss how the themes we have been discussing in relation to *progressivism* were emergent ones at the university, particularly with respect to the burgeoning social sciences. Duncan McArthur's progressive iterations of what constituted active learning, individualized instruction, and the correlation of school and society were comprehensive reformulations of ideas affected by these currents.

We shall begin with a dominant philosophical orientation related to idealism and to civic humanism—emphasizing both individual freedom and social conscience—that flourished, primarily under the influence of renowned philosopher John Watson. This orientation, particularly in the Canadian context, reflected a complexity of thought wherein two main streams were immediately compatible with the consensus values in Ontario at the time: individual responsibility to seek out a course in the world, and obligation to social well-being and development.[7] This intellectual cross-pollination of ideas reflected a "particularly Canadian . . . mixture of idealism and individualism thus posited a world in which the free will of man was untrammeled by the institutions around him,"[8] while the individual could only be fully realized through society. The liberal concern for the individual was thus restrained by the social needs, which "could override individual rights in the name of community."[9]

At a time when change and inconstancy seemed normal, "Watson offered students a solution to the problems of life in a complex intellectual and social world."[10] The importance of philosophical idealism in the context, Brian McKillop has noted, is related to the rise of Darwinism (social and anthropological/scientific) in the academy.[11] The new worldview propagated by evolutionary scientists provoked anxiety:

> Great fear arose that the views of the evolutionists would lead to a belief in the relativity of knowledge and ethics. Moral philosophers also feared that the new physiological psychology, wed to the British tradition of empiricism, would lead to sensationalism and a rejection of metaphysics.[12]

Idealism did not reject evolutionary science and Darwinism. It offered an alternative to a positivistic empiricism by embracing, redirecting, and revisioning Christian piety.[13] Rational, intellectual inquiry were not necessarily disparate matters from faith; the world was utterly rational and comprehensible:

> The philosophical creed which commends itself to my mind is what in the text I have called speculative idealism, by which I mean the doctrine that we are capable of knowing Reality as it actually is, and that Reality when so known is absolutely rational.[14]

The very idea that Watson's philosophical framework for inquiring into worldly phenomena could be called a "creed" is interesting for two reasons.

Not only does it reveal the spiritual and faith-based elements to the world-view, it reminds the modern historian of Dewey's first major progressive text, which was published a year earlier in 1897, *My Pedagogic Creed*. Watson's idealism embraced humanity as a moral species. Given choice, humans could deliberate and decide both justly and morally.

Idealism, as a philosophical system, was the most dominant and influential one at Queen's, and it appeared to provide a comprehensive approach to thinking about and examining a bewildering and complex world:

> Idealism was, first of all, a philosophical system that was confident in the face of the multiple forms of modern scientific investigation. It rejected the problematic dualism of common sense while affirming the moral nature of man. It provided a renewed sense of design in the natural and mental worlds, a sense of purpose, and . . . in fact, it sought to do nothing less, in Watson's formulation at least, than to provide a way of encompassing and understanding naturalistic science within the larger framework of the essential rationality of a moral universe, thereby circumscribing and taming it.[15]

Idealism met the needs of a changing age, but it also made an explicit effort to take philosophic and reflective inquiry out of a purely academic and abstract realm and apply it to matters of human and social experience or reality. In Watson's own words, philosophy was seen as having:

> Expanded into the nobler discipline of an interpretation of social and political life and institutions, of art and religion, as these developed into ever higher and more perfect forms in the great secular process of history . . . [which is] in no sense divorced from the concrete life of man.[16]

Idealism, in confronting lived experience, confronted the relationship between individuals and the society in which they lived. "The morality of Watson and other Ontario idealists was a social morality;" explained A. B. McKillop, "the freedom that flowed from it depended on a commitment to the larger good of the community."[17] What McKillop was pointing to is the way that John Watson's idealism seemed to embody and articulate, with regards to the individual within a social state, the "fundamental premises of early practitioners of social science in Ontario, and they inspired a generation and more of students to serve"[18] the communities in which they lived. The following explanation, from Watson's *An Outline of Philosophy* (1901), can help us see how a new group of social scientists, such as Duncan McArthur, was affected by the calls for intelligent inquiry and for social service:

> It is still true that only by identifying himself with a social good can the individual realize himself. And the reason is that in the community the idea of humanity as an organic unity is in process of realization . . . the

individual man can find himself, can become moral, only by contributing his share to its realization. He must learn that, to set aside his individual inclinations and make himself an organ of the community is tot be moral, and the only way to be moral.[19]

B. Anne Wood argued that under the influence of Watson and Queen's University's Principal Grant, the idealist spirit "infused Queen's at the time. It was a spirit characterized by a strong sense of commitment to the community and dedication to service for the public good."[20] In this environment, according to Watson, freedom was not the pursuit of personal pleasure; it entailed voluntarily doing "what one ought. But what ought one to do? We ought to aim at making ourselves and others perfect citizens, i.e., citizens who share in all that tends to make the life of a man a perfect whole."[21]

Principal Grant, just noted, combined "an evangelical spirit, a commitment to public service, and idealist principles in a highly active life"[22] that permeated the intellectual environment at Queen's. A distinct sense of Britishness and praise for the Empire as a force for promoting progress throughout the word, particularly through its parliamentary democracy, was another key component to the intellectual environment at Queen's. In the words of Principal Grant, "to be Canadian one had to be British."[23] The renewed faith in Empire and Commonwealth were inseparable from the themes of Christian Protestantism, which dominated the religious atmosphere of the university:

> Just as the union of the churches was the precondition for the Christianization of social order, so too the unity of the Empire was necessary to maintain a political power making for righteousness on earth. Both Christianity and imperialism called men to self-sacrifice and service; both required the allegiance to ideals and the denigration of the material and the flesh.[24]

The "sense of Anglo-superiority is associated with and, in part grew out of, the nineteenth-century Canadian imperialist movement," which bolstered the belief that Canada "was an advanced political entity . . . because of its Britishness."[25]

Principal Grant, like Duncan McArthur, stressed the importance for students to become active leaders in their community, to promote social change and improvement. He implored them to "study history, become leaders of public opinion, and, by means of these lessons form the past, direct the course of events."[26] This conscious development of an active model of citizenship, along with a strong sense of community and a sensibility to the interdependence of individuals characterized the environment at Queen's. Grant and Watson began extramural lectures in the community, which were "a model of service for future Queen's graduates, whose major duty, they considered, should be to direct public opinion on important social issues . . . [and] educate people so they could make intelligent decisions"[27] for their community.

These lectures, along with the general orientation towards social service and study, must be seen in relation to the growing influence of social scientific research within the university.[28] An emerging cohort of social scientists, amongst them Adam Shortt, who studied at Queen's and fell under the tutelage of Watson and the influence of Grant, would turn their attention, and that of their students—who included, in Shortt's case, Duncan McArthur—to social study. As these social scientists concentrated on understanding "aspects of the 'real' life of Canadian society," they were doing so with a commitment to serving the community and promoting moral citizenship. In the words of Shortt:

> The steady manifestation on the part of individuals, of self-control, self-respect and a strong sense of personal responsibility . . . the central feature in this development is the growing personality, or self, which in its more or less clear consciousness of a rational freedom, spontaneously recognizes its responsibility for conduct.[29]

J. H. Putman, who, like McArthur studied at Queen's and then burst onto the scene of progressive education as Chief Inspector for schools in Ottawa, wrote widely about social responsibility, schooling, and citizenship. These themes, translated into educationally progressive terms by Putman, have much in common with what is progressive educationally in McArthur's and others' thinking. This is particularly clear when Putman contrasts the *new* view on human development with the *old* idea of faculty psychology. The demise of mental disciplinarian's hold over the curriculum via faculty psychology has been discussed at length. In Putman's view: "Our minds are not like putty. They choose and select . . ." argued Putman, "it would be more correct . . . to compare the mind at birth to marble" than to a muscle.[30]

Putman, like Duncan McArthur, believed that the:

> Role of the teacher, like the role of the family, assumed archetypal proportions. The teaching function was magnified many times beyond its previous limited domain of keeping order, haring recitations, and preparing pupils for examination . . . only expert professionals with outstanding personalities could hope to survive in this higher idealistic plane.[31]

Now, returning to the importance of social science inquiry and educational reform in the context being described, it is necessary to discuss one of McArthur's best mentors and friends, who pioneered academic research into Canadian constitutional and economic history. In this field, which would occupy most of McArthur's academic research and shape the textbook that he would later write, he was the first economic historian to work as a professor in a Canadian university.[32] In this capacity, at Queen's, until 1908, Shortt was an unusually influential teacher, representing "the new breed of social analysts who were emerging at Canadian universities [and] provided detailed accounts of the impact of social change."[33]

As "one of the first to recognize the importance of economic and industrial efficiency,"[34] Shortt maintained that "Canadian society could deal with the economic problems and social justice issues by heeding social scientific reform principles and advocating state interventionism."[35] The idea that a social scientist was also a social engineer and specialist would be an influential one.[36] These men inevitably affected Duncan McArthur's ideas about institutional and educational reform, for it was "from Shortt [that] he learned the practical application to Canada of the 'economic interpretation of history.'"[37] McArthur was, later in his life, recognized as "probably one of the greatest of Shortt's disciples."[38]

Shortt, following the instruction of Queen's University's first course in political economy 1886:

> Built up a department of political and economic science and attracted a band of adepts who followed him in two major undertakings from 1890 to the Second World War. The first was to study, teach, and write about Canadian economic and political question using the tenets of the new political economy. The second was to move from commentary on to participation in national affairs by becoming senior federal servants. These two goals emerged from the intellectual and institutional environment of Canada and Queen's University in the period between 1890 and 1925.[39]

Shortt, like McArthur after him, had a firm conviction in the malleability of society and that study of the "trends of social change and the role of individuals"[40] was critical for the burgeoning social sciences. To this end, he turned to the study of history, a fact that made some of his contemporaries, such as Principal Grant, see him a retreating into "a narrow, empiricist approach that made him a dry expositor of historical issues, or . . . a 'Mr. Gradgrind'."[41]

And yet, for both Adam Shortt and Duncan McArthur, the study of history bore no relation to mere commentary on contextual or contingent tendencies and statistics. They believed that the historical approach to studying social development and life would allow them to approach the dominant themes of extant society with a sustained and systematic method. It was on the bases of such studies that a social scientist could intervene in society in order to reshape it. This Canadian turn to historical research as a necessary element of social study was perfectly consistent with "the mainstream of British and American social science as its younger practitioners at the end of the century turned to historical study."[42]

James Kloppenberg, having examined the transatlantic underpinnings of progressive thought, supports this claim, finding that social scientists following the turn of the century located "the foundations of knowledge in experience and [believed] that history provides a source of judgment more reliable, despite its uncertainties, than metaphysical or ideological doctrine."[43] In Shortt's own words:

> Not only therefore does a properly conceived presentation of historical facts afford an indispensable basis for the satisfactory answer to any intellectual question which arises, but it affords the only satisfactory data for political societies of the present day, and the consequent value of practical economic and political programmes which depend upon the soundness of these analysis.[44]

The emphasis on rational inquiry and the scope of study involving social groups hearkens back to Watson's explanations regarding the compatibility of idealism and intelligent study of social phenomena. Other important qualities here involve the emphases on self-direction, on rationality, and on responsibility. In fact, "like other historically oriented social scientists, Shortt allowed for a major portion of human intervention and control—a portion for individuality—within the social order."[45]

Shortt had believed that only by "redirecting humankind's purposes and politics . . . could conditions be altered and destinies changed."[46] In considering the social and interactive contexts of learning, for example, Shortt argued "the ordinary individual is the child of society, alike in his moral and social relations . . . [operating] in the daily intercourse of family and social life.[47] Putman also understood that "the school had an extremely important role to play in this process of self-realization."[48] This process envisaged "the social and business life of the community . . . [as] a starting point for the social life."[49] The importance on individual choice and direction was not only necessary for so-called *new liberals*, it left space within a context of remarkable social change, industrialism, and reform for the idealist faith in humanity to shape its future. Social scientists could be guides for democracy, but the institution was meant to facilitate "the realization by the individual of the liberty to think, to criticize, [and] to act."[50]

Adam Shortt's conception of an enfolding model of progress, which involved individual development through democratic institutions, was not, by any means, out of the ordinary. "The concept of progress as an unending evolution and the idea that human fulfillment was a function of that evolution informed both . . . economic accounts of progress . . . and history as unending growth,"[51] explained Barry Ferguson in relation to O. D. Skelton and faith that social science was a reliable means for studying and directing that 'progress.' Shortt, Skelton, and McArthur saw the interplay between individual fulfillment and social improvement as leading to development for both and "eternal progress with perfection as its goal."[52] The framing of progress in such evolutionary terms is, as noted in the introductory chapter, a consistent one throughout the interwar period.

From the perception of social science, intervention and guidance was necessary to direct the individual and to orient progress towards some common good. Social scientists, such as Adam Shortt and Duncan McArthur, who offered specialized knowledge and experience, were increasingly the providers of such guidance. The concern was not only for a reformation of the environment in which Canadians lived, but also of the individual's moral or spiritual self. Shortt, like George Munro Grant, President of Queen's University, concerned with present conditions and with the orientation of progress, couched explorations of personal rights and freedoms in terms of social responsibility and obligation.[53]

The social scientists in Ontario's intellectual currents increasingly brought to bear their analyses and methods of analysis on the problems of government and were increasingly relevant to the notion of *progressivism.* "Laissez-faire individualism was crumbling in the face of modern complexity," and, as a result, state involvement or intervention in matters "like urbanization, government efficiency, social dislocation, and industrialization"[54] was increasingly justified. It is in this sense that McArthur, an intellectual and an academic, would enter into provincial government with a reformist's attitude and be considered a progressive force. Applying the social scientific method and finding adequate responses to modern conditions could limit radicalism and guide the direction of a wide array of reforms.

Paralleling U.S. reforms, "Canadian historians have often employed the term *progressivism* to describe the variety of social reform movements that sprang up from within the middle class and the intellectual community in this period." The Canadian experience of industrialization and urbanization followed the American one and the terms for describing the corollary concern for reforms of government also ran parallel. As such, "Canadians were just beginning to urge serious reform of government at a time when American progressivism had already become mature and, some would say, decadent."[55] Yet, in both contexts, using terms like progressive to describe any individual educational reformer or academic, like Duncan McArthur, requires consideration of the increasing influence of social science for directing progressive matters in the social realm. For McArthur, associate of Ontario's first wave of social scientists such as Shortt and Skelton, and member of the Queen's community, a space of rich and diverse intellectual inferences, the prospect of leading the movement towards progressive schooling in the province must have been an incredibly enticing one.

In fact, McArthur's obituaries make clear that he took this commitment to public service seriously. A few days before his sudden death, it was reported, he had informed the media that he would do no political campaigning "but was remaining in public life in the hope that he could complete some reforms on which he had set his heart."[56] For years prior, "ill health had dogged him and impaired his powers for work,"[57] yet he was committed to continuing with his commitment to the Department. In fact, "overwork brought on" the serious illness, to which he eventually succumb.[58] McArthur had, it was openly recognized, never sought political honours before 1934, but he "eagerly embraced the opportunity for increased authority to promote school reforms"[59] when the opportunity was offered to him by Liberal Premier of Ontario Mitchell Hepburn.

McArthur was "never by temperament a revolutionary," but the opportunity to initiate "progressive reforms" in the province "proved irresistible."[60] This was particularly true in McArthur's case, since his 1934 appointment as Deputy Minister of Education, which wooed him from a Faculty position at Queen's, which he had held between 1917 and 1922,[61] also led to a position as Chief Director of the Ontario's schools several months later.[62] It was in 1940, following the passing of Leo Sampson that McArthur was appointed Minister of Education and former Chief Director George F. Rogers came back to the Department as his Deputy.[63]

Despite Sampson's de facto leadership of the Ministry from 1934–40, the sources are in agreement that McArthur was the driving force behind school initiative and reforms. Robert Stamp noted confidently "actual leadership was assumed by the new deputy minister . . . the outstanding educator Hepburn had been seeking for over a year . . . member of the Kingston Board of Education, and a man who had the respect of the province's teachers."[64] The expectation was that McArthur, "perhaps because of his professorial background, might make a difference."[65] His leadership would put an end to the "era of drift"[66] and usher in changes that promised to "be definitely for the better."[67] These changes, as progressive reforms of education, shall now be discussed in more particular domains with regards to McArthur and the battlegrounds upon which educational *progressivism* was waged.

Social Meliorism

We have seen quite evidently that the intellectual and spiritual environment at Queen's University, where Duncan McArthur had studied and worked, was heavily involved in the promotion of social service and communitarianism. This would influence McArthur's progressive educational agenda, which involved a heavy dose of social meliorism. Not only did his educational philosophy emphasize community and cooperative study, it advocated for the development of independent and critical thinking that would challenge, rather than acquiesce to, social matters. In a democratic state, one that would deal with the contingencies and precariousness of life intelligently, children needed to be given opportunity to exercise choice, which would build experiences using critical, rational thought. A curriculum of compulsion had to give way to one permitting self-direction and—activity. Both these qualities would be dominant features of the 1937 and 1938 revised program of studies for Ontario, for which McArthur's was largely responsible. The provision of electives and options for students in the province's high schools was one way of allowing for individualization of study. Other "improvements" to the curriculum included:

> Greater attention to English subjects; less number work in the primary grades, and a more practical course in arithmetic throughout other

grades; greater emphasis on health teaching; a closer correlation among subjects such as civics, history, and other social studies; more suitable completing courses for those who must leave school at the end of Grade IX or Grade X at the age of 16; more detailed outlines of the worked to be covered n each subject or group of subjects in each grade, and a closer grouping of subjects.[68]

The subjects, like the students themselves, could be grouped together in order to promote community and cooperation. The social studies, for example, integrated, as we have seen in a previous chapter, a number of humanities and social science subjects and marshaled them towards some goal relating to civics, citizenship, or democracy. At no point was the individual seen in isolation from the community in which he or she lived.

Providing learners with freedom and choice in the course of their studies promoted social responsibility, "the unquestioned basis of his standard of conduct, and hence of responsibility."[69] Further, the direction any individual student pursued in their studies was, in McArthur's judgment, never entirely divisible from the social welfare of all members of a community. Schools, he believed, had "permitted, too frequently, the place in the procession to be considered of greater consequence than the direction in which the procession is moving."[70] The rational and moral student operates within a social, interpersonal framework, developing standards and understanding "of practical morality."[71] The personal understanding of rights and responsibilities, then, is "diffused throughout the community, from class to class."[72]

A personal note retrieved from the Queen's University archives reveals that McArthur believed the most significant improvement in education in Ontario could be effected by overhauling the "wholly unnecessary and improper emphasis . . . placed on class standing, thus creating a thoroughly vicious system of competition."[73] From elementary school through high school, the atmosphere promoted by Ontario's schools encouraged the belief in students that it was their duty to beat and come ahead of their peers, "the consequences of this emphasis on standing and grades based on competition are seen in the creation of a distinctly anti-social outlook."[74] If schools did not teach the importance of social community and cooperation, as well as the importance of tending to the needs of others, the foundations of children's ability to live cooperatively would be destroyed:

Our present system encourages a ruthless individualism which extends frequently to a global delight and the misfortune of others. The creation of a social consciousness, of a sense of social responsibility, of justice and equity, must be laid in the social relationships of the school and the classroom. No more serious indictment can be brought against the present educational system in Ontario than its promotion of the spirit of unrestrained individualism through its encouragement of the spirit of competition in the school-room.[75]

The responsibilities of citizenship, McArthur believed, echoing Shortt's belief that a mature understanding of obligation to the greater good diffuses from class to class throughout society, begins with the individual and then spreads "to the community as at first represented by the school, and then the municipality, the Province, the Dominion, and, finally, the Empire."[76] This "gradually expanding sense of obligation" to the principles of "democratic living" follows the "British conception of the democratic way of life."[77] Duncan McArthur, in a number of addresses, praised the British Empire and for the role that it played in social and economic development across the Commonwealth. The Empire was, of course, still one of the major economic and military powers in the world. In an address to the Empire Club of Canada on November 28, 1940, McArthur reminded his audience of what he deemed the most significant contribution that their British heritage had made to the modern, progressive world. "First," McArthur explained, "I would place our democratic system of parliamentary self-government. This has been the bulwark of our civil liberties."[78] The parliamentary system, a fundamentally democratic method for responding to social change and instituting progressive policies that have been "adopted and approved by the duly chosen representatives of the people of the Kingdom,"[79] was a hallmark of civilization.

Regardless of "wealth, or ability, or learning, whether clever or stupid, good or bad,"[80] a democratic and progressive system of schools would be responsible for all. Besides the "democratic system of parliamentary self-government,"[81] the "British tradition of service"[82] is the most important privilege extended by the Empire to Canadians. This tradition was deemed vital because it is the "recognition of the unity of interest of the individual and the community, and the sense of obligation to serve the community"[83] that provides the essential counterpoint to the selfish insistence upon rights. Thus, the "recognition of obligation as the counterpart of privilege"[84] is what makes the democratic life worth living and defending. The "creation and development of an intelligent and enlightened Canadian citizenship", then, is closely associated with "the promotion of an attitude of intelligent loyalty and even devotion to our nation and to its institutions."[85]

The cultivation of intelligence was never to be strictly a selfish and strictly individualist pursuit, cautioned McArthur. It was with this mindset that he, when revising the system of departmental examinations in Ontario, relaxing the criteria that would make them necessary for all students regardless of their desired career or interest, defended his actions. Examinations were solitary and anti-social institutions, forcing fierce competition amongst students who should have been ideally cooperating to build learning. Departmental examinations were indicative of "a ruth-less individualism" that had:

> Been permitted to creep into our schools through practices designed originally to satisfy a thoroughly legitimate demand of parents to know the rate of progress of their children. Instead of measuring the extend of the development within the child of interest and initiative, of effort and appreciation, our system of gradation too frequently has become the men's of self-glorification of the child or of its parent, and the creation of an attitude of mind which is fundamentally selfish and anti-social.[86]

Examinations were in large part responsible for the creation of conditions that "encouraged, too greatly, the spirit of competition; the desire to 'come first' has provided, too frequently, a more powerful motive than the ambition to master a particular field of knowledge."[87]

It was not the solitary and solipsistic acquisition of knowledge that represented a progressive system of schooling, in other words. More important elements for the cultivation of democratic and meliorist habits of mind were individual choice and the realization of the need for social service. Fostering social interdependence required that the learner have the opportunity to exercise moral and rational judgment within the framework of social and political institutions. This idea is strongly echoed by McArthur, whose emphasis on democracy as an educational ideal was a constant throughout his leadership of Ontario's schools. His view of progress in education involved "the vital task of acquiring a broader view of human possibilities" and a "realization in public education of the new emphasis . . . given to the ideals of democracy and the broader conception of national life."[88]

McArthur understood the importance of developing the individual within a social community of schooling—as made evident in his perpetual reiteration of the need for choice in subject matter, personal activity, and correlation of subjects with mental development—yet he felt strongly that the cultivation of individualism needed limits. His awareness of the tensions between these interests is clear as he attempts to negotiate the two:

> The old wine of unrestrained individualism, of laissez faire, the "God's in His Heaven, all's well with the world" complacency of the Victorians will not be contained within the new bottles of respect for human rights of a planned economy, and of subordination of individual freedom to the well-being of the community. If the school of to-day is to discharge adequately its responsibilities, it must recognize that the old order has changed and prepare the new generation to adjust itself harmoniously in an independent and integrated society.[89]

McArthur's opposition to unfettered self-interest and individualism is another reminder that his progressive orientation to educational reforms was influenced by communitarian and meliorist currents. Years after Adam

Shortt had cautioned that only by "redirecting humankind's purposes and politics . . . could conditions be altered and destinies changed,"[90] McArthur would rejuvenate his mentor's concern for social responsibility transcending class boundaries. Speaking to the graduating class, he argued that "too much emphasis had been placed upon the laudation of people who attained wealth or influence through the selfish exercise of their powers of acquisitiveness."[91] "Forget yourselves in service to your fellow-men," McArthur implored the crowd before going on to argue that "most of the troubles" of the day "between capital and labor, between nation and nation [were] due to selfishness—the unwillingness of groups to understand and appreciate the problems of others."[92]

Students and citizens needed to cultivate the "ability to apply their scientific knowledge to interpretation of conditions and sound, accurate judgment based on minute observations."[93] The primary objective and mark of success for schools had to be:

> The creation of an understanding of the fundamental relationships subsisting between the individual and the community and the promotion of habits of mind which, against this background of understanding, will make possible the exercise of sound judgment in matters of public concern.[94]

Duncan McArthur realized quite early on that his educational *progressivism* would require, at the most basic level, the support of teachers in the classroom. No matter what policies were instituted by the Department of Education, and no matter what was reported in media and in teacher journals, the teacher was key to the actual implementation of an educationally progressive philosophy of education. As such, McArthur emphasized the importance of building a teaching corps that was committed to democratic principles of schooling and the promotion of reform for the improvement of all Ontario's schools, urban and rural. Teacher education, predictably, also became a subject of reforms. As a start, trainer-teachers were promised they would not feel as if they "sacrificed" their future by devoting themselves to the improvement of educator standards.[95] "You can easily bankrupt the community intellectually and spiritually," explained McArthur with consideration for the lot of the province's teachers, by too drastic reductions in teachers' salaries."[96]

In relation to teacher candidates themselves, McArthur announced that "more varied opportunities will be offered for observation and practice teaching, and permanent certificates will be granted only to those young teachers who, in the opinion of the inspectors, are doing creditable work."[97] Further, work in the Normal Schools would have to be "more closely linked to that of the public schools by a system of temporary exchange between inspectors and normal school masters."[98] McArthur, like Putman, his former colleague at Queen's and a staunch progressive in his own right, at the time, felt that the "role of the teacher, like the role of the family, assumed archetypal proportions . . . only expert professionals with outstanding personalities could hope to survive in this higher idealistic plane.[99]

Ontario's progressive educators needed to have a firm commitment to social service if they were to be able to nurture a spirit of social responsibility in the students that were in their charge. In an October 1934 article addressed to all of Ontario's teachers titled *Education for Democracy*, McArthur made this position clear:

> The associations of the school form the earliest social relationships of our boys and girls. If the influence of the school, either through the content or the method of its instruction, tends to glorify and encourage an unbridled individualism, we need not be surprised if the product of the school manifests little evidence of the recognition of social obligations. The attitude and outlook of the teacher becomes of fundamental importance, and with it the outlook of the university as the training ground for teachers.[100]

Responding to McArthur's quote, *The School* put out the following call to educators: "Whether you teach in a one-room rural school, or in a city collegiate institute, a future prime minister may be in one of your classes this morning. Future voters and fellow citizens are sure to be."[101]

Appropriate instruction, along with the development of a moral and democratic citizenry through the schools, put great stresses on the teacher. McArthur's speeches, as reported in the press, lay stress on the belief that teachers are key to the vision he held for schools. For starters, he cautioned in 1938 that Ontario was moving towards a scarcity of teachers and that "if school boards wished to secure good teachers, they must give them adequate remuneration."[102] McArthur, consequently established minimum salaries of $500 for educators in rural areas[103] and reinstated "the annual increment schedule for normal and model school teachers, which was suspended in 1931" due to the Depression.[104] The increased attention to elevating the standards of the teaching profession was a constant theme for McArthur, who also drafted a Bill of Rights for teachers. His concentration on the rural schools, moreover, bore heavily political notes, which necessarily address inequities between urban and rural schooling:

> There is no problem more significant in its bearing on the life of the people of this province than that of the rural school. For too many years, it has provided a training and experience for the larger centres. Until we can stop the drift of good teachers from the country to the town and city, we cannot do much by way of improving educational conditions in the country districts, and until such times as the salaries paid country school teachers can be raised to a position comparable to those received in the city, we cannot expect to make changes for the better in rural education. Moreover, until such time as we can make condition sin the country districts sufficiently attractive for the young men and women to remain there, we can look for little improvement.[105]

The responsibilities of teachers, involved not merely the "training of hands . . . [but, also] the training in accurate thinking."[106] Further, McArthur stressed "there is need not only for accuracy in thinking but for a capacity to understand human relations." This understanding resembled a spirit of empathy, and manifested itself in a concern for the lot of the entire community.

McArthur himself believed that "young people in our schools are not separate, self-contained persons; from the time they draw their first breath, they are social beings, members of a community."[107] This spirit of progressive thinking about education intimately relates to McArthur's views concerning democracy. These, it is clear, did not develop independently of others' in Ontario; they bear the hallmarks of service to community and the balance of rights and responsibilities, which we have seen earlier. These bear the contradictions implicit in the balancing of both the personal and the social—between individual and communitarian—interests. These views are related to the belief that schools are vital contributors to the development of a rational, moral, and democratic citizenry, who will use democratic media to be represented and to participate in social betterment.

McArthur agreed with Dewey[108] that the cultivation of democratic "habits of mind,"[109] begins in the schools, which are incredibly important for the development of moral and intelligent citizenship. "Democracy is essentially a thing of the spirit," announced McArthur. Yet, the cultivation of this democratic feeling needed to be managed and directed by the state, which would guide the students through a "process of intelligent direction, which is but another name for education" to recognize our human right to individual liberty within the parameters of "some understanding of the meaning of community."[110] Schools, then, had a responsibility to "drive home the truth that these rights cannot be enjoyed apart from the community."[111] McArthur went on to explain that:

> The habit of mind which gives recognition to the rights of others, along with other habits of mind, must first be formed in the school, in the ordinary, every-day relations which exist among the children, who are themselves the members of the community formed by the school. For that reason, I maintain that this most important field of human relationship be brought within the range of intelligent direction and control.[112]

Social Efficiency

The *progressivism* of Duncan McArthur's educational philosophy was not entirely free from concerns of social efficiency and management. Social scientists at the time did, as noted, see their role as studying social conditions, analyzing trends, and guiding or directing policy. We have also seen, most notably in the chapter on humanism, that the context for reform in Ontario during and immediately following the Depression was one where school subjects needed to demonstrate their utility in some capacity or risk being cut from an already congested curriculum. McArthur's concerns for efficiency in education were normal in the broader context and not merely concentrated upon training students to become industrial workers and trained, unthinking cogs in a machine. As with all aspects of his *progressivism*, McArthur was knitting together seemingly contradictory views on what constituted educational progress in an attempt to weave greater order and consistency out of them.

McArthur's position aimed to steer the Department of Education's reforms between any extreme position, such as the Scylla of utilitarian practicality and the Charybdis of extreme communitarianism. He openly "admitted that it is the function of the school to equip the young man and the young woman for the performance, in a creditable manner, of the tasks of life," yet, he felt that it was "equally true that the business of life is not conducted in a vacuum."[113] McArthur conceded, in other words, that he believed education needed closer correlation with social structures and realities, but not at the expense of individual interests or communitarianism:

> It is, therefore, an essential duty of the school not only to impart knowledge regarding the nature of the social structure and of the social relationship involved in membership in the community, but also to create that attitude of mind which will make it possible for the individual to adjust himself satisfactorily within the community, however extensive that community may be.[114]

McArthur's efforts to balance different progressive aims was necessarily part of the education Department's reformist aim regarding "unification" of Ontario's pedagogical interests and needs; to "boil it all down" in any context where progressives were not of one sort was, indeed, problematic.[115] While it was important for McArthur to make education "very closely related to the real needs of the people,"[116] he also worried about doing so with only utilitarian concerns in mind. Controversies inevitably arose. School trustee Clifford Howard, for example, declared that McArthur had committed a "breech of faith" by breaking "a verbal agreement" made in 1942 concerning grants for urban municipalities.[117] Over five years, the York Township Board of Education had faced, Howard argued, nearly three times the reduction in grants than what had been agreed. When progress— in this case, related to equalization of funding throughout the province— affected funding packages to any school group adversely, the frontal attacks on McArthur's policies were, not surprisingly, voluminous.

The financial concerns of school boards were not the only space of tension between local interests and overall reform concerns. Concern from the rural communities for the preservation and continuity of work on the farm forced the Department of Education had to arrange "for the release of school pupils early in April to permit them to assist in seeding and other farm duties."[118] Such arrangements, involving between 50,000 and 100,000 students, were no minor task. Minimum wages were set, examination dates were rescheduled, and communication needed to be established between the Department and farmers, dairies, cheese factories, canneries, and meatpacking houses.[119]

Such and other news stories circulating in the latter half of the 1930s and early 1940s relating the Department of Education's efforts to make schools more useful for particular communities while maintaining some general progressive orientation are reminders of the inherently complicated nature of educational reform. Centralizing administration and organization of schools promoted efficient management of the whole province's education, but it was not necessarily the best way addressing the needs of local communities. It is one thing for individuals such as McArthur to talk about educational systems that are both efficient and communitarian, but it is another thing to administer such systems.[120] As McArthur himself lamented, the basic requirement of a system of education—"directing the activities of" large numbers of students—had led to "a system of rigid control and minute regulation"[121] that also happened to be "the most depressing feature of education in Ontario in recent years [namely, it] has been an enslavement to a system with its all but complete suppression of individuality and initiative in both teachers and pupils."

The administration and reorganization of Ontario's schools certainly proved cumbersome, and consumed much of McArthur's attention. Dealing with the matter of raising and equalizing grants from the province to the schools proved an important issue, garnering the attention of the ratepayers associations, the media, and school administrators. Newspaper coverage of modifications to the tax and grant system announced Deputy Minister McArthur's intention to take "over the income tax" so as to be in a better position to provide "additional grants" to the schools boards as "warning" to High School principals that changes were on the horizon.[122] That is not to say that reforms were rushed into or taken lightly. McArthur, always a social scientist, initiated and participated in a number of committees; researching issues and aiming to take "complete survey and report on the entire system."[123] Even as late as a month before his death, he was "appointed chairman of the special committee charged with the administration of the Ontario Social Security and Rehabilitation Act", and immediately announced his intention to "convene the committee without delay."[124]

The reliance on committees to study extant conditions as necessary precursors to reform policies is enlightening. It reveals McArthur's faith in social scientific research to enlighten progressive reform and, more significantly, it demonstrates the increasing influence of social science analysis on industrial and governmental policy in Canada. Thorough research and the marshalling of statistics and trends as warrants for reforms were certainly also influenced by the Department's anticipation of educationist's potentially negative reactions to change. Following the Department of Education's first announcement of upcoming reforms, when McArthur stepped into the media light for an ailing Leo Sampson, it was reported that "not only did he represent a new government, but [McArthur] had already announced that very considerable changes would be made in the educational system of the province."[125] "It was hardly to be expected," the report continued, that he "could so soon announce many definite changes. Indeed, many people hoped that the Department of Education would reach decisions slowly, and after careful investigation."[126] During the same speech, McArthur put media and educators on notice, preemptively proclaiming that "before any important changes are made in the school system or in the courses of study, committees will make very thorough surveys and will receive suggestions from any who wish to offer them."[127]

Sometimes, his speeches had to settle the anxieties of a public fearing that the increased centralization and involvement of government would throw the system out of balance and that the drive for increasing efficiency would make schools less relevant to particular communities' interests or needs. There "will be no interference, says Deputy Minister" the subheading of one article in *The Globe*, for example, announced and went on to explain how McArthur effectively "calmed the fears of urban Trustees with regard to interference of Municipal Councils to school estimates, which they announced in a resolution."[128] A progressive system of schooling for McArthur would have "an increasingly graded school system, centralized consolidated schools with the resultant larger bureaucracy manned by experts," but, at the same time, he hoped "that class tensions would be reduced, middle-class values would be inculcated, and these more efficient institutions would eliminate social problems."[129] This challenge, McArthur felt, could not happen "over-night or even in a generation. It is important, however, that in the changes incidental to the growth of every living organism, we shall move in the right direction."[130]

This direction was, in large part, aimed at making schools more "practical," as the "correlation" amongst subjects and between those subjects and actual life was crucial.[131] The very comprehensive reforms introduced during the McArthur years at the Department of Education focused intensively, then, on the correlation of academic work with the realities of life. It was principally the "social significance of subjects"[132] and the ultimately utilitarian relation they bore to citizenship instruction that shaped the new courses of study in Ontario. Again, we have seen that this was an important theme for many efficiency progressives at the time. The inclusion of subjects in the Programme of Study was contingent on their utility and function concerning the correlation of school and society.

Language and arithmetic, for starters, were each defined as "essentially a social study,"[133] whose development charted the course of society's need to communicate and to explain. If "children could be made aware of the social significance of language and numbers, the approach to the more complex problems of social organization would become much less difficult,"[134]

McArthur avowed. Courses in civics, economics, and current events were useful means for

> The creation of an intelligent interest in social organization and in extending the social horizon of the pupil. The value of such courses depends, in large measure, however, on the adequacy of the foundation of knowledge and experience on which they are established.[135]

Despite McArthur's assessment that history and geography, as taught in schools, were some of the least interesting subjects for students to study, he believed that "the value of such essentially social studies as history and geography in the promotion of social consciousness is inestimable."[136] Geography, in particular, needed to be humanized. This meant building understanding of the senses that in human history "places cannot readily be dissociated from people" and that "no instruction can demonstrate more satisfactorily the essential interdependence of nation and racial groups than the study of geography."[137]

Even the study of music and the visual arts could be contextualized as fundamentally social entities. These, like others subjects, needed to be presented in ways that demonstrated their relation to and correlated to students' real lives. The new course of study needed, also, to demonstrate the organic unity of all study:

> with an adequate insight into the nature of the course of instruction not only should the teacher be capable of making the subject of greater interest, but the ill effects of the tendency to departmentalize knowledge would be reduced and encouragement given to present the essential unity of subject-matter of all instruction.[138]

McArthur was willing to make subjects accountable to some criterion of utility, then, but what made distinguished his criteria from some of the more extreme efficiency progressive perspectives we have already seen was the breadth of his vision. Subjects were not only deemed useful if they led to efficient maintenance of an industrial and economic order. Cultivating democratic cooperation and fostering citizenship were also worthwhile aims for Ontario's schools.

Child Study

With regards to child study and developmental psychology, there were two relevant currents that dominated McArthur's progressive educational vision. The first involved his interest in building an activity curriculum that related more intimately to the development of students. The second involved a commitment to allowing for greater choice in the course of study for students, so that the curriculum could relate more to an individual learner's interests.

Both currents shall be discussed here, beginning with McArthur's aim to correlate school studies more with children's "own personal experience" and "the ordinary process of their growth."[139] A progressive educational system would consider the individual interests of children and provide learning experiences that would "have meaning for them"[140] as they pursued studies.

It was the belief that personal development and interest were important motivational aspects that proved particularly influential in McArthur's decision to begin loosening the language requirements for university admission. The reform, which would be a death knell for the study of Latin in Ontario, stipulated that students with "secondary school work in one foreign language rather than two such languages"[141] could apply to postsecondary institutions. The role that Duncan McArthur would play in the demise of classical studies in Ontario was already discussed in the chapter discussing humanist educators in the province. He, A. B. McKillop noted, "championed French as opposed to Latin in the province's high schools. Soon Latin was denied to students in the first year in the secondary school . . . [and] students were allowed to choose between Latin and mathematics as the language of entry into university."[142]

McArthur "was convinced that the greatest service that could be rendered . . . the study of these languages was to make them optional rather than compulsory."[143] Further, "he was doubtful of the preservation of the cultural values of the humanities by compelling students to study them."[144] The reform was also consistent with the Department of Education's aim to consider the usefulness of subjects in actual life. As early as 1934, McArthur had announced that experiments would "be conducted in the teaching of French to determine whether more emphasis should be laid on ability to read a second language, and less emphasis on grammar and oral work."[145]

These experiments would extend to the study of Latin and, despite the critique of professors, including J. F. Macdonald from University College, who confronted McArthur during his address at the College and Secondary Department at the Ontario Educational Association, he remained steadfast in his belief that students should be given options regarding coursework and that compulsory subjects needed to loosen their hold on the course of study. A snippet of Macdonald's remarks, as presented in an article in the *Globe and Mail*, represented him as both sexist and archaic:

> I cannot help feeling that the culture is being handed over to the women of this country. I am always being asked to address women's organizations but never men's. It seems that only practical subjects appeal to the men. Now we are going to aggravate that condition by allowing students to enter university with only one foreign language. Here we are a very virile people with a very effeminate literature.

The discussion was a heated one, but we do know, as discussed in an earlier chapter, that it prompted Ontario's humanist educationists to strike a committee that would later issue a less vitriolic and more rational defense of

Latin and Greek. McArthur's retort to Macdonald, as reported, represented him as an immanently progressive voice of reform and reason. For starters, McArthur argued that his opponent's way of thinking was both old-fashioned and out of touch. "It does not matter what you teach, as long at is unpleasant,"[146] he began. Then in reference to a mental disciplinarian approach to schooling explained: "That educational psychology is absolutely antiquated."[147] Ontario's schools were not lagging behind others, McArthur explained, they were leading progressive and forward-looking:

> I'm afraid that Professor Macdonald has rather given away his case by stating that only women are interested in the humanities. That's the contribution the humanities have made in the culture of this Province during the last 30 years. I would like to point out that the universities in the Province are more rigid in their foreign language demands than those of Oxford, Cambridge, and Aberdeen.[148]

The time for study of classics, which were not relevant to contemporary life, for McArthur, had passed. It is with some irony, then, that A. B. McKillop noted that McArthur was, himself, a graduate in "honour classics" and still, perhaps for political reasons, was a fierce critic of the humanities.[149] It is true that the political climate in Ontario stressed the need for developing a relevant and practical group of subjects for study, and this is certainly part of McArthur's motivation. But his adamancy regarding the importance of providing choice in the course of study so that the new progressive curriculum would be more relevant to each individual's interests and chosen path should not be understated. Only 10 percent of students, he would note, proceeded to study in the university, yet all students were compelled to pursue an academic curriculum; instead of catering to the minority and to the universities' demands for classics, the course of studies should be interesting and relevant to at least 90 percent of the population.[150]

> This is basically the most sweeping change that should be made in the course of instruction. More specifically, the student who does not wish to go to a university should not be compelled to spend three or four years in the study of Latin. He could become much more intimately familiar with the classics through good translations in English. A central core of compulsory subjects could be prescribed such as English, Literature and Composition, Mathematics, History, Geography, Natural Science, Health. The student should be allowed the right of selecting certain options in accord with his interest which might include Latin and French, Economics, Household Science, Commercial training and handicraft.[151]

It is, in large part, for similar reasons that McArthur spearheaded fundamental changes in Ontario's system of departmental examinations. A reduction in the stress upon external exams would liberate the teachers and students to pursue learning that was not tightly restricted and confined. In fact, the enforcement of departmental examinations also tethered teachers to the kinds of teaching that provoked discordance between their authentic knowledge of children's achievements and the means of assessment:

> To escape this condition, formal examinations should be reduced to a minimum. The teacher should make himself familiar with the progress of each child from day to day. Instruction should be individual rather than in the mass. Consideration should be given to the mental capacity of each pupil and credit given for progress as well as for actual achievement. As a general rule, the good teacher does not need examinations to test the knowledge of the pupils. They are required only to comply with our system of regulation and regimentation.[152]

In the emphatic words of Dr. George Rogers, member of McArthur's staff and part of the Committee on High and Vocational Courses of Study that made a survey of the examination systems in the province: "I don't think examinations in English composition have been worth anything—they have been a total loss"[153] because they do not give information regarding student's interest in the subject or their actual use of it in real life Students, it was argued, needed to proceed through the years of school based on the recommendations of their teachers and principals, not based on examinations.[154]

Consistent with his position on Latin and examinations, the hegemony of a single, authorized textbook was condemned during McArthur's tenure at the Department of Education. McArthur advised educationists in 1934: "The relaxation of the examination system may prove to be of definite encouragement to teachers to promote reading beyond the limits of prescribed texts."[155] Textbook learning, he continued, is not only narrow; its mandate enforced a compulsion on teachers to push through it at the peril of ignoring broad student interest, activity, and exploration:

> The system of authorizing special text-books for courses of study has likewise led to the encouragement of the formation of habits of mind which cannot be regarded as otherwise than undesirable. The authorizing of a particular book as a text gives to the printed word within the book a literal inspiration. It becomes easy for the student to assume that all of the truth relating to a subject is contained within the covers of the book.[156]

Further, the data contained within textbooks, once "committed to memory are soon forgotten. The information temporarily acquired is seldom related to the structure of knowledge or experience possessed by the pupil."[157]

Of all McArthur's progressive and reformist perspectives, and despite the consistency of these with his advocacy for loosening of examination requirements, McArthur's attack on textbook instruction is amongst the most interesting in light of the fact that McArthur wrote and then published a history textbook in 1931 for high school study. Following some relatively aggressive marketing, the text was, as the inside cover notes, "*authorized* for use in the schools of Nova Scotia, Manitoba, Saskatchewan, and British Columbia."[158]

The apparent discrepancy between McArthur's rhetorical and de facto orientations towards textbooks can be reconciled by appealing to his constantly unfolding conceptualization of self-activity, his belief that subjects had to be taught in a relevant manner, and his desire that teachers be allowed the freedom to make the curriculum interesting for their students. While many teachers undertake "to do work which might be better left to the pupils themselves" by overly depending on data to be examined as the bases of instruction, the "habit of independence of thought and judgment is not encouraged as completely as possible by reason of this condition."[159] Facts can be the starting point of instruction, but the use of these to develop proper habits of mind is more important. Consequently:

> Having provided our prospective citizen with something to think about in relation to his duties as a citizen, it is of importance that he should be taught how to think. The first duty of the school to the community is to train its youth to think accurately and to assist in the formation of sound judgments.[160]

Schools, it follows, cannot depend entirely upon external aids in order to teach students how to develop capacities for intelligent citizenship. Overreliance on textbooks can provoke passivity of mind, whereas education should be more concerned with the promotion and "the encouragement of initiative in thought and independence in judgment."[161] Instruction that merely pursues the "presumed necessities of examinations . . . is degraded to the mere reciting of the facts set forth on the pages of the text."[162]

Further, McArthur's Preface to his own textbook seemed to justify his work because it represented a *new history* that broke with the "general tendency, which has prevailed for many years in the writing of the history of Canada, to emphasize unduly constitutional development."[163] McArthur's text "endeavoured to stress the progress of settlement and the economic and social problems which have arisen from the efforts of the people."[164] It was, perhaps, more acceptable as a source in the new order of progressive education because it could better support the revolution in schooling that he supported. This revolution in the teaching of history, McArthur stated, was necessary in light of evidence indicating "that the course in history is now one of the least interesting studies in the curriculum of our schools, whereas it is capable of being made and is being made by teacher a subject of intense interest."[165]

This transformation, beginning with textbooks such as the one that he wrote, which brought out the essentially social qualities of the discipline, had marked a shift in "emphasis from military and constitutional history to the revelation of significant social and economic relationships. History is essentially a study in the record of citizenship, of the behaviour of individuals as members of social groups."[166] It is, it seems, that McArthur's attacks were not aimed at textbooks themselves, but at educators' tendency to treat them like authoritative annals of facts to be memorized and recited in isolation from their relationship to human social life:

> It is very questionable whether uniform courses or uniform text-books would be blessings. They might lead to unprogressive conservativism rather than progress, for the course for the book to which everybody will agree is likely to be old fashioned or mediocre.[167]

The teacher and student should use many sources, some of which were better at promoting a progressive mindset than others were. If authorization of textbooks was to be undertaken, there should be more than one option. Key, at all times, was the provision of learning that is interesting and relevant to the actual lives and experiences of Ontario's children. Whether it concerned the authorization of textbooks or the authority of departmental examinations, the encouragement of learning that was not related to authentic experiences and the cultivation of critical thought was regressive and restraining:

> A further and serious defect in our present system, likewise a product of over-examination, is the emphasis placed on the memorization of facts at the expense of the cultivation of the powers of reasoning and thinking. So long as the formal examination is maintained as the test of achievement in education, the cultivation of the memory will be encouraged in preference to the capacity for thinking. To this extent, the education of the child is being neglected. In the solution of the problems of life the exercise of the memory will not prove a substitute for the use of the powers of reason.[168]

Realizing these ideals meant more than a change in orientation, it required complete revision of the curriculum. The new course of studies would have a number of influences, including the child study movement in education and the corollary field of developmental psychology. As such, McArthur's first public announcement concerning reforms to the elementary and secondary curricula at the Ontario Educational Association 1934 gathering signaled the Department's intention to correlate the subjects of study more closely with "the mental development of pupils."[169] To this end, "pupils should be promoted to the high schools, as far as possible, on the recommendation of their teachers," who are more familiar with the particular and individual development of children than administrators guided only by data from departmental examinations. The British Hadow Reports, cited by the revised courses of studies (as opposed to John Dewey's progressive educational doctrines), signal not only a political move and an extension to the British Empire (as opposed to the United States),[170] but also an acknowledgement of the rising importance of developmental psychology within educational circles.[171]

These Hadow reports had emerged from an organization in Great Britain of the Association for Education in Citizenship that initially aimed to be a clearing house for teachers concerned with fostering citizenship and developing richer understanding of children's development in terms of ideas and experiences. Sir Henry Hadow was president of the Association.[172] *The Education of the Adolescent* (1926), usually called *The Hadow Report* after its recently deceased chairman, recommended that: "At the end of the school year in which he reached the age of 11, every child should be transferred from the primary school into some sort of post-primary school."[173] The adolescent child was a qualitatively different learner, and an intermediate school was a progressive measure that school boards needed to take in order to align instruction greater with the development of learners. The province's intermediate schools, which had begun to be organized during the Depression, became an important part of Ontario's educational agenda. Greater concern for the "adolescent" child, in particular, were stressed:

> Reorganization of the elementary school system of England on the basis of recommendations of the Hadow Report on the Education of the Adolescent appears to be making satisfactory progress. According to the latest Report of the Board of Education for England and Wales, on March 31, 1933, approximately 50 per cent of pupils aged 11 and over were in reorganized schools, corresponding roughly to what are known in Canada as Intermediate Schools, and in the United States as Junior High Schools.[174]

The Hadow report, throughout the province, was praised as "progressive" and thoroughly "forward-looking document"[175] along lines advocated for by child study advocates.

Reforms to the course of study in the province, consistent with this orientation, would create "a central core of subjects to be open to all pupils. These might include English, geography, history and civics, one science, mathematics and a second language."[176] The provision of freedom for students to choose subjects that were interesting and relevant to their own stage of thinking and learning necessarily extended "beyond this group of subjects, options might be offered in a wider range of subjects than is at present available."[177] It is not only the provision for, but also the expansion upon, options of study that would be later characterized as a defining characteristic of progressive reform initiatives across North America.

> In determining the structure and function of an organization for the purposes of education it is imperative to have a clear conception of the related importance of the different "areas" in the educational world. The are, first—the child; second the teacher; third—the official. The activities of the official are futile unless they are reflected in an improvement in

the character of instruction provided by the teacher; the energies of the teacher are wasted unless they instruct and inspire the pupil.[178]

Ultimately, it was the positing of learners at the centre of Ontario's educational organization that concerned McArthur most.

McArthur's progressive reforms manifested a firm conviction to weave together and manage seemingly contradictory visions of reform into a coherent and comprehensive vision. He, for his part, openly acknowledged the coexistence of contradictory viewpoints and perspectives on pedagogical reform. McArthur felt that "a great deal of the clamoring for changes" in schools "could be interpreted as a sign of the times, and had no doubt been stimulated by the change in Government."[179] He felt the effort to "coordinate . . . opinions . . . so varied and diversified"[180] would be immense. It would be "a tremendous problem" for the Department of Education to "understand the contradictory views expressed on many things" and produce "some satisfactory practical change."[181]

McArthur's educational perspectives would contain seemingly contradictory or divergent visions of progress. Progressive curricula and policies influenced in large measure by developmental psychology and the democratic orientation towards free choice, would sweep into the province. Yet, these reform currents never resembled a flood of unrestrained individualism, as they would be restrained by a faith in the importance of maintaining standards of efficiency, building social service, and fostering democratic citizenship. The complexity of intellectual currents examined reflects the very complicated and contradictory constitution of progressive education, which is the main interest of my study. Examining the case, albeit briefly, of Duncan McArthur's educational *progressivism* allows for different *progressivisms* to be seen as they existed: tangled and enmeshed.

In conclusion, it seems fitting to revisit an obituary article written by James F. Kenney in honour of Duncan McArthur that was published in *The Canadian Historical Review* following the Minister of Education's passing in London, Ontario on July 20, 1942. Kenney expresses ambivalence about McArthur's reforms even as he praises his late friend's contributions to education as a teacher, professor, and public servant. His comments on the subject of McArthur's move from the academic to the political sphere are particularly enlightening:

It may long be debated whether his transfer from academic to political life was a loss or a gain. It may be debated whether the radical reforms in education which he was pressing forward would have been for better or for worse. But the transfer was inevitable, for, fundamentally, McArthur was not the pure scholar. His primary interest was in the great forces, the pressing problems, of Canadian political and social life today; and his primary interest in history was because of the light it threw on the genesis and development of those forces.[182]

Not only did Kenney view McArthur's reforms as "radical," he saw fit to comment on the formative influence of social science and historical study in shaping his approach to educational *progressivism*.

McArthur's attention to education was "inevitable," and that he was somehow fated to reform Ontario's schools. A. E. Prince, Professor of English History at Queen's and a former colleague of McArthur's, believed that McArthur, also, shared the feeling that "events were not fortuitous happenings; they developed according to a predestined divine plan, through laws whose application could be worked out in practice."[183] What was generally agreed upon, despite all tensions or contradictions, is that "his lodestar of education was guiding him."[184]

Notes

1. Duncan McArthur, "A New Deal in Education in Ontario," handwritten note retrieved from *Duncan McArthur Fonds (1929–1940)*, Q73-3, location 1059, Queen's University Archives.
2. A previous version of this chapter was published in the journal *Paedagogica Historica*, and the author wishes to acknowledge Dr. Ian Grosvenor, the journal's editor, for generously granting permission. See Theodore Christou, "The Complexity of Intellectual Currents: Duncan McArthur and Ontario's Progressivist Curriculum Reforms," *Paedagogica Historica* 49, no. 5 (2013), pp. 677–697.
3. Item is located in F 2154–3, container B115809.
4. Following a presentation of this chapter at the Canadian History of Education Association Biennial Conference (October 24, 2008), an archivist employed at the Archives of Ontario corrected the database.
5. "Notes and News," *The School* (September, 1934), pp. 65–66.
6. Herbert Kliebard, *The Struggle for the American Curriculum, 1893–1958* (New York and London: RoutledgeFalmer, 2004).
7. Doug Owram, *The Government Generation: Canadian Intellectuals and the State, 1900–1945* (Toronto: University of Toronto Press, 1986), p. 6.
8. Ibid., p. 7.
9. Ibid., p. 8.
10. A. B. McKillop, *A Disciplined Intelligence: Critical Inquiry and Canadian Thought in the Victorian Era* (Kingston and Montreal: McGill-Queen's University Press, 1979), p. 189.
11. Ibid., pp. 172–182.
12. B. Anne Wood, *Idealism Transformed: The Making of a Progressive Educator* (Kingston and Montreal: McGill-Queen's University Press, 1985), p. 31.
13. Ibid.
14. Barry Ferguson, *Remaking Liberalism: The Intellectual Legacy of Adam Shortt, O. D. Skelton, W. C. Clark and W. A. Mackintosh* (Montreal and Kingston: McGill-Queen's University Press, 1993), p. 3.
15. Ibid., pp. 188–189.
16. John Watson, "Edward Caird as Teacher and Thinker," *Queen's Quarterly* 1 (June, 1909), pp. 304–305.
17. McKillop, *Matters of Mind*, p. 191.
18. Ibid.
19. John Watson, *An Outline of Philosophy* (Glasgow: James Maclehose and Sons, 1901), p. 232.

20. Wood, *Idealism Transformed*, p. 27.
21. John Watson, "The University and the State," *Queen's University Journal* 2 (November 26, 1898), pp. 25–26.
22. McKillop, *Matters of Mind*, p. 197.
23. Wood, *Idealism Transformed*, p. 20.
24. Carl Berger, *The Sense of Power: Studies in the Ideas of Canadian Imperialism, 1867–1914* (Toronto: University of Toronto Press, 1970), p. 32.
25. Philip Massolin, *Canadian Intellectuals, the Tory Tradition, and the Challenge of Modernity, 1939–1970* (Toronto: University of Toronto Press, 2001), p. 6.
26. Wood, *Idealism Transformed*, p. 21.
27. Ibid., p. 28.
28. Watson, *An Outline of Philosophy*, p. vi.; Anne Wood, *Idealism Transformed*, p. 28.
29. Adam Shortt, "Legislation and Morality," *Queen's Quarterly* (1901), p. 354, cited in Anne Wood, *Idealism Transformed*, p. 28.
30. J. H. Putman, "Inspector's Report" (1922), cited in Anne Wood, *Idealism Transformed*, p. 32.
31. Wood, *Idealism Transformed*, p. 34.
32. W. A. Mackintosh, "Adam Shortt, 1859–1931," *Canadian Journal of Economics and Political Science* 4, no. 2 (May, 1938), pp. 164–176.
33. Massolin, *Canadian Intellectuals, the Tory Tradition, and the Challenge of Modernity, 1939–1970*, p. 29.
34. Ibid., p. 110.
35. Ibid., p. 240.
36. Ibid., p. 32.
37. James F. Kenney, "Duncan McArthur (1885–1943)," *The Canadian Historical Review* 24 (Toronto: University of Toronto Press, 1943), p. 450.
38. Ibid., p. 449.
39. Ferguson, *Remaking Liberalism*, p. 3.
40. Ibid., p. 53.
41. Ibid.
42. Ibid.
43. James Kloppenberg, *Uncertain Victory: Social Democracy and Progressivism in European and American Thought, 1870–1920* (New York: Oxford University Press), p. 6.
44. Adam Shortt, "The Significance for Canadian History of the Work of the Board of Historical Publications," *Proceedings and Transactions, Royal Society of Canada*, Series 3, no. 13 (1919), pp. 104–105, cited in Ferguson, *Remaking Liberalism*, pp. 54–55.
45. Ferguson, *Remaking Liberalism*, p. 55.
46. Massolin, *Canadian Intellectuals, the Tory Tradition, and the Challenge of Modernity, 1939–1970*, p. 32.
47. Shortt, "Legislation and Morality," p. 358.
48. Anne Wood, *Idealism Transformed*, p. 33.
49. J. H. Putman, "The Teacher: An Essential Qualification for His Success," *The Ottawa Citizen*, February 21, 1913, p. 3.
50. Adam Shortt, "Some Aspects of the Social Life of Canada," *Canadian Magazine* 11 (1898), p. 7.
51. Ferguson, *Remaking Liberalism*, p. 112.
52. Adam Shortt, "The Influence of Daily Occupations and Surroundings on the Life of the People," *Sunday Afternoon Addresses* (Kingston: Queen's University, 1893) cited in Owram, *The Government Generation*, p. 8.
53. Doug Owram, *The Government Generation*, pp. 14–17.
54. Ibid., p. 77.
55. Ibid., p. 78.
56. "Hon. Duncan McArthur," *The Globe and Mail* (Toronto), Wednesday, July 21, 1943, p. 1.

57. Ibid.
58. "Death of Dr. Duncan McArthur," *Journal of the Royal Astronomical Society of Canada*, 37 (1943), p. 343.
59. Ibid.
60. Ibid.
61. Ibid.
62. Robin S. Harris, *Quiet Evolution: A Study of the Educational System of Ontario* (Toronto: University of Toronto Press, 1967), p. 110.
63. Ibid.
64. Robert Stamp, *The Schools of Ontario, 1867–1967* (Toronto: University of Toronto Press, 1982), p. 155.
65. Ibid.
66. "School Estimates Not Under Control of Urban Councils," *The Globe* (April 25, 1935), p. 60.
67. *Saturday Night* (July 28, 1934), cited in Stamp, *The Schools of Ontario*, p. 155.
68. "Elementary Schools' Courses Overhauled, Simpson Announces," *The Globe and Mail* (March 31, 1937), p. 10.
69. Ibid.
70. Duncan McArthur, "Education for Citizenship," *The Canadian School Journal* (October, 1935), p. 299.
71. Shortt, "Legislation and Morality," p. 354.
72. Wood, *Idealism Transformed*, p. 28.
73. Duncan McArthur, "Method of Instruction," handwritten note retrieved from *Duncan McArthur Fonds (1929–1940)*, Q73-3, location 1059, Queen's University Archives.
74. Ibid.
75. Ibid.
76. Wood, *Idealism Transformed*, p. 28.
77. Ibid., p. 214.
78. Duncan McArthur, "Education and the Empire," in *The Empire Club of Canada Speeches* (Toronto: The Empire Club of Canada, 1941), p. 214.
79. Ibid.
80. Ibid.
81. Ibid., p. 213.
82. Ibid., p. 214.
83. Ibid.
84. Ibid., p. 215.
85. Duncan McArthur, "The Teaching of Canadian History," in *Papers and Records, Volume XXI* (Toronto: The Ontario Historical Society).
86. McArthur, "Education for Citizenship," p. 299.
87. Ibid.
88. Ibid.
89. Ibid.
90. Massolin, *Canadian Intellectuals, the Tory Tradition, and the Challenge of Modernity, 1939–1970*, p. 32.
91. "McArthur Raps Praise of Rich," *The Globe and Mail* (May 28, 1937), p. 11.
92. Ibid.
93. Ibid.
94. McArthur, "Education for Citizenship," p. 299.
95. Ibid.
96. Duncan McArthur, "Press Extracts From Addresses," *The Canadian School Journal* (March, 1935), p. 87.
97. "Dr. D. McArthur at the O.E.A.," *The School* (June, 1935), p. 834.
98. Ibid.
99. Wood, *Idealism Transformed*, p. 34.
100. "Editorial Notes," *The School* (November, 1934), p. 186.

101. Ibid.
102. "States School Grants Raised to Cut Taxes," *The Globe and Mail* (April 21, 1938), p. 19.
103. "Dr. D. McArthur at the O.E.A.," p. 834.
104. "Restoration of Pay Scale Announced," *The Globe and Mail* (March 31, 1937), p. 10.
105. "Dr. D. McArthur at the O.E.A.," pp. 834–835.
106. "McArthur Stresses Importance of Technical School Courses," *The Globe and Mail*, May 20, 1937, p. 1.
107. McArthur, "Education and the Empire," p. 213.
108. Most famously, in *Democracy and Education*.
109. McArthur, "Education and the Empire," p. 213.
110. Ibid.
111. Ibid.
112. Ibid.
113. Ibid.
114. Ibid.
115. Ibid.
116. Wood, *Idealism Transformed*, p. 41.
117. "Breech of Faith Seen in School Grant Cut," *The Globe and Mail* (April 27, 1943), p. 16.
118. "Want 100,000 School Pupils to Aid Farmers," *The Globe and Mail* (February 26, 1943), p. 15.
119. Ibid.
120. Robert D. Gidney, "Centralization and Education: The Origins of an Ontario Tradition," *Journal of Curriculum Studies* 7, no. 4 (November, 1972), p. 46.
121. McArthur, "A New Deal in Education in Ontario."
122. "States School Grants Raised to Cut Taxes," *The Globe and Mail* (April 21, 1938), p. 19.
123. "School Estimates Not Under Control of Urban Councils," *The Globe* (April 25, 1935), p. 1.
124. "Minister Head of Committee," *The Globe and Mail* (June 18, 1943), p. 8.
125. "Dr. D. McArthur at the O.E.A.," p. 833.
126. Ibid.
127. Ibid.
128. Ibid.
129. Wood, *Idealism Transformed*, p. 41.
130. McArthur, "Education for Citizenship," p. 264.
131. "50,000 Students Must Undergo Basic Training," *The Globe and Mail* (Tuesday, May 12, 1942), p. 4.
132. McArthur, "Education for Citizenship," p. 285.
133. Ibid., p. 286.
134. Ibid., p. 285.
135. Ibid., p. 286.
136. Ibid.
137. Ibid.
138. Ibid.
139. McArthur, "Education and the Empire," p. 213.
140. Ibid.
141. "McArthur Would Cut Language Requirement," *The Globe and Mail* (March 30, 1940), p. 5.
142. McKillop, *Matters of Mind*, p. 462.
143. Ibid.
144. Ibid.

145. "Dr. D. McArthur at the O.E.A.," p. 834.
146. "McArthur Would Cut Language Requirement," p. 5.
147. Ibid.
148. Ibid.
149. McKillop, *Matters of Mind*, p. 462.
150. McArthur, "Organization".
151. Ibid.
152. McArthur, "Method of Instruction."
153. "Fewer Exam Papers in Schools Proposed," *The Globe and Mail* (March 31, 1937), p. 10.
154. Ibid.
155. Ibid., p. 268.
156. Ibid.
157. Ibid.
158. Duncan McArthur, *History of Canada for High Schools* (Toronto: W.J. Gage & Co., Limited, 1931), my italics.
159. McArthur, "Education for Citizenship," p. 267.
160. Ibid.
161. Ibid.
162. Ibid.
163. McArthur, *History of Canada for High Schools*, p. v.
164. Ibid.
165. McArthur, "Education for Citizenship," p. 300.
166. Ibid., p. 267.
167. "Editorial Notes: Canadian Educational Association," *The School* (October, 1936), p. 93.
168. McArthur, "Method of Instruction."
169. "Dr. D. McArthur at the O.E.A.," p. 833.
170. Stamp, *The Schools of Ontario, 1867–1967*, p. 179.
171. Patrice Milewski, "'The Little Gray Book': Pedagogy, Discourse, and Rupture, 1937," *History of Education* 37, no. 1 (2008), pp. 91–92.
172. "The Association for Education in Citizenship," *The School* (October, 1934), p. 95.
173. M. A. Cameron, "The Spens Report," *The School* (September, 1939), pp. 3–5.
174. "Notes," *The School* (October, 1934), p. 96.
175. Cameron, "The Spens Report," pp. 3–5.
176. "Dr. D. McArthur at the O.E.A.," p. 834.
177. Ibid.
178. McArthur, "A New Deal in Education in Ontario," emphasis in original text.
179. "O.E.A. Study of Curricula Now Planned," *The Globe* (April 26, 1935), p. 1.
180. Ibid.
181. Ibid.
182. Kenney, "Duncan McArthur (1885–1943)," p. 450.
183. A. E. Prince, "The Honourable Duncan McArthur: A Tribute," *The Queen's Review* (Kingston, 1943), p. 162.
184. Ibid.

6 Ontario in the Twenty-first Century

Progressive Educational Rhetoric, Redux

Teachers adopt modern instructional practices, including the teaching of 21st Century competencies, integrating technology with pedagogy, harnessing the power of social media for learning and offer learners interconnected learning experiences, choices, and opportunities.

Faculties of Education in Canada adopt 21st Century learning based pre-service teaching standards and integrate ICT into their own pedagogies and classrooms.

Provinces adopt 21st Century teaching standards for in-service teachers and provide the tools, resources and training required for teachers to be innovative, teach 21st Century competencies, integrate technology with pedagogy and better engage their learners.[1]

Progressive education has been a tour de force over the last century with respect to public education, wrestling with humanism for control of curriculum and educational policy.[2] We are in the midst of a progressivist educational tide. I argue that progressive education is at once a response to modernity and an aspect of modernity. As a response to modernity, it manifests our existential angst about the accelerated rate of change affecting the social landscape of life. As an aspect of modernity, it accelerates our alienation from the constantly changing world in which we live.

Progressivist educational ideology as articulated historically and contemporaneously concentrates on three aims: a) focus on the individual learner's aptitudes and interests rather than upon a rigid curriculum developed in a bygone age; b) engage the learner actively in the construction of knowledge, a process prohibited by the memorization and examination of content; and, c) commit to relating school life to the modern world and its concerns, not to the affairs of a world of the past. In other words, progressives seek to focus on the individual child as an emerging being rather than upon a traditional curriculum, they endeavour to make schooling adaptive to the needs of these individuals with a world wrought with flux, and they are committed to relating school life to the modern, evolving, and rapidly transforming realities of social existence. Schools as conceived and as constructed historically are no longer relevant to a modern age.

Ronald Wright's 2004 Massey Lecture, *A Short History of Progress* develops a two-pronged argument. The first is relatively uncontroversial: the social world that we inhabit is changing. The second is bolder, but also more exciting: the social world that we inhabit is changing at an increasingly accelerated rate, which renders the taken-for-granted world unrecognizable to us with alarming quickness. From the Palaeolithic era to the end of the last ice age, a span consuming 99.5 percent of human existence, tools and cultural ideals replicated themselves, evolving at a staggeringly slow pace.

> Nowadays, Wright argues, we have reached such a pass that the skills and mores we learn in childhood are out-dated by the time we're thirty, and few people past fifty can keep up with their culture—whether in idiom, attitudes, taste, or technology—even if they try.[3]

The first progressivist wave overtook Canada during the interwar period, intensifying in the years following the Depression. Half a decade after Alberta introduced of a revised *Programme of Studies* for public schools in 1936, every province in Canada had transformed its formal curriculum, infrastructure, and examination structures. A new and progressive age was on the horizon, and it demanded that school life adjust to meet the needs of a contemporary world. This world was altered by the transformative effects of modern warfare, as experienced in the trenches of Europe, as well as by immigration, industrialization, and urbanization.

The second wave of progressive education followed the first by approximately 35 years; an indicative example is Ontario's *Living and Learning* document, which was submitted to the public in 1968. More commonly referred to as the Hall-Dennis Report, a name associated with the two chairs of the committee that drafted the document, *Living and Learning* offered a wide set of recommendations, which challenged educationists to focus on the individual learner's inclination towards self-discovery and exploration, to limit competition, to re-vision classroom spaces, and to abolish corporal punishment. Educationists wrestled to make sense of new technologies in the classroom, such as television programming, and conceptions of individual rights and responsibilities.

The third wave of progressivist thinking, 21st Century Learning, is a tidal force in education today. Whilst mediated within a discourse that concentrates upon the transformative influence of technology on our existence, the rhetoric of 21st Century Learning is thoroughly progressivist in its philosophical orientation towards the place of schools in society. Curriculum revisions are undertaken across Canada, in most cases concentrating on disciplinary thinking rather than content memorization and on the alignment between school learning and life beyond the classroom. The debate surrounding Ontario's new Health and Physical Education curriculum is indicative of a century-long tension between progressivist and traditionalist thought. The former, as noted previously, explicitly aims to modernize education, while the latter resists the impetus to jump at various provocations that modernity advances.

Throughout the history of Canadian public education, progressivists have largely defined the pedagogical aims that they espouse in opposition to tradition; tradition, in this sense, bears a definitively negative connotation. According to progressivist sensibilities, noted above, extant school structures were derived in, and are associated with, a bygone and obsolete social context. The schools of today should help students understand and live in a modern world rather in a world that has passed. Nearly nine decades ago, John Dewey (1938) articulated a challenge to progressivist educators that still resonates; he felt that the dichotomy of "traditional" and "progressive" schools is problematic.[4]

Dewey dared progressivists to be more critical of their own pedagogical principles and claims, but also to articulate an educational philosophy that was not defined primarily in opposition to another set of ideas, which is generally depicted in caricature.

Progressive educators who had proceeded according to this principle of continuity had neglected questions central to the pedagogical project. Dewey was noting a reactive element to reformist rhetoric, which exposed an instinctual response to the present.

Even as it acknowledges its internal inconsistencies, progressivist rhetoric drives forward an agenda that yokes progress to skill development that relates to the marketplace as depicted in its present place and as projected into the future. This is consistent historically.[5] What distinguishes 21st Century Learning is its concentration upon information and computer technologies. This concentration is not led entirely by educational associations, as technology corporations are intimately involved as partners. One might consider, as a case in point, *Canadians for 21st Century Learning and Innovation*, or *C21*. Ten of the 12 founding members of *C21* are corporations.[6] It is unsurprising that producers of technology products will argue that their commodities are essential to the future of education, yet educational stakeholders' rhetoric is not misaligned.

The Ontario Public School Boards Association (OPSBA) has also called upon the province to embrace the call for 21st Century Learning, and to commit to greater integration of technology:

> This paper is a call for the Government of Ontario and the Ministry of Education to lead the way in establishing a vision for Learning and Teaching in a Digital Age. Student and teacher use of technology in their everyday lives and the possibilities this creates for expanding the integration of 21st century skills into our learning and our instructional practices is at a tipping point.
>
> Many other jurisdictions have moved vigorously ahead to define a vision to guide education well into the 21st century and we urge Ontario, which is a leader in student achievement and in education in so many

spheres, to take up this challenge. This call is not inspired by consider-ations of funding but by a conviction that it is critical to define how we will move to keep pace with rapidly evolving technology to ensure our students are globally competitive. This is a matter of public confidence in our education system. Students, teachers, parents, school boards—all our education stakeholders—are ready to embrace this vision.[7]

If this final assertion is true, then there are immediate implications for all these stakeholders with respect to the ways that they conceptualize and structure teachers' professional development. The OPSBA argues that Ontario is lagging behind the times and that, as a consequence, it risks losing the public trust whilst simultaneously compromising the competitiveness of its students in an increasingly progressive world. This plea depicts a future in which Ontario's future is bleak and the province is out of pace:

> It is tempting to turn this on its head and speculate about what will hap-pen if we do not embrace change. A graphic illustration of this would be the North American automotive sector which in 2008 has revealed itself to be a dinosaur that has ignored its environment and failed, not only to anticipate what its customers would want, but even to respond to them when they made their wants known through their defection to small, environment-friendly automobiles made in Asia and Europe.[8]

OPSBA's call, further, challenges the province to take action on an educational vision that is enthusiastically accepted by all of Ontario's educationists. The public is associated with the customer and the province as the service provider. The former party desires educational reform, and the province must deliver. There is a great deal of propaganda at play in progressivist rhetoric. The OPBSA does not offer warrants for its claims that the public supports educational reform, if the public supports the financial investment in technologies, or if keeping pace with society is even possible. The context is established rhetorically, not empirically. Yet, educators may question the ways that this rhetoric affects the ways that they pursue professional development opportunities and the opportunities that they have to disagree with the OPBSA's vision for instruction.

Looking to Ontario's past, the rhetoric of progressive education was equally concerned with the relationship that schools had with modern, contempo-rary society. Rather than looking towards technology as a means of deal-ing with the future, educationists turned to other innovations and program revisions, including the introduction and elaboration of technical education, domestic science, and vocational guidance.[9] This sparked somewhat more of a backlash from traditionalists who felt that education was reforming too much and too quickly in its effort to keep pace with modernity. The cur-riculum had survived social evolution in the past, and it could be a bulwark that would help Ontarians deal with their future.[10]

Progressive schools were depicted as having an important role to play in the promotion of commercial, technical, and industrial progress in society.[11] With this in mind, students needed to learn many of the basic principles of industry, including business ethics, retail practice, contracts, taxation, and banking.[12] Progressive education was thus characterized as the adjustment of educational facilities to give students training in the skills they would need in their vocations.[13] If school learning was to be more closely related to life in business or industry, the business model was an apt one for school organization.[14] While today's popular imagining of the future conjures a world that is wired, digital, and negotiated by technological means, particularly in the workplace, Ontarians between the two World Wars saw their future in industry.

If technology is today's metaphor for social progress, as well as the principal means by which we could reform schools to address this progress, industry was both the medium and the message for many Ontarians during the interwar period.[15] The depiction of schools as a factory and children as resources is entirely consistent with many efficiency progressivists' characterizations of the educational process.

Revisiting twenty-first-century rhetoric, one notes the echo of a historical anxiety about school's relationship to contemporary society with respect to vocation and industry; as a group called Action Canada reports:

> Fuelled primarily by technological advancements and geopolitical developments, the pace of change in the twenty-first century exceeds even that of the Industrial Revolution . . . In order to remain competitive in an increasingly sophisticated and integrated global economy, Canadian industries must be able to efficiently and effectively adjust to emerging technologies, practices, and environments. This places new demands on the labour market for a dynamic workforce that is highly adaptable in the face of change. But the implications of accelerated change are by no means limited to the economic context. The consequences of historically unprecedented shifts in areas such as climate, technology, and demography are—at a minimum—tantamount to those in the global economy. By extension, they too demand resilient societies capable of adapting to new situations.[16]

The Hamilton-Wentworth School Board has published an extensive report on its plans to reform education. This thoroughly progressivist claim is rooted in a concern that society is "changing at an unprecedented rate," and "our current education system is based on an out-dated industrial model."[17] The District argues that it has an important role to play in securing that students are prepared for the future, and that technology, along with a new emphasis upon social learning, have made traditional modes and media of learning, including textbooks, dubious.

The Hamilton-Wentworth School Board's testament to educational reforms that could prepare students to face the future is a clear echo of early Ontarian progressivist claims. This testament makes a set of historical claims, which ought to be seen in their entirety:

> Schooling today continues to be based on an out-dated, industrial-aged model that does not meet the needs of 21st century learners. Historically schools have been very traditional and slow to innovate. Our models of curriculum delivery; our school calendar; and our organizational structures date back to the beginning of the 1900's. Schools have been modelled [sic] on the Scientific Management theory that reflected the assembly line method of production. (e.g. a subject specialist teacher, teaching the same material in successive periods; students sitting at desks; schools as primary 'sorters' of future career roles). The idea was, much like a car on an assembly line, to create a model of students that would be able to enter the workforce with the same skills. Although in other primary areas of society such as health care, transportation, and communication there has been dramatic changes since 1900, education systems remain essentially unchanged.
>
> Often the best rational we can offer for current practice is "we've always done it this way." Consider the 10-month school calendar. It is based on a time when young people were needed in the summer to help harvest crops. Despite the fact that that agricultural model is only needed in some rural pockets of our society, we continue, year after year, with the 10-month school calendar.
>
> There is a need for schools to remain in sync with the world around them and the learners within them. Students need to be involved in real, relevant experiences that recognize how they learn.[18]

The School Board's historical claims are made entirely without warrants. These are pursued by another unwarranted claim, which, in Lamarckian character, argues that students' brains have evolved as a result of their engagement with the digital age. What Darwin described as a slow, generational process of evolution is hastened to fit within a decade:

> Digital Age students are profoundly different than those who graduated only 10 to 15 years ago. . . . Student brains are different than those of their teachers, administrators, parents and employers—most of whom graduated before the digital age. To harness their current gifts—gifts deemed necessary to compete in the global economy—we must change how we educate on every level.[19]

The Ottawa Catholic District School Board corroborates the claim that students today are qualitatively different than anyone else. In its own statement, Ottawa Catholic District School Board states that schools are unsuitable means of educating students, whose digital brains are qualitatively unique:

Today's students are different from the students that our system was created to educate. The new digital learners are immersed in technology and they expect to use digital tools as part of their educational experience. Brain based research provides evidence that today's generation of students are "wired" differently than previous generations. Instructional strategies are evolving to reflect the needs of 21st century learners. The question we need to ask is not about what equipment to purchase or install, but rather what skills do our students need to succeed. The class of 2020 is currently sitting in our primary classrooms. These students will graduate from a learning environment and culture that espouses 21st century skill sets and tools.[20]

The argument is thoroughly progressivist. Extant schools are obsolete and educationists must look to the world of tomorrow in order to decide what skills and development will be useful. Nearly eight decades earlier, Joseph McCulley, noted progressivist and Headmaster of Pickering College argued:

Children must be freed from any authoritative concepts or any blind worship of tradition or the status quo. In their school days they must have some opportunity to learn how to choose,—to choose between opposed alternatives that path which will ultimately be good for the maximum good of all. Biological structures and civilizations themselves which have shown an inability to adapt to new conditions have perished; the school of tomorrow must, above all things, turn out citizens who are capable of facing their very different problems intelligently, courageously and with sympathy for all living beings.[21]

McCulley identified conflicts relating to religious surety, moral codes, financial stability, political faith, and the breakdown of a strong agricultural community as sources of tensions in society that reflect upon schools. Further, he argued that

Security in all these areas and many others has been shattered by our rapidly changing age . . . no longer is the classical and traditional curriculum carefully divided off into subject matter areas, sufficient to provide any understanding of the problems of modern life.

McCulley is concerned with schools as a driving force in social life and with progressive education as a means of affecting social evolution.

The twin forces of evolution and revolution are thus invoked iteratively in the rhetoric of progressive education. This is apparent, once more, in the OPBSA's position:

A high proportion of teachers in Ontario classrooms graduated from teacher education programs in an era when technology, if it was a factor

154 Ontario in the Twenty-first Century

at all, was seen as an esoteric bell or whistle. Many have incorporated some of the advantages of the wired world into their personal lives and from there into their professional practice in the classroom. Many have not. Most faculties of education have not rushed to embed the resources of technology in their programs and professional development offerings for teachers, more often than not, adhere to traditional class and workshop modalities. Technology as part of teacher education was not on the agenda four years ago. Faculties are realizing they need to help teachers be better prepared. The notion of elective courses on use of technology is old school thinking. The pressure is to embed technology in effective classroom strategies.

A common challenge for faculties of education is that their preservice candidates do not often have access to hook up notebooks in their practicum schools where the host teachers are teaching in a traditional manner.[22]

Society has evolved; education needs a revolution. Teacher education and, by broader implication, all teachers' ongoing professional development, are called to abandon "traditional" notions of teaching and learning. Teachers who serve as mentors for teacher candidates are the exemplars of tradition. The implication is clear: professional development should concentrate on technology, and educational institutions should "rush" to embed technological resources into their infrastructure. Thus, the generational gap is not only one that separates specially-evolved children who are in the classroom today from their teachers, but it also divides teacher candidates from practicing teachers.

Teachers who are practicing today must develop fluency with current digital technologies or, one presumes, make space for teachers who will. Professional development, it follows, must concentrate upon the twenty-first century. Uxbridge Public School, for instance, notes:

In Ontario, we are educating a generation of children and youth who have no memory of a world without the Internet, without instant access to information, and without an array of media at their fingertips. Effective learning in school engages students in modes of thinking, exploration and, knowledge-building that are relevant to their experiences growing up in the 21st Century.[23]

Teachers are challenged to adapt to the new age but not to problematize the new age or to ask what it means to be human in a world that seems new and peculiar. The Uxbridge Public School pursues its argument by citing Dewey as the standard bearer of this progressivist agenda:

The school-based inquiry process at Uxbridge Public School reorients teacher professional development using a contemporary version of

Dewey's (1965) idea of creating "intensive, focused opportunities to experiment with aspects of practice and then learn from that experience". More to the point of this inquiry was, what did we, as educators, learn from students about 21st Century learning with visual technology that could improve our current professional practice in the classrooms of our school.[24]

Dewey's pragmatist framework and his articulation of the need to act intelligently in the present as a means of developing habits of mind that will be useful in an uncertain future resonate in contexts ripe with rapid social change. John Dewey's *My Pedagogic Creed* claimed education "is a process of living and not a preparation for future living."[25] He was keenly aware to the social realities that were radically changing in North America, particularly after the First World War.

John Dewey was, in the words of Lawrence Cremin, "sensitive to the movement of things around him"; he "wanted schools to use the stuff of reality to educate men and women intelligently about reality. His notion of adjustment was an adjustment of conditions, not to them."[26] As a pragmatist, Dewey invoked an active approach to learning that helped students find the best solution to the problem at hand.[27] Solutions to future problems could not be derived today. It was only possible to practice intelligent and authentic problem solving today and cultivate those habits and practices that will be useful tomorrow. This necessitated a careful and deep understanding of contemporary social life. Education had a social role to play, which:

> Requires a searching study of society and its moving forces. That the traditional schools have almost wholly evaded consideration of the social potentialities of education is no reason why progressive schools should continue the evasion, even though it be sugared over with aesthetic refinements. The time ought to come when no one will be judged to be an educated man or woman who does not have insight into the basic forces of industrial and urban civilization. Only schools which take the lead in bringing about this kind of education can claim to be progressive in any socially significant sense.[28]

Preparing students to deal with the uncertain world of the future entails engaging them thoughtfully with present, uncertain world. Professional development for teachers, then, within a Deweyan framework, would indeed concentrate educationists' attention upon the world at hand. This would involve thinking upon the world as it is, and studying it. This does not entail transforming teachers' brains, but their habits of mind and practice. By concentrating upon the world around them thoughtfully, teachers can then deal with the world of the future, whatever that may be.

Dewey's response to the problems of modernity is consistent with the very problems of modernity. It is, perhaps, a very part of modernity. We cannot know the future, yet we must concern ourselves with this future and its social realities howsoever they manifest themselves within particular contexts. There are no eternal truths and persistent solutions, but there is a pressing concern to deal with the present, as this is the only means of facing the future intelligently and well.

How, then, ought educationists to position their work, intellectual and pedagogical, in an age where progressivism constitutes orthodoxy? Perhaps, in light of the history of educational rhetoric surrounding teachers and schools, educators must endeavour to be aware of the ongoing tension between progressivist and traditional rhetoric, which has polarized discussions about teaching, learning, and policy. Returning to Dewey's *Experience and Education* may be helpful, as this text opposes the dichotomy that emerges between the two ideological camps. So-called traditional education, for Dewey, lacks a holistic conception of the learner and focuses instruction on content with disregard for process. Progressive schools, on the contrary, tend to be reactionary and concentrate on activity and process at the expense of disciplinary thinking. The either-or thinking characterized by each extreme form of education is contextualized in the broader history of educational theory, which is "marked by opposition between the idea that education is development from within and that it is formation from without."[29] This opposition, he continues: "so far as practical affairs of the school are concerned, tends to take the form of contrast between traditional and progressive education."[30]

The dichotomy between presentations and conceptions of *traditional* and *progressive* schools is problematic:

> The general philosophy of the new education may be sound, and yet the difference in abstract principles will not decide the way in which the moral and intellectual preference involved shall be worked out in practice. There is always the danger in a new movement that in rejecting the aims and methods of that which it would supplant, it may develop its principles negatively rather than positively and constructively.[31]

Progressive educators who had proceeded "on the basis of rejection, of sheer opposition" had neglected questions central to the pedagogical project, including: [32]

> What is the place and meaning of subject-matter and of organization *within* experience? How does subject-matter function? Is there anything inherent in experience which tends towards progressive organization of its contents? What results follow when the materials of experience are not progressively organized?[33]

These questions, I wish to argue, should be the fundamental ones in the composition and orientation of teachers' professional development. Technology, as a means to an end, may facilitate the posing of questions and the articulation of answers. It is, perhaps, of secondary concern. According to Dewey, educational experiences are the bases of learning, but experience is not inherently meaningful or necessarily educative for everyone. The pedagogical value of any professional development experience is instead, judged by its effect upon an individual learner's present and future, and the degree to which it enables him or her to contribute positively to the world around them as an educator.

Progressivists must be sufficiently critical of their own underlying principles. It does not suffice to say that the world has changed and that, as a consequence, educationists must reform schools. What does social evolution mean for education? How might we live a good life within a world that seems to be spinning evermore quickly on its axis? How might professional development help educationists understand, make sense of, and challenge the extant state of society, rather than just adjust to it? Deprived of these prima facie questions, professional development in a progressive world will be, in Dewey's words, "as dogmatic as ever was the traditional education which it reacted against."[34]

Notes

1. Canadians for 21st Century Learning and Innovation, *Shifting Minds: A Vision and Framework for 21st Century Learning in Canada* (2012), pp. 17–18. Accessed at: www.c21canada.org.
2. Theodore Christou, "We Find Ourselves in the World of the Present: Humanist Resistance to Progressive Education in Ontario," *History of Education Quarterly 55*, no. 3 (2015), pp. 273–293.
3. Roland Wright, *A Short History of Progress* (Toronto, ON: House of Anansi Press, 2004), p. 14.
4. John Dewey, *Experience and Education* (New York: Touchstone, 1938), p. 20.
5. Theodore Christou, "Progressivist Rhetoric and Revised Programmes of Study: Weaving Curricular Consistency and Order Out of Diverse Progressivist Themes in Ontario, Canada," *Curriculum History 13*, no. 1 (2014), pp. 61–82.
6. These corporations include: a) one that arranges for educational excursions internationally, but also online language learning, Education First; b) five publishers, Scholastic Education, Pearson, Oxford, McGraw-Hill/Ryerson, and Nelson; and c) four from the technology industry, Dell, Microsoft, SMART Technologies and IBM.
7. Ontario Public School Boards Association, *A Vision for Learning and Teaching in a Digital Age*, p. 1. Accessed at: www.opsba.org/files/OPSBA_AVisionFor Learning.pdf.
8. Ibid., p. 16.
9. "Vocational Training and Vocational Guidance," *The Canadian School Journal* (November, 1932), p. 371.
10. Theodore Michael Christou, *Progressive Education: Revisioning and Reforming Ontario's Public Schools, 1919–1942* (Toronto, ON: University of Toronto Press, 2012).
11. See, for example, "Vocational Education," *The School* (January, 1929), pp. 425–426.
12. J. L. Jose, "Is Business Practice Meeting the Community Needs?" *The School* (January, 1941), pp. 389–391.

13. "Education of 90% of the Pupils for 10% of the Jobs," *The Canadian School Journal* (July, 1929), p. 1.

14. J. Ferris David, "Secondary Schools and their Relation to Business," *The Canadian School Journal* (April, 1933), p. 28.

15. Kieran Egan, *Getting It Wrong From the Beginning: Our Progressivist Inheritance From Herbert Spencer, John Dewey, and Jean Piaget* (New Haven, CT and London, UK: Yale University Press, 2002), p. 2.

16. Action Canada, *Future Tense: Adapting Canadian Education Systems for the 21st Century*, p. 4. Accessed at: www.actioncanada.ca/wp-content/uploads/2014/04/TF2-Report_Future-Tense_EN.pdf.

17. Hamilton-Wentworth District School Board, *Education for the 21st Century: Here, Now and Into the Future*, p. 1. Accessed at: www.hwdsb.on.ca/aboutus/strategic-directions/education/documents/Full-Report.pdf.

18. "Education for the 21st Century: Here, Now and into the Future," p. 2.

19. Ibid., p. 3. See also, F. Kelly, T. McCain, and I. Jukes, *Teaching the Digital Generation: No More Cookie-Cutter High Schools* (Thousand Oaks, CA: Corwin, 2008), p. 20.

20. Ottawa Catholic School Board, *Toward 2020: Connecting With Our Students*, p. 1. Accessed at: www.ottawacatholicschools.ca/images/learningtech/oc-schools-pdf-towards2020.pdf.

21. Joseph McCulley, "Education in an Age of Insecurity," *The Canadian School Journal* (April, 1937), p. 140.

22. Ontario Public School Boards' Association, *What If? A 21st Century Classroom Scenario*, p. 11. Accessed at: www.opsba.org/files/WhatIf.pdf.

23. Uxbridge Public School, *21st Century Learning*. Accessed at: http://uxbridgeps.ddsbschools.ca/21st-century-learning.html.

24. John Dewey, "The Relation of Theory to Practice in Education," in M. Borrowman (Ed.), *Teacher Education in America: A Documentary History* (New York: Teachers College Press, 1965), pp. 140–171.

25. John Dewey, "My Pedagogic Creed," *The School Journal* 54, no. 3 (January 16, 1897), pp. 77–80.

26. Lawrence A. Cremin, "John Dewey and the Progressive-Education Movement, 1915–1952," *The School Review* 67, no. 2 (Summer, 1959), p. 170.

27. John Dewey and Evelyn Dewey, *Schools of To-Morrow* (New York: E. P. Dutton & Co., 1915), p. 249.

28. John Dewey, "How Much Freedom in New Schools?" *New Republic* 63 (1930), p. 206.

29. Dewey, *Experience and Education*, p. 17.

30. Ibid.

31. Ibid., p. 20.

32. Ibid., p. 21.

33. Ibid., p. 20.

34. Ibid., p. 22.

Conclusion
A Path Revisited: Historical Research in Education Reviewed

The most popular new ideas were associated with progressive education, which represented a revolt against existing formal and traditional schooling. It also meant expansion of the school's purpose and curriculum through emphasis upon the child's place in the larger society. New pedagogical ideas founded on research and growth in psychology were central to the changes of the progressives. Within this broad framework, however, there were many variations and differences in philosophy of practice.[1]

The liberal order, Ian McKay argues, both encouraged and sought to "extend across time and space a belief in the epistemological and ontological primacy of the category 'individual.' "[2] This is "more akin to a secular religion or totalizing philosophy than an easily manipulated set of political ideas," and it represented a great shift from the principles of Tory communitarianism or civic humanism that were prominent in Ontario's Victorian social order and were key to the classical curriculum and a liberal arts education.[3] The spread of progressivist ideas across educational spaces echoes "the implantation and expansion over a heterogeneous terrain of a certain politico-economic logic—to wit, liberalism."[4]

Modernity and progress, then, in schools as in society, when viewed as the extension and application of ideological orders, represents a very complex process that disintegrates and dissolves old ways and structures, pedagogical and other.[5] It is the way that ideologies reach out to and affect public opinion, directly and indirectly, via "libraries, schools, associations and clubs of various kinds, even architecture and the layout and names of streets."[6] The liberal order stressed the primacy of the individual within society, swept over Canadian institutions and organizations, transforming them in its wake. This progressive modernization of the country affected the schools and, more generally, educational thought.

Yet, even as a potential link between progressivism and liberalism may be useful to future scholarship, I do worry about arguments that are "inescapably structural."[7] That is, historians' concepts are not constructed to reduce complex events into static categories that portray a false "fixity of the past."[8] But by categorizing, periodizing, and describing, do historians compartmentalize and restrict, or mask, complexity? Certainly, intellectual debates surrounding all kinds of progress, including educational progressivism, are prone to inconsistencies and variances. I have been inconsistent in the ways that I have considered the themes of progressive education in the province of Ontario's interwar history. No matter how much I return to these themes, I cannot escape the pervasive sense that I have missed something analytical, that there is more evidence to frame, that I have to cycle back and start anew.

This research has modeled its approach on the seminal work of Herbert Kliebard, whose examination of American educational progressivism assumed from its inception a certain complexity about the past. By conceptualizing the ideological debates on school curricula as a struggle, Kliebard necessarily set up a dynamic wherein interest groups—three of which make up a typology of progressivism in this study—vie for control over schools. He likened curriculum to a battlefield. I have tested that hypothesis in the Canadian context and found it wanting. Progressives all wanted schools to change. They insisted that the curriculum was out of date, ignored the individual child, and promoted passive and uninteresting pedagogical approaches. Progressives still want schools to change, largely for the same reasons. In light of the complexity inherent in progressivism and despite the apparently consistent reformist message that progressivists share, I do not believe that any uniformly happy, agreeable, and cohesive vision for the future of schooling was ever a reality. Curriculum will always be contested. That is precisely why it matters.

The discussion bears this out. Case in point is the fundamentally different interpretations about what it meant for schools to focus on the individual. Developmentalists argued that individualized instruction entailed directing school activities to a learner's psychological stage of development. Efficiency advocates justified mental testing as a means of ascertaining a child's learning, level of understanding, and potential socio-economic place in the world. Social meliorists argued that centering instruction on the child had to involve elements of equity and social justice.

Yet, as the study of Duncan McArthur demonstrates, there is a fluidity to these contexts that belies any effort to box up any individual educationist into a particular category. At no point was it possible for me to say that any McArthur or anyone else was strictly an efficiency advocate or solely a developmentalist. Such rigid compartmentalization would ignore the changes in perspective or attitude displayed over time. The progressive movement in Ontario was far less fixed and far more fluid than that.

This is not an argument that history is mired in a state of "inexpungeable relativity."[9] We have moved past the crisis of the linguistic turn, where relativity was linked to the postmodern understanding of language as self-referential, having no extra-linguistic reality.[10] History is not fiction, and the "dissolution of the materiality" of language has not led to "the dissolution of history."[11] Rather, values, interpretation, and language are "an inherent part of critical inquiry."[12] This account, like all "accounts of social reality are not only value-impregnated but value-impregnating, not only practically-imbued but practically-imbuing."[13]

Further language is, to paraphrase Christopher Lorenz, a necessary and *enabling* constraint.[14] This seemingly oxymoronic phrase "is intended to flag a necessary tension rather than a contradiction. Complex unities are simultaneously rule-bound (constraining) and capable of flexible, unanticipated possibilities (enabling)."[15] In other words, description and research is simultaneously constrained by and enabled by language. This study is thus inevitably:

a. partial—there can be no complete interpretation of anything;
b. perspectival—all interpretation is interpretation from a particular point of view embedded within a particular tradition; and
c. revisable—all interpretation is open to later revisions.[16]

Yet, I argue that in Ontario, educational reform discourse could have been stimulated from a number of positions including, but not limited to, disillusionment with the present state of affairs, or an optimistic zeal for a sense of disappointment and disillusionment pervaded and stimulated reform initiatives. A concept like social meliorism has a different potency when viewed in relation to Depression-era vagrancy, labour unrest, hunger, and unemployment in the heart of Toronto than it might in a rural one-room schoolhouse situated in a community booming because of the pulp-and-paper industry explosion in the early 1920s. In the former case, the concept would be a priority for individuals whose children, hypothetically speaking, had to quit school in order to find work or leave home in order to cease being a financial burden. In the latter case, the meliorist spirit might have invigorated a feeling of *brotherhood* and led to cooperation, unionization, or fellowship. The meaning in any particular context of any concept is personal and negotiated, but historical work in education is far from a subjective, literary creation.

Notes

1. Robert Patterson, "Society and Education During the Wars and their Interlude: 1914–1945," in J. Donald Wilson, Robert M. Stamp, and Louis-Philippe Audet (Eds.), *Canadian Education: A History* (Toronto: Prentice-Hall, 1970), p. 373.
2. Ian McKay, "The Liberal Order Framework: A Prospectus for a Reconnaissance of Canadian History," *The Canadian Historical Review* 81, no. 4 (2000), p. 623.
3. Ibid., p. 624.
4. David Forgacs, Ed., *The Antonio Gramsci Reader: Selected Writings 1916–1935* (New York: New York University Press, 2000), pp. 380–381.
5. See, for instance, Philip Massolin, *Canadian Intellectuals, the Tory Tradition, and the Challenge of Modernity, 1939–1970* (Toronto: University of Toronto Press, 2001), p. 4.

6. Ibid., p. 381.
7. Elizabeth Fox-Genovese, "Literary Criticism and the Politics of the New Historicism," in Keith Jenkins (Ed.), *The Postmodern History Reader* (New York: Routledge, 1997), p. 86.
8. Gertrude Himmelfarb, "Telling It as You Like It: Postmodernist History and the Flight From Fact," *The Postmodern History Reader*, p. 158.
9. Hayden White, "Historical Emplotment and the Problem of Truth," *The Postmodern History Reader*, p. 392.
10. Jacques Derrida, *Of Grammatology* (Baltimore: The Johns Hopkins University Press, 1976).
11. Gabrielle Spiegel, "History, Historicism and the Social Logic of the Text in the Middle Ages," *The Postmodern History Reader*, p. 184.
12. Benedicta Egbo, "Emergent Paradigm: Critical Realism and Transformative Research in Educational Administration," *McGill Journal of Education* 40, no. 2 (2005), p. 274.
13. Roy Bhaskar, "Facts and Values: Theory and Practice/Reason and the Dialectic of Human Emancipation/Depth, Rationality and Change," in M. Archer, R. Bhaskar, A. Collier, T. Lawson and A. Norrie (Eds.), *Critical Realism: Essential Readings* (London: Routledge, 1998), p. 409.
14. Chris Lorenz, "You Got Your History, I Got Mine," *Österreichische Zeitschrift für Geschichtswissenschaften* 10, no. 4 (1999), pp. 563–584.
15. Brent Davis, David Sumara, and Rebecca Luce-Kapler, Rebecca, *Engaging Minds: Learning and Teaching in a Complex World* (New York: Routledge, 2008), p. 193.
16. Lorenz, "You got Your History," p. 573.

References

"21st Century Learning." *Uxbridge Public School*. Accessed June 28, 2017. www.ddsb.ca/school/uxbridgeps/SchoolInformation/21stCenturyLearning/Pages/default.aspx.

"The 1934 Convention." *The Canadian School Journal* (March, 1934): 85–86.

"50,000 Students Must Undergo Basic Training." *The Globe and Mail*, Toronto, May 12, 1942.

An Action Canada Task Force Report. "Future Tense: Adapting Canadian Education Systems for the 21st Century." *Action Canada*. Accessed February, 2013. www.actioncanada.ca/wp-content/uploads/2014/04/TF2-Report_Future-Tense_EN.pdf.

"The Aims of Education." *Canadian School Board Journal* (June, 1928): 4–6.

Aitken, W.E.M. "The Use of a High School Library." *The School* (March, 1931): 613–615.

Alexander, Charles A. "The Teacher's Place in the New Health Programme." *The Canadian School Journal* (January, 1935): 28.

Althouse, J. G. *Addresses By J. G. Althouse: A Selection of Addresses By the Late Chief Director of Education for Ontario, Covering the Years 1936–1956*. Toronto: W. J. Gage Limited, 1958.

Anglin, R. W., Hooper, A. G., Husband, A. G., Jennings, W. A., and Levan, I. M. "Report of the High School Inspectors." In *Report of the Minster of Education for the Year 1932*. Toronto: The Queen's Printer for Ontario.

"Association for Childhood Education." *The Canadian School Journal* (January, 1932): 39.

"The Association for Education in Citizenship." *The School* (October, 1934): 95.

Axelrod, Paul. "Beyond the Progressive Education Debate: A Profile of Toronto Schooling in the 1950s." *Historical Studies in Education* 17, no. 2 (2005): 227–241.

———. *Making a Middle Class: Student Life in English Canada During the Thirties*. Montreal and Kingston: McGill-Queen's University Press, 1990.

Baskerville, Peter A. *Ontario: Image, Identity, and Power*. Toronto: Oxford University Press, 2002.

Berger, Carl. *The Sense of Power: Studies in the Ideas of Canadian Imperialism, 1867–1914*. Toronto: University of Toronto Press, 1970.

Berhardt, K. S. "A Prophet Not Without Honour: The Contribution of William E. Blatz to Child Study." In *Twenty-Five Years of Child Study: The Development of the Programme and Review of the Research at the Institute of Child Study, University of Toronto, 1926–1951*, edited by Karl S. Bernhardt, Margaret I. Fletcher,

Frances L. Johnson, Dorothy A. Millichamp, and Mary L. Northway, 3–17. Toronto: University of Toronto Press, 1951.

Bhaskar, Roy. "Facts and Values: Theory and Practice/Reason and the Dialectic of Human Emancipation/Depth, Rationality and Change." In *Critical Realism: Essential Readings*, edited by M. Archer, R. Bhaskar, A. Collier, T. Lawson, and A. Norrie. London: Routledge, 1998.

Bissell, Electa. "Developing a Sense of Responsibility in the Grade II Child." *The School* (November, 1929): 224–226.

Blatz, William E. *Human Security: Some Reflections*. Toronto: University of Toronto Press, 1966.

———. *Understanding the Young Child*. New York: William Morrow & Co., 1944.

———. "Security." *The School* (February, 1941): 499–503.

———. *Hostages to Peace: Parents and the Children of Democracy*. New York: William Morrow & Co., 1940.

———. "William E. Blatz to G. J. Hecht: Personal Correspondence." *William E. Blatz Fonds*, Thomas Fisher Rare Book Library, Box 1, Number 43, April 2, 1930.

———. *University of Toronto Monthly: June*. Toronto: University of Toronto, 1926.

Blatz, William, and Bott, Helen MacMurchy. *Parents and the Pre-School Child*. New York: William Morrow & Co., 1929.

———. *Parents and the Pre-School Child*. Toronto: J. M. Dent and Sons Ltd., 1928.

———. "An Intelligence Test for Fathers." *William E. Blatz Fonds*, Thomas Fisher Rare Book Library, Box 1, Number 43, n.d.

———. "List of Publications By the Staff of the Institute of Child Study." *William E. Blatz Fonds*, Thomas Fisher Rare Book Library, Box 28, Number 1.

Bobbitt, Franklin. *The Curriculum*. Boston: Houghton Mifflin, 1918.

———. *How to Make a Curriculum*. Boston: Houghton Mifflin, 1913.

Bode, Boyd H. *Modern Educational Theories*. New York: Macmillan, 1927.

Bothwell, Robert. *The Penguin History of Canada*. Toronto: Penguin, 2006.

Bott, Helen. *Bulletin of the Institute, No. 50*. Toronto: Institute of Child Study, 1951.

"Breech of Faith Seen in School Grant Cut." *The Globe and Mail*, Toronto, April 27, 1943.

Brehony, Kevin J. "A New Education for a New Era: The Contribution of the Conferences of the New Education Fellowship to the Disciplinary Field of Education, 1921–1938." *Paedagogica Historica* 40, no. 5 (2004): 733–755.

Brittain, Horace L. "Some Views of Administration of Public Education." *The Canadian School Journal* (December, 1934): 406–407.

Brough, T. A. "Revising the Curriculum in British Columbia." *The School* (October, 1936): 101–105.

Brown, J. W. "The School Library." *The Canadian School Journal* (January, 1934): 6.

Bruno-Jofré, Rosa. "To Those in 'Heathen Darkness': Deweyan Democracy and Education in the American Interdenominational Configuration." In *International Standing Conference for the History of Education, July 2007*. Hamburg: University of Hamburg, 2008.

———. "Citizenship and Schooling in Manitoba: 1918–1945." *Manitoba History* (1998/1999): 26–36.

Burpee, Lawrence J. "The Work of the International Joint Commission." *The School* (February, 1937): 467–472.

Burt, Cyril. *The Young Delinquent*. London: The University of London Press, 1925.

Burton, C. L. "Business as an Objective." *The Canadian School Journal* (October, 1932): 340–343.

Bury, J. B. *The Idea of Progress: An Inquiry into Its Origin and Growth*. New York: Dover Publications, Inc., 1932.

Cameron, M. A. "The Spens Report." *The School* (September, 1939): 3–5.

Canadian Council on Learning. *Changing Our Schools: Implementing Successful Educational Reform*. January, 2009. www.edu.gov.on.ca/eng/policyfunding/memos/jan2009/LessonsinLearning.pdf.

"The Canadian Education Association." *The School* (December, 1936): 281–285.

"Canadian Federation of Kindergarten, Nursery School, and Kindergarten-Primary Department." *The Canadian School Journal* (January, 1932): 97–98.

"Changing the Educational Emphasis." *The Canadian School Journal* (March, 1933): 83–84.

Charters, Werrett W. *Curriculum Construction*. New York: Macmillan, 1923.

———. *Teaching the Common Branches*. Boston: Houghton Mifflin, 1913.

———. *Methods of Teaching: Developed From a Functional Standpoint*. Chicago: Row, Peterson & Co., 1909.

Chittick, Rae. "The Place of the Teacher in a Mental Hygiene Programme." *The School* (March, 1940): 568–572.

Christou, Theodore M. "We Find Ourselves in the World of the Present: Humanist Resistance to Progressive Education in Ontario." *History of Education Quarterly* 55, no. 3 (2015): 273–293.

———. "Progressivist Rhetoric and Revised Programmes of Study: Weaving Curricular Consistency and Order out of Diverse Progressivist Themes in Ontario, Canada." *Curriculum History* 13, no. 1 (2014): 61–82.

———. "The Complex of Intellectual Currents: Duncan McArthur and Ontario's Progressivist Curricular Reforms." *Paedagogica Historica* 49, no. 5 (2013): 677–697.

———. "Schools Are No Longer Merely Educational Institutions: The Rhetoric of Social Efficiency in Ontario Education, 1931–1935." *History of Education* 42, no. 5 (2013): 566–577.

———. *Progressive Education: Revisioning and Reframing Ontario's Public Schools, 1919–1942*. Toronto: University of Toronto Press, 2012.

Coe, George A. *A Social Theory of Religious Education*. New York: Charles Scribner's Sons, 1927.

Cohen, David K. "Dewey's Problem." *The Elementary School Journal* 98, no. 5 (1998): 427–446.

Commachio, Cynthia. *The Infinite Bonds of Family: Domesticity in Canada, 1850–1940*. Toronto: University of Toronto Press, 1999.

Committee of the Classical Section of the Ontario Educational Association. "The Report on Latin." *The School* (June, 1935): 865–871.

"Conference vs. Debate." *The Canadian School Journal* (March, 1932): 93.

Conn, Henry. "Measuring Aptitude for School Work." *The School* (April, 1931): 717–723.

"The Convention of 1933." *The Canadian School Journal* (May, 1933): 163.

Cook, John A. "Co-operation in Education." *The Canadian School Journal* (November, 1933): 446–447.

Cooke, H. M. "Secondary Education." *The Canadian School Journal* (November, 1932): 381–383.

Cooper, William John. "Educational News." *The Canadian School Journal* (November, 1933): 403–405.

Corbett, E. A. "Adult Education and the School." *The School* (September, 1938): 18–20.

———. "Can the Radio Be Used Effectively in University Extension Work?" *The School* (October, 1935): 93–97.

Counts, George S. "Dare Progressive Education be Progressive?" *Progressive Education* 4, no. 9 (1932): 257–263.

———. *Dare the School Build a New Social Order.* New York: John Day, 1932.

———. *The American Road to Culture: A Social Interpretation of Education in the United States.* New York: John Day, 1930.

Cremin, Lawrence. *American Education: The Metropolitan Experience, 1876–1980.* New York: Harper & Row, 1988.

———. "John Dewey and the Progressive Education Movement, 1915–1952." In *Dewey on Education,* edited by Reginald D. Archambault, 160–173. New York: Random House, 1961.

———. "John Dewey and the Progressive-Education Movement, 1915–1952. *The School Review* 67, no. 2 (1959): 160–173.

Cross, Wilbur. *Twenty-Five Years After: Sidelights on the Mental Hygiene Movement and Its Founders.* New York: Doubleday, 1934.

Cuban, Larry. *Inside the Black Box of Classroom Practice: Change Without Reform in American Education.* Cambridge: Harvard Education Press, 2013.

Curtis, Bruce, Livingston, D. W., and Smaller, Harry. *Stacking the Deck: The Streaming of Working-Class Kids in Ontario Schools.* Toronto: Our Schools/Our Selves Education Foundation, 1992.

Dain, Norman. *Clifford W. Beers: Advocate for the Insane.* Pittsburgh: University of Pittsburgh Press, 1980.

Davis, Brent, Sumara, David, and Luce-Kapler, Rebecca. *Engaging Minds: Learning and Teaching in a Complex World.* New York: Routledge, 2008.

"Death of Dr. Duncan McArthur." *Journal of the Royal Astronomical Society of Canada* 37, (1943): 343.

Deeley, Charles F. "Two Thoughts on Projects." *The School* (January, 1941): 405–407.

Derrida, Jacques. *Of Grammatology.* Baltimore: The Johns Hopkins University Press, 1976.

"Despair or Courage." *The Canadian School Journal* (January, 1933): 5.

Dewey, John. "The Relation of Theory to Practice in Education." In *Teacher Education in America: A Documentary History,* edited by M. Borrowman, 140–171. New York: Teachers College Press, 1965.

———. *Experience and Education.* New York: Touchstone, 1938.

———. "How Much Freedom in New Schools?" *New Republic* 63 (1930): 204–206.

———. "Whither Humanism." *The Thinker* 2 (1930): 9–12.

———. "Why I Am for Smith." *New Republic* 56 (1928): 320–333.

———. *The School and Society.* Chicago: University of Chicago Press, 1907.

———. "My Pedagogic Creed." *The School Journal* 54, no. 3 (1897): 77–80.

Dewey, John, and Dewey, Evelyn. *Schools of To-Morrow.* New York: E. P. Dutton & Co., 1915.

Dickie, Donalda. "Education Via the Enterprise: The Task of Education." *The School* (September, 1940): 3–9.

Duncan McArthur. "Press Extracts From Addresses." *The Canadian School Journal* (March, 1935): 87.

Dunlop, Florence S. "The School Psychologist." *The School* (May, 1940): 753–756.

Durkheim, Émile. *The Evolution of Educational Thought: Lectures on the Formation and Development of Secondary Education in France.* London: Routledge and Kegan Paul, 1977.

Durrant, C. R. "The Search for an Educational Ideal." *The Canadian School Journal* (April, 1934): 123–124.

Easterbrook, W. T., and Aitken, H.G.J. *Canadian Economic History*. Toronto: University of Toronto Press, 1990.

Editorial. "Below Average." *The School* (February, 1942): 463.

———. "High Marks Still Count." *The School* (March, 1942): 557.

———. "There Is a Tomorrow." *The School* (May, 1942): 741.

———. "This Is Our Country." *The School* (June, 1942): 833.

———. "Working Together." *The School* (February, 1941): 497–498.

———. "A Dilemma." *The School* (April, 1941): 683.

———. "School and Society." *The School* (September, 1941): 1.

———. "Editorial: Education Week." *The School* (November, 1941): 181.

———. "Educational News: Democracy." *The School* (November, 1941): 200.

———. "The Coming Triumph of Humanity." *The School* (December, 1941): 275–276.

———. "Work." *The School* (November, 1940): 185–186.

———. "Schools and Democracy." *The School* (February, 1939): 9–10.

———. "As a Man Thinks." *The School* (December, 1939): 283–284.

———. "The Social Sciences." *The School* (January, 1936): 363.

———. "Editorial Notes: Canadian Educational Association." *The School* (October, 1936): 93.

———. "President Butler and Democracy." *The School* (October, 1936): 94–95.

———. "Dr. D. McArthur at the O.E.A." *The School* (June, 1935): 833–855.

———. "Academic Freedom." *The School* (September, 1935): 2–3.

———. "Survey of Experiments in Social-Economic Education." *The School* (November, 1935): 181–182.

———. "Notes and News." *The School* (September, 1934): 65–90.

———. "Control of Expenditures for Education." *The Canadian School Journal* (October, 1932): 339.

———. "Vocational Education." *The School* (January, 1929): 425–426.

"Editorial Notes." *The School* (November, 1934): 185–187.

"Editorial Notes: Democracy at War." *The School* (October, 1939): 95–96.

"Editorial Notes: Education for Citizenship." *The School* (June, 1936): 823–824.

"Editorial Notes: Indoctrination." *The School* (April, 1936): 641–643.

"Editorial Notes: New Approaches to the Social Studies." *The School* (April, 1937): 645–647.

"Editorial Notes: Progress in Education." *The School* (November, 1930): 213–215.

"Editorial Notes: The School and Society." *The School* (May, 1933): 737–738.

"The Editor's Page." *The Canadian School Journal* (January, 1935): 3.

"Education for Character." *The School* (October, 1934): 95.

"Education of 90% of the Pupils for 10% of the Jobs." *The Canadian School Journal* (July, 1929): 1.

"Educational Experiments, Research, and Progress in Canada." *The School* (December, 1940): 278.

"Educational News." *The Canadian School Journal* (November, 1933): 403–405.

"Educational News: Ontario." *The School* (April, 1942): 723–724.

"Educational Progress in Canada: Vocational Education." *The School* (June, 1942): 871–872.

Egan, Kieran. *Getting It Wrong From the Beginning: Our Progressivist Inheritance From Herbert Spencer, John Dewey, and Jean Piaget*. New Haven, CT: Yale University Press, 2002.

Egbo, Benedicta. "Emergent Paradigm: Critical Realism and Transformative Research in Educational Administration." *McGill Journal of Education* 40, no. 2 (2005): 267–284.

"Elementary Schools' Courses Overhauled, Simpson Announces." *The Globe and Mail*, Toronto, March 31, 1937.

Ellis, Jason. "'Backward and Brilliant Children': A Social and Policy History of Disability, Childhood, and Education in Toronto's Special Education Classes, 1910–1945." Ph.D. diss., York University, 2011.

Ferguson, Barry. *Remaking Liberalism: The Intellectual Legacy of Adam Shortt, O. D. Skelton, W. C. Clark and W. A. Mackintosh*. Montreal and Kingston: McGill-Queen's University Press, 1993.

Ferguson, Howard. *Report of the Minister of Education, Province of Ontario for the Year 1929*. Toronto: The Legislative Assembly of Ontario, 1929.

Ferris, David J. "Secondary Schools and their Relation to Business." *The Canadian School Journal* (April, 1933): 128–129.

"Fewer Exam Papers in Schools Proposed." *The Globe and Mail*, Toronto, March 31, 1937.

Fletcher, B. A. "Some General Principles of Education." *The School* (January, 1939): 371–377.

Foster, George E. "The League of Nations." *The School* (March, 1928): 645–651.

Fox-Genovese, Elizabeth. "Literary Criticism and the Politics of the New Historicism." In *The Postmodern History Reader*, edited by Keith Jenkins, 84–102. London: Routledge, 1997.

Fullan, Michael. "Great to Excellent: Launching the Next Stage of Ontario's Education Agenda (2012)." *Michaelfullan*. Accessed June 26, 2017. www.michaelfullan.ca/wp-content/uploads/2013/09/13_Fullan_Great-to-Excellent.pdf.

Fyfe, W. H. "Science in Secondary Education." *The School* (April, 1934): 652–660.

———. "Inaugural Address." *W.H. Fyfe Papers*, Box 2, File 9, Queen's University Archives, October 24, 1930.

Gavin, F. P. "Recent Social Changes and the Schools." *The Canadian School Journal* (May, 1935): 134–135.

Gemmell, Katie. "The Impact of Progressive Education on Roman Catholic Schools in the Archdiocese of Vancouver, 1924–1960." PhD diss., University of British Columbia, 2015.

Gidney, Robert D. "Centralization and Education: The Origins of an Ontario Tradition." *Journal of Curriculum Studies* 7, no. 4 (November, 1972): 33–48.

Gidney, Robert D., and Millar, W.P.J. *How Schools Worked: Public Education in English Canada, 1900–1940*. Montreal and Kingston: McGill-Queen's University Press, 2012.

Gleason, Mona. *Normalizing the Ideal: Psychology, Schooling, and Family in Postwar Canada*. Toronto: University of Toronto Press, 1999.

Goldring, C. C. "The School and Business." *The Canadian School Journal* (January, 1935): 10–12.

———. "Manual Training or the General Shop?" *The School* (February, 1935): 470–471.

———. "Educational News." *The Canadian School Journal* (November, 1935): 325.

———. "Some Possible Phases of Vocational Guidance in Canadian Schools." *The School* (June, 1933): 841–844.

———. "The Work of a Principal." *Educational Courier* (June, 1933): 8–10.

Goode, Marion E. "The Function of Guidance." *The School* (November, 1940): 192–194.

———. "The Methods of Guidance." *The School* (December, 1940): 288–318.

Goode Hodgins, Marion. "Permanent Values in Education." *The School* (May, 1942): 760–762.

Gould, Margaret S. "Education at the Expense of Health." *The Canadian School Journal* (October, 1934): 343–344, 366.

Green, W.H.H. "The Vocational School and the Community." *The School* (November, 1940): 211–213.

Greer, C. W. "Two Sides to a Question: If Teachers Are to Devote More Time to Exceptional Children, to What Intelligence Group Should Most of the Additional Attention Be Given? To Pupils of Superior Intelligence." *The School* (February, 1942): 465.

Griffin, J. D. "News and Comments." *The Canadian School Journal* (December, 1933): 446.

Hall, Stanley G. *Adolescence*. New York: Appleton, 1904.

———. "Ideal School Based on Child Study." *Journal of Proceedings and Addresses of the National Education Association* (1901): 474–488.

Hamilton-Wentworth District School Board. "Education for the 21st Century: Here, Now and into the Future." *Hwdsb.on.ca*. Accessed June 27, 2017. www.hwdsb. on.ca/wp-content/uploads/2012/09/Strategic-Directions-Education-in-HWDSB-Full-Report.pdf.

Hannan, Angela A. "Canadian Leaders Deserve Respect." *The School* (September, 1941): 11–14.

Harris, Robin S. *Quiet Evolution: A Study of the Educational System of Ontario*. Toronto: University of Toronto Press, 1967.

Hayes, William. *The Progressive Education Movement: Is It Still a Factor in Today's Schools?* New York: Rowman & Littlefield Education, 2006.

"Health Education." *The School* (March, 1936): 550–551.

Henderson, Viola. "The School Child's Lunch." *The Canadian School Journal* (September, 1932): 296–297.

Henry, George S. *Report of the Minister of Education for the Year 1932*. Toronto: The Legislative Assembly of Ontario, 1932.

Herd Thompson, John, and Seager, Allen. *Canada, 1922–1939: Decades of Discord*. Toronto: McClelland and Stewart, 1985.

Hess, Frederick M., ed. *When Research Matters: How Scholarship Influences Education Policy*. Cambridge: Harvard Education Press, 2008.

Hildreth, Gertrude. *Psychological Service for School Problems*. Yonkers-on-Hudson, NY: World Book Company, 1930.

Hill, A.S.H. "Is Democracy Worth Fighting For?" *The School* (May, 1940): 750–752.

Hill, Harold W. "Above-Average and Below-Average Students." *The School* (December, 1940): 327–330.

Himmelfarb, Gertrude. "Telling It as You Like It: Postmodernist History and the Flight From Fact." In *The Postmodern History Reader*, edited by Keith Jenkins, 158–174. London: Routledge, 1997.

Hincks, C. M. "Do You Know? Do You Believe?" *The Canadian School Journal* (February, 1934): 55.

Holland, Fern. "To-morrow." *The Canadian School Journal* (September, 1934): 316–317.

"The Home and School Movement." *The Canadian School Journal* (March, 1933): 85–86.

"Hon. Duncan McArthur." *The Globe and Mail*, Toronto, July 21, 1943.

Honour Classics in the University of Toronto. Toronto: University of Toronto Press, 1929.

Hooper, H. Ruth, and Lancaster, Edna. "Classes for More Intelligent Pupils." *The School* (December, 1940): 352–355.

Husband, A. J. "The Teaching of History in the Secondary School." *The School* (December, 1931): 308–314.

"The Institute of Child Study: The School Reporter Takes a Chance." *The School* (April, 1941): 692–699.

Johnson, Frances L. "Activities and Aims of Parent Education." In *Twenty-Five Years of Child Study: The Development of the Programme and Review of the Research at the Institute of Child Study, University of Toronto, 1926–1951*, edited by Karl S. Bernhardt, Margaret I. Fletcher, Frances L. Johnson, Dorothy A. Millichamp, and Mary L. Northway, 39–45. Toronto: University of Toronto Press, 1951.

Jose, J. L. "Is Business Practice Meeting the Community Needs?" *The School* (January, 1941): 389–391.

Keillor, James. "High School Civics." *The School* (January, 1927): 492–495.

———. "High School Civics." *The School* (September, 1926): 59–61.

Keirstead, W. C. "Indoctrination in Education." *The School* (May, 1940): 743–748.

Kelly, F., McCain, T., and Jukes, I. *Teaching the Digital Generation: No More Cookie-Cutter High Schools*. Thousand Oaks, CA: Corwin, 2008.

Kenney, James F. "Duncan McArthur (1885–1943)." *The Canadian Historical Review* 24. Toronto: University of Toronto Press, 1943.

Kidd, E. E. "The Guidance Programme at Scarborough Collegiate Institute." *The School* (May, 1941): 834–837.

Kirkconnell, Watson, and Woodhouse, A.S.P., eds. *The Humanities in Canada*. Ottawa: The Humanities Research Council of Canada, 1947.

Kliebard, Herbert. *The Struggle for the American Curriculum, 1893–1958*. New York: Routledge Falmer, 2004.

———. "Why History of Education?" *The Journal of Educational Research* 88, no. 4 (1995): 194–199.

———. *Forging the American Curriculum: Essays in Curriculum History and Theory*. New York: Routledge, 1992.

Kloppenberg, James. *Uncertain Victory: Social Democracy and Progressivism in European and American Thought, 1870–1920*. New York: Oxford University Press, 1986.

Labaree, David F. "Progressivism, Schools and Schools of Education: An American Romance." *Paedagogica Historica* 41, nos. 1 and 2 (2005): 275–288.

Laird, A. M., and Durrant, J. E. "An Occupational Survey of a Small City." *The School* (April, 1939): 655–661.

Lavell, Alfred E. "Abstract of an Address on 'Home, School, and the Prevention of Crime." *The Canadian School Journal* (April, 1932): 148.

Laycock, S. R. "Helping the Below-Average Pupil." *The School* (February, 1942): 466–470.

———. "Helping the Bright Pupil." *The School* (March, 1942): 561–565.

———. "Extra-Curricular Activities in the Modern School." *The School* (October, 1941): 93–103.

———. "The Diagnostic Approach to Problems of Pupil Adjustment." *The School* (February, 1939): 461–467.

Lemisko, Lynn S., and Clausen, Kurt W. "Connections, Contrarieties, and Convulsions: Curriculum and Pedagogical Reform in Alberta and Ontario, 1930–1955." *Canadian Journal of Education* 29, no. 4 (2006): 1097–1126.

Line, W., and Griffin, J.D.M. "Education and Mental Hygiene." *The School* (April, 1937): 647–649.

Lipmann, Walter. *Drift and Mastery*. New York: Macmillan, 1914.

Littleproud, J. R. "School Savings: A Project in Citizenship." *The Canadian School Journal* (January, 1934): 9–11.

Long, John A. "The Construction and Use of New-Type Tests." *The School* (October, 1940): 95–102.

———. "A Review of the Year, 1935." *The School* (February, 1936): 466–467.

Lorenz, Chris. "You Got Your History, I Got Mine." *Österreichische Zeitschrift für Geschichtswissenschaften* 10, no. 4 (1999): 563–584.

Lowther, Arthur A. "A Vocational School Literature Course." *The School* (September, 1926): 53–57.

Mackintosh, W. A. "Adam Shortt, 1859–1931." *Canadian Journal of Economics and Political Science* 4, no. 2 (May, 1938): 164–176.

Macklem, R. H. "The Community School." *The School* (April, 1942): 656–663.

MacPhee, E. D. "The Value of the Classics." *The School* (October, 1927): 111–120.

Macrae, Angus. *Talents and Temperaments*. London: Nisbet & Co., 1946.

Martin, W. G. "Education and Citizenship." *The Canadian School Journal* (May, 1932): 194–199, 206.

Massolin, Philip. *Canadian Intellectuals, the Tory Tradition, and the Challenge of Modernity, 1939–1970*. Toronto: University of Toronto Press, 2001.

McAllister, Ted V. *Revolt Against Modernity: Leo Strauss, Eric Voegelin & The Search for Postliberal Order*. Lawrence, KS: University Press of Kansas, 1996.

McArthur, Duncan. "Education and the Empire." In *The Empire Club of Canada Speeches*, 212–224. Toronto: The Empire Club of Canada, 1941.

———. "Education for Citizenship." *The Canadian School Journal* (October, 1935): 299–302.

———. *History of Canada for High Schools*. Toronto: W.J. Gage & Co., Limited, 1931.

———. "Method of Instruction." Handwritten note retrieved from *Duncan McArthur Fonds (1929–1940)*, Q73-3, location 1059, Queen's University Archives, n.d.

———. "A New Deal in Education in Ontario." Handwritten note retrieved from *Duncan McArthur Fonds (1929–1940)*, Q73-3, location 1059, Queen's University Archives, n.d.

———. "Organization." Handwritten note retrieved from *Duncan McArthur Fonds (1929–1940)*, Q73-3, location 1059, Queen's University Archives, n.d.

———. "The Teaching of Canadian History." In *Papers and Records, Volume XXI*. Toronto: The Ontario Historical Society, n.d.

"McArthur Raps Praise of Rich." *The Globe and Mail*, Toronto, May 28, 1937.

"McArthur Stresses Importance of Technical School Courses." *The Globe and Mail*, Toronto, May 20, 1937.

"McArthur Would Cut Language Requirement." *The Globe and Mail*, Toronto, March 30, 1940.

McClenahan, D. R. "Observations on Rural Public Health Work in Ontario." *The Canadian School Journal* (December, 1932): 314–315.

McCulley, Joseph. "Education and the War." *The School* (February, 1940): 471–478.

———. "Education in an Age of Insecurity." *The Canadian School Journal* (April, 1937): 148–155.

———. "Education in a Changing Society." *The Canadian School Journal* (January, 1932): 58–62.

McDonald, F. J. "Character Training and Citizenship." *The Canadian School Journal* (June, 1934): 238–241.

McKay, Ian. "The Liberal Order Framework: A Prospectus for a Reconnaissance of Canadian History." *The Canadian Historical Review* 81, no. 4 (2000): 617–645.

McKillop, A. B. *Matters of Mind: The University in Ontario, 1791–1951*. Toronto: University of Toronto Press, 1994.

———. *A Disciplined Intelligence: Critical Inquiry and Canadian Thought in the Victorian Era*. Kingston and Montreal: McGill-Queen's University Press, 1979.

McNally, G. Fred. "Curricula for Canadian High Schools." *The School* (January, 1935): 377–380.

Milewski, Patrice. "Positivism and Post-World War I Elementary School Reform in Ontario." *Paedagogica Historica* 48, no. 5 (2012): 728–743.

———. "'The Little Gray Book': Pedagogy, Discourse, and Rupture, 1937." *History of Education* 37, no. 1 (2008): 91–111.

Millichamp, Dorothy A. "The Organization of the Institute and Its Place in the Community." In *Twenty-Five Years of Child Study: The Development of the Programme and Review of the Research at the Institute of Child Study, University of Toronto, 1926–1951*, edited by Karl S. Bernhardt, Margaret I. Fletcher, Frances L. Johnson, Dorothy A. Millichamp, and Mary L. Northway, 18–38. Toronto: University of Toronto Press, 1951.

Millichamp, Dorothy A., and Fletcher, Margaret I. "Goals and Growth of Nursery Education." In *Twenty-Five Years of Child Study: The Development of the Programme and Review of the Research at the Institute of Child Study, University of Toronto, 1926–1951*, edited by Karl S. Bernhardt, Margaret I. Fletcher, Frances L. Johnson, Dorothy A. Millichamp, and Mary L. Northway, 30–36. Toronto: University of Toronto Press, 1951.

"Minister Head of Committee." *The Globe and Mail*, Toronto, June 18, 1943.

Ministry of Education, Ontario. "21st Century Teaching and Learning, 2014." *EduGains*. Accessed June 27, 2017. www.edugains.ca/resources21CL/WhatsNew/21stCTeachingandLearning_QuickFacts_Winter2014.pdf.

Minkler, Frederick. "The Progressive Education Conferences in Hamilton and Windsor." *The School* (January, 1939): 378–383.

Motyer Raymond, Jocelyn. *The Nursery World of Dr. Blatz*. Toronto: University of Toronto Press, 1991.

Murray, R. S. "The Problem of Teaching." *The Canadian School Journal* (December, 1934): 415–416.

Mustard, Thornton. "The New Programme of Studies." *Educational Courier* (October, 1937): 8–10.

Neatby, Hilda. *So Little for the Mind*. Toronto: Clarke, Irwin, 1953.

"The N.E.F. Conference." *The School* (May, 1937): 741–742.

"News From Home and Abroad." *The Canadian School Journal* (June, 1935): 196.

Northway, Mary L. "Postscript." In *Human Security: Some Reflections*, 123–131. Toronto: University of Toronto Press, 1966.

————. "Preface." In *Human Security: Some Reflections*, edited by William E. Blatz, ix–xiv. Toronto: University of Toronto Press, 1966.

"Notes and News: Ontario." *The School* (May, 1935): 811–812.

"O.E.A. Study of Curricula Now Planned." *The Globe*, Toronto, April 26, 1935.

Oliver, Hugh, Holmes, Mark, and Winchester, Ian., eds. *The House that Ryerson Built: Essays in Education to Mark Ontario's Bicentennial*. Toronto: OISE Press, 1985.

Ontario Department of Education. *Programme of Studies for Grades 1 to 6 of the Public and Separate Schools*. Toronto: The King's Printer, 1937.

Ontario Public School Boards' Association. "A Vision for Learning and Teaching in a Digital Age." *Opsba.org*. Accessed June 27, 2017. www.opsba.org/SiteCollection Documents/OPSBA_AVisionForLearning.pdf.

Ontario Public School Boards' Association. "What If? A 21st Century Classroom Scenario." *Opsba.org*. Accessed June 27, 2017. www.opsba.org/SiteCollectionDocu ments/WhatIf.pdf#search=What%20if%3F%20A%2021st%20Century%20 Classroom%20Scenario.

Osborne, Ken. "Teaching History in Schools: A Canadian Debate." *Journal of Curriculum Studies* 35, no. 5 (2003): 585–626.

Ottawa Catholic School Board. "Toward 2020: Connecting With Our Students." *Opsba.org*. Accessed June 27, 2017. www.ocsb.ca/images/learningtech/oc-schools-pdf-towards2020.pdf.

Owram, Doug. "The Government Generation: Canadian Intellectuals and the State, 1900–1945." *The Canadian Historical Review* 68, no. 3 (1987): 465–468.

Patterson, Robert. "The Implementation of Progressive Education in Canada, 1930–1945." In *Essays on Canadian Education*, edited by N. Kach, K. Mazurek, R. S. Patterson, and I. DeFavery, 79–93. Calgary: Detselig, 1986.

————. "Society and Education During the Wars and their Interlude: 1914–1945." In *Canadian Education: A History*, edited by J. Donald Wilson, Robert M. Stamp, and Louis-Philippe Audet, 379–380. Toronto, ON: Prentice-Hall of Canada, 1970.

Peat, Donald. "Two Sides to a Question: If Teachers Are to Devote More Time to Exceptional Children, to What Intelligence Group Should Most of the Additional Attention Be Given? To Below-Average Pupils." *The School* (February, 1942): 464.

Phair, John T., Power, Mary, and Roberts, Robert H. "An Experiment in Health Teaching in the Schools of Ontario." *The School* (September, 1936): 6–11.

————. "School Medical Inspection." *The Canadian School Journal* (September, 1932): 295.

Plato. "Meno." In *Plato, IV*, trans. W. R. M. Lamb. Cambridge: Harvard University Press, 1924.

Plumptre, H. P. "Education for World Citizenship." *The Canadian School Journal* (September, 1935): 247–250, 257.

Prince, A. E. "The Honourable Duncan McArthur: A Tribute." *The Queen's Review* (1943): 162.

————. "The Teacher: An Essential Qualification for His Success." *The Ottawa Citizen*, Ottawa, February 21, 1913.

"Restoration of Pay Scale Announced." *The Globe and Mail*, Toronto, March 31, 1937.

Ridenour, Nina. *Mental Health in the United States: A Fifty Year History*. Cambridge: Harvard University Press, 1961.

Roberts, R. H. "Health Education." *The School* (October, 1935): 98–104.

Robertson, J. E. "An Educational Survey." *The Canadian School Journal* (March, 1932): 120.

Rodgers, Daniel. *Atlantic Crossings: Social Politics in a Progressive Age.* Cambridge, MA: Harvard University Press, 1998.

Rogers, G. F. "Present Day Problems in Education." *The Canadian School Journal* (May, 1933): 173–177.

Ross, Edward A. *Social Control: A Survey of the Foundations of Order.* New York: Macmillan, 1901.

Rugg, Harold. *Now Is the Moment.* New York: Duell, Sloan and Pearce, 1943.

Russell, David H. "Subject Matter Disabilities." *The School* (February, 1942): 471–475.

———. "Education for Critical Thinking." *The School* (November, 1941): 188–194.

Russell, David H., and Tyler, Fred T. "Special Education in Canada." *The School* (June, 1942): 882–890.

Russell, Olive. "Is Vocational Guidance Feasible?" *The School* (March, 1939): 559–568.

"*Saturday Night* (July 28, 1934)." In *The Schools of Ontario, 1867–1967,* edited by Robert Stamp. Toronto: University of Toronto Press, 1982.

Schneider, Jack. *From the Ivory Tower to the Schoolhouse: How Scholarship Becomes Common Knowledge in Education.* Cambridge: Harvard Education Press, 2014.

"School Administration and School Finance in Ontario: Can They Be Improved?" *The Canadian School Journal* (May, 1932): 187, 190–192.

"School Estimates Not Under Control of Urban Councils." *The Globe,* Toronto, April 25, 1935.

"The Schools and the War of Machines: A Report of the Work of the Vocational Schools of Ontario." *The School* (February, 1941): 504–506.

Scott, Ernest F. "The Effects of the War on Literature and Learning." *Queen's Quarterly* 27 (December, 1919): 147–153.

Sears, Alan. "Historical Thinking and Citizenship Education: It Is Time to End the War." In *New Possibilities for the Past: Shaping History Education in Canada,* edited by Penney Clarke, 344–364. Vancouver: UBC Press, 2011.

"Secondary School Costs." *The Canadian School Journal* (January, 1933): 13–15.

Sertran, David P. "Morality for the 'Democracy of God': George Albert Coe and the Liberal Protestant Critique of American Character Education, 1917–1940." *Religion and American Culture* 15, no. 1 (2005): 107–144.

Sharpe, Frank T. "What Would I Do If I Left School Under Present Conditions?" *The Canadian School Journal* (October, 1933): 355–358.

"Shifting Minds: A Vision and Framework for 21st Century Learning in Canada, 2012." *Canadians for 21st Century Learning and Innovation.* Accessed June 23, 2017. www.c21canada.org.

Shortt, Adam. "The Significance for Canadian History of the Work of the Board of Historical Publications." *Proceedings and Transactions, Royal Society of Canada* 3, no. 13 (1919): 103–109.

———. "Some Aspects of the Social Life of Canada." *Canadian Magazine* 11, no. 1 (1898): 3–11.

———. "The Influence of Daily Occupations and Surroundings on the Life of the People." In *Sunday Afternoon Addresses,* 3rd Series, 58–69. Kingston: Queen's University, 1893.

Silcox, S. "The Teacher's Book Shelf." *The School* (March, 1930): 560–562.

Sinclair, S. B. "How Rural School Trustees Can Select an Efficient Teacher." *The Canadian School Journal* (March, 1932): 94–95.

Snider, Colonel F. E. "How Shall We Achieve Greater Efficiency in Our Schools." *The Canadian School Journal* (September, 1935): 251–253.

Spencer, Herbert: "Progess: Its Law and Causes." *The Westminster Review* 67 (April, 1857): 445–465.

Spiegel, Gabrielle. "History, Historicism and the Social Logic of the Text in the Middle Ages." In *The Postmodern History Reader*, edited by Keith Jenkins, 260–273. London: Routledge, 1997.

Spring, Joel. *Education and the Rise of the Corporate State*. Boston: Beacon Press, 1972.

Stamp, Robert. *Ontario Secondary School Program Innovations and Student Retention Rates: 1920s–1970s*. Toronto: Ministry of Education, 1988.

———. *The Schools of Ontario, 1867–1967*. Toronto: University of Toronto Press, 1982, p. 155.

"Standards in the Middle School: A Discussion of Methods in Measurements in Matriculation Subjects." *The School* (March, 1941): 619–623.

"States School Grants Raised to Cut Taxes." *The Globe and Mail*, Toronto, April 21, 1938.

Stewart, W.A.C. *The Educational Innovators: Progressive Schools, 1881–1967*. New York: St. Martin's Press, 1968.

"Supplement: Reports on Educational Progress in Canada and Newfoundland, 1940–1941." *The School* (June, 1941): 907–930.

Sutherland, Neil. "The Triumph of 'Formalism': Elementary Schooling in Vancouver From the 1920s to the 1960s." *BC Studies*, nos. 69 and 70 (Spring–Summer, 1986): 175–210.

———. *Children in English-Canadian Society: Framing the Twentieth Century Consensus*. Toronto: University of Toronto Press, 1976.

Taylor, B. C. "The Latin Society—I." *The School* (September, 1941): 40–43.

Taylor, Frederick W. *The Principles of Scientific Management*. New York: Harper & Brothers, 1911.

"Teachers and the Trades and Labour Congress." *The School* (December, 1935): 272–273.

Thompson, John H., and Seager, Allen. *Decades of Discord, 1922–1939*. Toronto: McClelland and Stewart, 1985.

Tomkins, George S. *A Common Countenance: Stability and Change in the Canadian Curriculum*. Vancouver: Pacific Educational Press, 2008.

Transom, E. J. "Time Off for Thinking." *The School* (February, 1941): 507–513.

———. "Time Off for Thinking." *The School* (March, 1941): 607–613.

Tröhler, Daniel. "The 'Kingdom of God on Earth' and Early Chicago Pragmatism." *Educational Theory* 56, no. 1 (2006): 89–105.

Tyack, David. *The One Best System: A History of American Urban Education*. Cambridge, MA: Harvard University Press, 1974.

"Vocational Training and Vocational Guidance." *The Canadian School Journal* (November, 1932): 371–372.

von Heyking, Amy. *Creating Citizens: History and Identity in Alberta's Schools, 1905 to 1980*. Calgary: University of Calgary Press, 2006.

"Want 100,000 School Pupils to Aid Farmers." *The Globe and Mail*, Toronto, February 26, 1943.

Watson, John. "Edward Caird as Teacher and Thinker." *Queen's Quarterly* 1 (June, 1909): 304–305.

———. *An Outline of Philosophy*. Glasgow: James Maclehose and Sons, 1901.

White, Hayden. "Historical Emplotment and the Problem of Truth." In *The Postmodern History Reader*, edited by Keith Jenkins, 392–412. London: Routledge, 1997.

Wilson, J. Donald, Stamp, Robert M., and Audet, Louis-Philippe, eds. *Canadian Education: A History*. Toronto: Prentice-Hall of Canada, 1970.

Winters, E. A. "Harold Rugg and Education for Social Reconstruction." PhD diss., University of Wisconsin, 1968.

Wood, B. Anne. *Idealism Transformed: The Making of a Progressive Educator*. Kingston and Montreal: McGill-Queen's University Press, 1985.

Woods, D. S. "Trends in the High School Curriculum: General Courses and University Requirements." *The School* (April, 1940): 658–662.

Woodworth, Robert S., and Sheehan, Mary R. *Contemporary Schools of Psychology*. New York: Ronald Press, 1964.

"The Work of Voluntary Agencies." *The School* (November, 1933): 188–189.

Wright, Roland. *A Short History of Progress*. Toronto: House of Anansi Press, 2004.

Young, Gordon. "Optional Subjects." *The Canadian School Journal* (December, 1933): 427–445.

Index